PROBLEMS AND PERSPECTIVES IN HISTORY

EDITOR: H. F. KEARNEY MA PHD

The Theory of Capitalist Imperialism

PROBLEMS AND PERSPECTIVES IN HISTORY

EDITOR: H.F. KEARNEY MA PHD

The Theory of Capitalist Imperialism

D. K. Fieldhouse

BEIT LECTURER IN COMMONWEALTH HISTORY
AND FELLOW OF NUFFIELD COLLEGE, OXFORD

LONGMAN

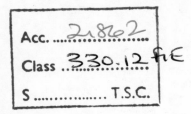
LONGMAN GROUP LIMITED
London
*Associated companies branches and representatives
throughout the World*

© D. K. Fieldhouse 1967

First published 1967
New impression 1977

ISBN 0 582 31362 7

*Printed in Hong Kong by
Commonwealth Printing Press Ltd*

Editor's Foreword

'Study problems in preference to periods' was the excellent advice given by Lord Acton in his inaugural lecture at Cambridge. To accept it is one thing, to put it into practice is another. In fact, in both schools and universities the teaching of history, in depth, is often hindered by certain difficulties of a technical nature, chiefly to do with the availability of sources. In this respect, history tends to be badly off in comparison with literature or the sciences. The historical equivalents of set texts, readings or experiments, in which the student is encouraged to use his own mind, are the so-called 'special periods'. If these are to be fruitful, the student must be encouraged to deal in his own way with the problems raised by historical documents and the historiography of the issues in question and he must be made aware of the wider perspectives of history. Thus, if the enclosure movement of the sixteenth century is studied, the student might examine the historiographical explanations stretching from More's *Utopia* and Cobbett to Beresford's *Lost Village of England*. At the same time he might also be dealing with selected documents raising important problems. Finally he might be encouraged to realize the problems of peasantries at other periods of time, including Russia and China in the nineteenth and twentieth centuries. In this particular instance, thanks to Tawney and Power, *Tudor Economic Documents*, the history teacher is comparatively well off. For other special periods the situation is much more difficult. If, however, the study of history is to encourage the development of the critical faculties as well as the memory, this approach offers the best hope. The object of this series is to go some way towards meeting these difficulties.

The general plan of each volume in the series will be similar, with a threefold approach from aspects of historiography, documents and editorial consideration of wider issues, though the structure and balance between the three aspects may vary.

A broad view is being taken of the limits of history. Political history will not be excluded, but a good deal of emphasis will be placed on economic, intellectual and social history. The idea has in fact grown out of the experience of a group of historians at the University of Sussex, where the student is encouraged to investigate the frontier areas between his own and related disciplines.

H. KEARNEY

TO
MAX HARTWELL

Contents

CONTENTS

Acknowledgements

We are grateful to the following for permission to reproduce copyright material:

Académie royale des Sciences d'Outre-Mer for 'Lettre du Duc de Brabant du 26 juillet 1863' from *Documents d'Histoire precoloniale belge* (1861–1865) ed. L. Le Febve de Vivy (trans. by D.K.F.); George Allen & Unwin Ltd for extracts from *The Economic Foundations of Society* by A. Loria, *The Evolution of Modern Capitalism* by J. A. Hobson and *Capitalism, Socialism and Democracy* by J. A. Schumpeter; G. Bell & Sons, Ltd for an extract from *The War of Steel and Gold* by H. M. Brailsford; Basil Blackwell & Mott Ltd and Oxford University Press, New York for an extract from *Patterns of Trade and Development* by Ragnar Nurkse; Cambridge University Press for an extract from *Home and Foreign Investment* by A. K. Cairncross; The University of Chicago Press for an extract from *War and the Private Investor* by E. Staley; Columbia University Press for an extract from *The Pattern of Imperialism* by E. M. Winslow; Howard Fertig, Inc. Publisher, New York for an extract from *Imperialism and World Economy* by N. I. Bukharin (New Edition 1967); Hamish Hamilton Ltd for 'Hobson's Misapplication of the Theory' from *Englishmen and Others* by A. J. P. Taylor; Harper & Row, Publishers, Inc. for 'Bases of a New National Imperialism' from *A Generation of Materialism 1871–1900* by Carlton J. H. Hayes, Copyright 1941 by Harper & Row, Publishers, Inc.; Macmillan & Co. Ltd for an extract from *Africa and the Victorians* by R. E. Robinson and J. A. Gallagher; The Macmillan Company of New York for an extract from *Imperialism and World Politics* by P. T. Moon, Copyright The Macmillan Company 1926: Renewed 1954 by Alice Moon; James Nisbet & Co. Ltd for an extract from *The War in South Africa* and from *Imperialism, A Study* by J. A. Hobson; North-Holland Publishing Company for an extract from *Hobson and Underconsumption* by E. E. Nemmers; Oxford University Press for an extract from *Capital Investment in Africa* by S. H. Frankel, and from Appendix I of *Survey of British Commonwealth Affairs, Vol. II—Problems and Economic Policy 1918–1939, Part I* by W. K. Hancock (published under the auspices of the Royal Institute of International Affairs); Routledge & Kegan Paul Ltd for an extract from *The Accumulation of Capital* by Rosa Luxembourg; Verlag

ACKNOWLEDGEMENTS

J. H. W. Dietz Nachf, GmbH for an extract from *Finance Capitalism* by R. Hilferding, and the author for an extract from *Economic Imperialism* by Leonard Woolf.

We regret that we have been unable to trace the copyright owners in *Patriotism and Empire* by J. M. Robertson, and would welcome any information that would enable us to do so.

Introduction

Much of the confusion surrounding the character of 'imperialism' results from the fact that the same word is commonly used to describe several quite distinct things. It is, for example, sometimes used to indicate a set of historical events: thus the events of the period before 1914 which resulted in the extension of European empires overseas may be described as imperialism, irrespective of the motives for this territorial expansion. Alternatively, imperialism may refer to the impulses behind this territorial expansion rather than to the events. Thus we can talk of 'popular imperialism' as a special form of nationalism, and argue that this was a main cause of colonial expansion. Again, imperialism has a special meaning for Marxists. Following the definition given by Lenin, imperialism is a technical word indicating a particular stage in the evolution of any capitalist society. Such an imperialist state has a number of special features, one of which is a propensity to acquire or control dependent societies; and this tendency is not restricted to any particular period of time.

To talk constructively about imperialism it is therefore necessary to decide which of these meanings is adopted. The basic division is, in fact, between the first meaning and the other two: between imperialism as shorthand for a particular set of historical events and imperialism as a name given to the forces which lay behind imperial expansion. Yet such a distinction is only the start of the problem. The reason why imperialism as a set of facts has been so much debated is that the facts, particularly during the period after about 1870, are so surprising that they gave rise to a number of complex explanations, each of which constitutes a theory of imperialism. Let us consider first the facts and then look at some of the theories which resulted from them.

The facts of imperialism are surprising mainly because events between about 1870 and 1914 seemed to some contemporaries to be unique. During the earlier part of the nineteenth century Europe's overseas empires had been expanding steadily, but so gradually that in retrospect this seemed to be an age of 'anti-imperialism'. Moreover in this period relatively few European states were concerned with overseas expansion – Britain, France, Russia and the Netherlands. Spain and Portugal also had overseas empires, but these were small and apparently derelict. No other continental power belonged to the imperial club. By marked contrast the period after about 1870 seemed one of very rapid colonization. In the thirty-six years after 1878 Europe and the United States acquired about 17·4 per cent of the world's land surface at an average rate of some 240,000 square miles a year. By 1914 there were very few countries which were not under European rule or onetime colonies which had seized their independence. Moreover, during the same years, Germany, Italy, Belgium, the United States and Japan had joined the ranks of the empire-owners. These developments were certainly striking: they forced historians and others to explain why this expansion should have taken place at that particular time and to that extent. The result has been the proliferation of theories of imperialism, each of which provides a different answer to these questions.

It is not the purpose of the documents reproduced in this book to survey the vast field of explanatory theories of imperialism so that the reader may take his pick. This has been done in other collections. We are concerned here only with one of these explanations, the Theory of Capitalist Imperialism,[1] which, for reasons which will be explained later, stands apart from all the rest. But, in order to clarify the problem, a brief survey of the most common explanations of imperialism may be given.

All such explanations fall into one of two broad categories: they either concentrate on Europe and ask what motives Europeans had for acquiring overseas dependencies; or they concentrate on other parts of the world and ask whether situations existed there which may have induced Europe to impose its rule on them. Or, to use convenient labels, there are 'Eurocentric' and 'peripheral' theories of imperialism. Eurocentric theories are most common, and the Theory of Capitalist Imperialism is one of them. To consider this group of theories first, we can identify three distinct types. One concentrates attention on European statesmen and explains the acquisition of colonies in political terms. Statesmen like Bismarck and Salisbury annexed colonies after about 1880 because they thought them necessary as strategic bases, to preserve 'vital' lines of communication, or even as diplomatic bargaining counters. Another theory concentrates on European public opinion, and explains imperialism as a popular and emotional concern for national prestige and power. A third takes its stand on the commercial needs of European states. The growing industries of the later nineteenth century, it has been argued, needed overseas markets, but found that

[1] The term 'capitalist imperialism' comes from Lenin. Capitals are used throughout this book merely to distinguish this from all other theories of imperialism.

the growth of high protective tariffs in most 'civilized' countries other than Britain was tending to close nearby markets to their imports. At the same time Europe needed more raw materials, particularly those which came from the tropics. Colonies were therefore needed both as markets and sources of primary products, and this accelerating need explains the sudden rush for tropical colonies after about 1870. Finally there is the Theory of Capitalist Imperialism. This will be considered in detail later, but it comes within the general heading of Eurocentric theories of imperialism because it concentrates attention almost entirely on Europe and sees colonization as a direct result of Europe's need to invest surplus capital overseas.

'Peripheral' theories of imperialism are different in kind. They focus interest on the non-European world, and do not attempt to prescribe an overall answer to the question why colonies were acquired. Some peripheral situations were common enough to provide useful initial lines of investigation. For example, existing European colonies had always tended to expand into their own surroundings, whether this was due to European settlers wanting more land or non-European labour, or because the existing frontiers were politically unstable and annexation seemed to promise greater security. Again, especially in the nineteenth century, it was common for quite small groups of Europeans who lived in the peripheral world – missionaries, planters, labour recruiters, explorers and so on – to undermine the fabric of indigenous societies and governments, often without intending to do so. When this happened the European state from which they came might eventually be obliged, either for moral reasons or to protect substantive interests such as trade or investments, to step in and to provide a framework of political stability. There were, of course, many other peripheral situations which might lead to the imposition of European rule on indigenous societies; but all have this in common, that they provide a satisfactory explanation of at least certain parts of European expansion after 1870 without the need to assume a positive imperialist movement within Europe. Hence a peripheral approach to imperialism may lead to interpretations of this second expansion of Europe very different from a theory which begins in Europe itself.

At first sight the Theory of Capitalist Imperialism may seem to be merely one of many comparable ways of explaining European expansion, and it has frequently been treated in this way. Why, then, should it be made the subject of this collection of documents? There are two main grounds for giving it special attention. First, it has proved in many ways the most influential of all these theories or historical explanations, and remains dogma throughout a large part of the world. Second, it is in fact different in kind from all other theories of imperialism. Those we have mentioned, whether 'Eurocentric' or 'peripheral', have one thing in common: they are pragmatic. Starting with some readily observed facts – the acquisition of colonies, the need for markets, crises on the circumference and so on – they attempt to provide some explanation of these facts. Thus they are all deductive theories, working from facts or assumed facts to theories deduced from them. Superficially the Theory of Capitalist Imperialism may seem to do the same thing, taking as its starting point the fact of colonial expansion and the fact of European investment overseas, and proceeding to link these as effect and cause. Yet to assume this is to misunderstand this most complex and influential of all theories of imperialism. It is the purpose of Parts One and Two of these documents to show that the Theory was not merely an *ad hoc* response to the facts of colonization after about 1870, but that it derived from a body of highly theoretical economic concepts, dating back to the eighteenth century, which were eventually adopted and adapted in the late nineteenth and early twentieth centuries to explain historical events. In short, this was an inductive theory whose theoretical basis existed long before those events which it was eventually used to explain.

The Theory of Capitalist Imperialism is best known in the forms eventually given to it by two men – J. A. Hobson, an English Liberal, and V. I. Lenin, the founder of Russian Communism. They have therefore commonly been credited with having formulated the theory, the one in terms appropriate to the tradition of liberal opposition in Britain to colonization, the other according to the economic principles laid down by Marx. Yet in fact neither can claim so much originality. They were both essentially publicists who succeeded in applying established economic principles and current ideas to a particular set of events in a way which appeared to their readers to be particularly clear and convincing. The Theory of Capitalist Imperialism would have existed (though it might not have gained as much publicity) in much the same form if neither had written. To understand it we must therefore examine its evolution over nearly a century and a half before Lenin published his work in 1917.

Part One of this collection is concerned with the theoretical concepts on which the eventual Theory in its applied form was built. By about 1850 they already provided an argument that could be used to explain the expansion of European economic influence, and possibly also European political control, before the rapid expansion of the years after 1870 occurred. The argument can be summarized as follows. Capitalist societies tend to save money and to invest these savings as capital in order to produce more goods in the future. This accumulation of capital is essential if society is to progress, for otherwise production would be static. Yet accumulation will take place only if those who possess savings think that the profits they are likely to make on new investments will be a sufficient reward. Hence capital accumulation depends ultimately on the general level of profits remaining above the point at which capitalists would prefer to consume their savings rather than to invest them. So much was generally agreed; and this leads on to the vital question whether profit rates in capitalist societies will tend to rise or decline over a period of time. The roots of the Theory of Capitalist Imperialism lie in the general, but not unanimous, opinion of nineteenth-century economists, that the normal tendency of the rate of profit in industrialized societies was to decline over a long period.

Why should the rate of profit decline, and what relevance could this have to colonization? To the first question the writers represented in Part One put forward various answers; but all agreed that, in certain circumstances profits must tend to decline as time went on. The link between a declining profit rate and colonization emerges from some of the solutions or temporary palliatives suggested by some of these theorists. Although for different reasons (because of their differing explanation of the declining tendency of profits), all suggested that if part of the savings of the industrialized countries of Europe were invested overseas instead of at home, the moment when the rate of profit dropped below the minimum required to encourage capitalists to invest would be postponed. There were many possible forms this overseas investment might take, and there was no theoretical reason why it should be invested in European colonies rather than in other places. This fact is important, for it means that these economists saw no necessary connection between the economic problems of Europe and the creation of colonial empires. Yet some at least thought that colonies were preferable to other foreign countries. For example, E. G. Wakefield argued along these lines, giving as two of his reasons the additional profitability of investing money in the fertile virgin lands of new colonies, such as Australia, and the advantage of good colonial government as compared with the often indifferent standard of government to be found elsewhere. Thus the theory of the declining tendency of the rate of profit could perfectly well evolve into an argument for colonization. It could also be used to explain why colonies were being acquired, provided there was reason to think that their acquisition was in some way connected with the export of European capital.

Why, then, did these earlier economists not go further and produce the Theory of Capitalist Imperialism in its generally accepted form? The answer is primarily that, at the time at which they wrote – that is, before the 1870s (even Marx, who produced a parallel theory based on his rather different first principles, died in 1883) – there seemed no reason to think that the export of capital was resulting in the annexation of colonies. Colonies were being acquired, and capital was being exported; but they were not apparently linked as cause and effect, for much of the capital was going to independent states such as the U.S.A., and the annexation of most of the new colonies of this period, such as Burma, Fiji or Australasia, could be accounted for in other ways. Thus in the 1870s there existed a number of parallel theories which postulated the need of Europe to export capital if capitalism itself was to progress indefinitely; but it remained for others to argue that the necessary consequence of this export of capital was the acquisition of colonies.

Part Two traces some of the main steps by which the existing theory of capital exports became the Theory of Capitalist Imperialism. There were many more links in the chain than can be included here, but the more significant stages are represented. Note that application of the economists' concepts took two forms, one prospective or apologetic, the other retrospective and critical. The earlier is that represented by practical statesmen, such as Leopold II and Jules Ferry (but also many others), who used the principle that capitalism needed to export capital as an argument in favour of colonies they had already annexed or which they wished to acquire. The second form of application came later, and reflected the now obvious fact that annexation of colonies had taken place on a large scale since about 1880. It was possible in the 1880s and 1890s for men like Engels to argue tentatively that there was nothing surprising about such expansion. The economists had said that capital must be exported; capital certainly was being exported, some at least of it to places such as Egypt, Tunis and the Transvaal, all of which were duly annexed as colonies by one power or another. Imperialism – the word commonly used in England from the mid-1870s for the tendency to extend European possessions, whatever the motive or cause – was therefore clearly the product of the economic needs of capitalism. Therefore this process of annexing colonies was, what Lenin eventually called it – Capitalist Imperialism.

The stages by which this connection between economic theory and the facts of colonization was made, and the various forms the ultimate theory took, are the theme of the remaining documents in Part Two. Detailed study of the evolutionary process is necessary because only by seeing how the Theory grew can we fully understand its final form. Yet it is not enough for the historian merely to study the evolution of such an argument. His duty is to evaluate it: to ask whether it is logically sound and whether it really fits the historical facts as he knows them. Part Three is intended to show how such questions can best be applied to the Theory of Capitalist Imperialism and to indicate lines along which it can be evaluated. It is not suggested that these are the only lines of approach to the Theory, nor that all the critics are necessarily correct. But at least they provide models for the dissection of this and similar inductive methods of explaining historical events.

There remains the question of how the historian should handle such a theory when telling his story of events. The extracts in Part Four are chosen to show how four historians handled the Theory of Capitalist Imperialism. Although they are not necessarily representative of all historians writing on this theme at particular times, they reflect well enough the various stages since Lenin's book was published in 1916: first, almost complete acceptance of the Theory; then partial modification, and finally almost complete rejection, as the process of dissection by critics and the accumulation of new historical data combined to demonstrate its weaker points.

The theme of these documents, then, is the birth, growth and maturing of an economic concept which ended up as a quasi-historical theory used to explain some of the major events of the forty years before 1914. In the first instance the main interest lies in observing the process of evolution, irrespective of its historical relevance; for ideas have a life of their own divorced from historical facts, and these particular ideas lay at the heart of the new science of economics. Thereafter the interest centres on the historian's question: Is the Theory a correct explanation of the events it attempts to explain? Even if the conclusion is that the Theory is defective, the process of understanding it is worth the effort, for it has proved one of the most influential and enduring concepts prevalent in the twentieth century.

Part One

THE ROOTS OF THE THEORY

The Economists and the declining Tendency of the Rate of Profit

---

The Theory of Capitalist Imperialism is normally regarded as a product of the first two decades of the twentieth century and of Marxist economic principles. In some degree – particularly in matters of detail and in its direct application to recent historical events – this is true. But those who constructed the mature Theory built on concepts developed by economists and others during the previous century, and could thus claim respectable ancestry for at least the ground-work of their argument. The most important idea they inherited was the doctrine of the declining tendency of the rate of profit on capital. This was present in almost all the classical economists, though the reasons they assigned for this phenomenon varied. Adam Smith put it down to the excessive competition of capital within any one country; Malthus to the declining profitability of investment in marginal lands as population strained food resources; Sismondi to overproduction by capitalists and to the reduced capacity of the workers to buy industrial products as mechanization proceeded; Marx to the declining proportion of 'variable capital' (the fund set aside by the capitalist to pay wages) to 'constant capital' (the fund invested by the capitalist in machines and raw materials etc.). E. G. Wakefield and J. S. Mill, adopting the arguments of the pre-Marxist theorists, suggested that colonization, by attracting surplus capital from Europe, was probably the best way of sustaining the rate of profit there. All these writers were pessimistic about the future of capitalism if such an outlet for surplus capital could not be found: only Ricardo, following Say, insisted that production always created consumers, and so optimistically held that the rate of profit could be sustained without capital export, provided the level of wages did not rise.

I

1 The Competition of Stock
ADAM SMITH

Adam Smith (1723–90) is normally regarded as the founder of modern economic theory, and his Wealth of Nations, published in 1776, provided many of the basic ideas which were later adopted or modified by the classical economists. His theory that the rate of profit in a developed country must decline as a result of the competition of capital (he called it stock) was not entirely new, and was later seen to be oversimplified. But it formed the starting point of all later examination of the problem of surplus capital.

The rise and fall in the profits of stock depend upon the same causes with the rise and fall in the wages of labour, the increasing or declining state of the wealth of the society; but those causes affect the one and the other very differently.

The increase of stock, which raises wages, tends to lower profit. When the stocks of many rich merchants are turned into the same trade, their mutual competition naturally tends to lower its profit; and when there is a like increase of stock in all the different trades carried on in the same society, the same competition must produce the same effect in them all. . . .

In our North American and West Indian colonies, not only the wages of labour, but the interest of money, and consequently the profits of stock, are higher than in England. . . . High wages of labour and high profits of stock, however, are things, perhaps, which scarce ever go together, except in the peculiar circumstances of new colonies. A new colony must always for some time be more under-stocked in proportion to the extent of its territory, and more under-peopled in proportion to the extent of its stock, than the greater part of other countries. They have more land than they have stock to cultivate. What they have, therefore, is applied to the cultivation only of what is most fertile and most favourably situated. . . . Stock employed in the purchase and improvement of such lands must yield a very large profit, and consequently afford to pay a very large interest. Its rapid accumulation in so profitable an employment enables the planter to increase the number of his hands faster than he can find them in a new settlement. Those whom he can find, therefore, are very liberally rewarded. As the colony increases, the profits of stock gradually diminish. When the most fertile and best situated lands have been all occupied, less profit can be made by the cultivation of what is inferior both in soil and situation, and less interest can be afforded for the stock which is so employed. . . .

The acquisition of new territory, or of new branches of trade, may sometimes raise the profits of stock, and with them the interest of money, even in a country which is fast advancing in the acquisition of riches. The stock of the country not being sufficient for the whole accession of business, which such acquisitions present to the different people among whom it is divided, is applied to those particular branches only which afford the greatest profit. Part of what had before been employed in other trades, is necessarily withdrawn from them, and turned into some of the new and more profitable ones. In all those old trades, therefore, the competition comes to be less than before. The market comes to be less fully supplied with many different sorts of goods. Their price necessarily rises more or less, and yields a greater profit to those who deal in them, who can, therefore, afford to borrow at a higher interest. For some time after the conclusion of the late war, not only private people of the best credit, but some of the greatest companies in London, commonly borrowed at five per cent who before that had not been used to pay more than four, and four and a half per cent. The great accession both of territory and trade, by our acquisitions in North America and the West Indies, will sufficiently account for this, without supposing any diminution in the capital stock of the society. . . .

The diminution of the capital stock of the society, or of the funds destined for the maintenance of industry, however, as it lowers the wages of labour, so it raises the profits of stock, and consequently the interest of money. By the wages of labour being lowered, the owners of what stock remains in the society can bring their goods at less expense to market than before, and less stock being employed in supplying the market than before, they can sell them dearer. Their goods cost them less, and they get more for them. Their profits, therefore, being augmented at both ends, can well afford a large interest. . . .

In a country which had acquired that full complement of riches which the nature of its soil and climate, and its situation with respect to other countries, allowed it to acquire; which could, therefore, advance no further, and which was not going backwards, both the wages of labour and the profits of stock would probably be very low. In a country fully peopled in proportion to what either its territory could maintain or its stock employ, the competition for employment would necessarily be so great as to reduce the wages of labour to what was barely sufficient to keep up the number of labourers, and, the country being already fully peopled, that number could never be augmented. In a country fully stocked in proportion to all the business it had to transact, as great a quantity of stock would be employed in every particular branch as the nature and extent of the trade would admit. The competition, therefore, would everywhere be as great, and consequently the ordinary profit as low as possible.

But perhaps no country has ever yet arrived at this degree of opulence. [pp. 87, 92–5]

When the capital stock of any country is increased to such a degree, that it cannot be all employed in supplying the consumption, and supporting the productive labour of that particular country, the surplus part of it naturally disgorges itself into the carrying trade, and is employed in performing the same offices to other countries. The carrying trade is the natural effect and symptom of great national wealth; but it does not seem to be the natural cause of it. . . .

The extent of the home-trade and of the capital which can be employed in it, is necessarily limited by the value of the surplus produce of all those distant places within the country which have occasion to exchange their respective productions with one another. That of the foreign trade of consumption, by the value of the surplus produce of the whole country and of what can be purchased with it. That of the carrying trade, by the value of the surplus produce of all the different countries in the world. Its possible extent, therefore, is in a manner infinite in comparison of that of the other two, and is capable of absorbing the greatest capitals. [p. 354]

The establishment of the European colonies in America and the West Indies arose from no necessity: and though the utility which has resulted from them has been very great, it is not altogether so clear and evident. It was not understood at their first establishment, and was not the motive either of that establishment or of the discoveries which gave occasion to it; and the nature, extent, and limits of that utility are not, perhaps, well understood at this day. . . .

A project of commerce to the East Indies . . . gave occasion to the first discovery of the West. A project of conquest gave occasion to all the establishments of the Spaniards in those newly discovered countries.

4

The motive which excited them to this conquest was a project of gold and silver mines; and a course of accidents, which no human wisdom could foresee, rendered this project much more successful than the undertakers had any reasonable grounds for expecting. . . .

The stock . . . which has improved the sugar colonies of France, particularly the great colony of St Domingo, has been raised almost entirely from the gradual improvement and cultivation of those colonies. It has been almost altogether the produce of the soil and of the industry of the colonists, or, what comes to the same thing, the price of that produce gradually accumulated by good management, and employed in raising a still greater produce. But the stock which has improved and cultivated the sugar colonies of England has, a great part of it, been sent out from England, and has by no means been altogether the produce of the soil and industry of the colonists. [*Note. The West India merchants and planters asserted, in 1775, that there was capital worth £60,000,000 in the sugar colonies and that half of this belonged to residents in Great Britain.*] The prosperity of the English sugar colonies has been, in a great measure, owing to the great riches of England, of which a part has overflowed, if one may say so, upon those colonies. . . .

The policy of Europe, therefore, has very little to boast of, either in the original establishment, or, so far as concerns their internal government, in the subsequent prosperity of the colonies of America. . . . The government of Spain contributed scarce anything to any of them. That of England contributed as little towards effectuating the establishment of some of its most important colonies in North America.

When those establishments were affectuated, and had become so considerable as to attract the attention of the mother country, the first regulations which she made with regard to them had always in view to secure to herself the monopoly of their commerce; to confine their market, and to enlarge her own at their expense, and consequently, rather to damp and discourage, than to quicken and forward the course of their prosperity. In the different ways in which this monopoly has been exercised, consists one of the most essential differences in the policy of the different European nations with regard to their colonies. The best of them all, that of England, is only somewhat less illiberal and oppressive than that of any of the rest.

In what way, therefore, has the policy of Europe contributed either to the first establishment, or to the present grandeur of the colonies of America? In one way, and in one way only, it has contributed a good deal. Magna virum Mater! It bred and formed the men who were capable of achieving such great actions, and of laying the foundation of so great an empire; and there is no other quarter of the world of which the policy is capable of forming, or has ever actually and in fact formed such men. The colonies owe to the policy of Europe the education and great views of their active and enterprising founders; and some of the greatest and most important of them . . . owe to it scarce any thing else.

Such are the advantages which the colonies of America have derived from the policy of Europe.

What are those which Europe has derived from the discovery and colonization of America? . . .

The general advantages which Europe, considered as one great country, has derived from the discovery and colonization of America, consists, first, in the increase of its enjoyments; and secondly, in the augmentation of its industry.

The surplus produce of America, imported into Europe, furnishes the inhabitants of this great continent with a variety of commodities which they could not otherwise have possessed, some for conveniency and use, some for pleasure, and some for ornament, and thereby contributes to increase their enjoyments.

The discovery and colonization of America . . . have contributed to augment the industry, first, of all the countries which trade to it directly; such as Spain, Portugal, France and England; and, secondly, of all those which, without trading to it directly, send, through the medium of other countries, goods to it of their own produce. . . . All such countries have evidently gained a more extensive market for their surplus produce, and must consequently have been encouraged to increase its quantity. . . .

The exclusive trade of the mother countries tends to diminish, or, at least, to keep down below what they would otherwise rise to, both the enjoyments and industry of all those nations in general, and of the American colonies in particular. . . . By rendering the colony produce dearer in all other countries, it lessens its consumption, and thereby cramps the industry of the colonies, and both the enjoyments and the industry of all other countries, which both enjoy less when they pay more for what they enjoy, and produce less when they get less for what they produce. By rendering the produce of all other countries dearer in the colonies, it cramps, in the same manner, the industry of all other countries, and both the enjoyments and the industry of the colonies. . . . The surplus produce of the colonies, however, is the original source of all that increase of enjoyments and industry which Europe derives from the discovery and colonization of America; and the exclusive trade of the mother countries tends to render this source much less abundant than it otherwise would be. . . . [pp. 525, 531, 554-8]

The most advantageous employment of any capital to the country to which it belongs, is that which maintains there the greatest quantity of productive labour, and increases the most the annual produce of the land and labour of that country. But the quantity of productive labour which any capital employed in the foreign trade of consumption can maintain, is exactly in proportion . . . to the frequency of its returns. . . .

The monopoly of the colony trade, so far as it has operated upon the employment of the capital of Great Britain, has in all cases forced some part of it from a foreign trade of consumption carried on with a neighbouring, to one carried on with a more distant country, and in many cases from a direct foreign trade of consumption to a round-about one. . . .

In a trade of which the returns are very distant, the profit of the merchant may be as great or greater than in one in which they are very frequent and near; but the advantage of the country in which he resides . . . must always be much less. [pp. 565, 568]

The effect of the colony trade in its natural and free state, is to open a great, though distant market for such parts of the produce of British industry as may exceed the demand of the markets nearer home. . . . In its natural and free state, the colony trade, without drawing from those markets any part of the produce which had ever been sent to them, encourages Great Britain to increase the surplus continually, by continually presenting new equivalents to be exchanged for it. . . . The new market, without drawing any thing from the old one, would create . . . a new produce for its own supply; and that new produce would constitute a new capital for carrying on the new employment, which in the same manner would draw nothing from the old one.

The monopoly of the colony trade, on the contrary, by excluding the competition of other nations, and thereby raising the rate of profit both in the new market and in the new employment, draws profit from the old market and capital from the old employment. . . . It keeps down the revenue of the inhabitants of that country, below what it

7

would naturally rise to, and thereby diminishes their power of accumulation. It not only hinders, at all times, their capital from maintaining so great a quantity of productive labour as it would otherwise maintain, but it hinders it from increasing so fast as it would otherwise increase, and consequently from maintaining a still greater quantity of productive labour. [p. 574]

The Wealth of Nations (1776); ed. E. Cannan, New York, The Modern Library, 1937.

2 The Pressure of Population on Land

T. R. MALTHUS

Malthus (1766–1834) is famous mainly for his pessimistic theory (which was not itself original) that population would always tend to outstrip production of food; so that limitation of the size of families was essential. From this basis he worked out the principle of diminishing returns from investment in land or industry which provided a better explanation of the tendency of the rate of profit to decline than Smith's theory. This was adopted by Ricardo and became an integral part of classical economics. The Essay on Population was first published in 1798, but the extract comes from the second edition of 1803. The Principles of Political Economy was first published in 1820 and shows the influence of Ricardo.

The principal object of the present essay is to examine the effects of one great cause intimately united with the very nature of man; which, though it has been constantly and powerfully operating since the commencement of society, has been little noticed by the writers who have treated this subject. . . .

The cause to which I allude is the constant tendency in all animated life to increase beyond the nourishment prepared for it. . . .

It may safely be pronounced . . . that population, when unchecked, goes on doubling itself every twenty-five years, or increases in a geometrical ratio.

The rate according to which the productions of the earth may be supposed to increase, it will not be so easy to determine. Of this, however, we may be perfectly certain, that the ratio of their increase in a limited territory must be of a totally different nature from the ratio of the increase of population. A thousand millions are just as easily doubled every twenty-five years by the power of population as a thousand. But the food to support the increase from the greater number will by no means be obtained with the same facility. Man is necessarily confined in room. When acre has been added to acre till all the fertile land is occupied, the yearly increase of food must depend upon the melioration of the land already in possession. This is a fund, which, from the nature of all soils, instead of increasing, must be gradually diminishing. But population, could it be supplied with food, would go on with unexhausted vigour; and the increase of one period would furnish the power of a greater increase the next, and this without any limit. [I, pp. 5, 8]

It may be fairly pronounced, therefore, that, considering the present average state of the earth, the means of subsistence, under circumstances the most favourable to human industry, could not possibly be made to increase faster than in an arithmetical ratio.

The necessary effects of these two different rates of increase, when brought together, will be very striking. . . . Taking the whole earth, instead of this island, emigration would of course be excluded; and, supposing the present population equal to a thousand millions, the human species would increase as the numbers, 1, 2, 4, 8, 16, 32, 64, 128, 256, and subsistence as 1, 2, 3, 4, 5, 6, 7, 8, 9. In two centuries the population would be as to the means of subsistence as 256 to 9; in three centuries as 4096 to 13, and in two thousand years the difference would be almost incalculable. [I, pp. 10–11]

A country which excels in commerce and manufactures may purchase corn from a great variety of others; and it may be supposed, perhaps, that, proceeding upon this system, it may continue to purchase an increasing quantity, and to maintain a rapidly increasing population, till the lands of all the nations with which it trades are fully cultivated. As this is an event necessarily at a great distance, it may appear that the population of such a country will not be checked from the difficulty of procuring subsistence till after the lapse of a great number of ages.

There are, however, causes constantly in operation which will occasion the pressure of this difficulty long before the event here contemplated has taken place, and while the means of raising food in the surrounding countries may still be comparatively abundant.

In the first place, advantages which depend exclusively upon capital and skill, and the present possession of particular channels of commerce, cannot in their nature be permanent. . . . It is unreasonable . . . to expect that any one country, merely by the force of skill and capital, should remain in possession of markets uninterrupted by foreign competition. But, when a powerful foreign competition takes place, the exportable commodities of the country in question must soon fall to prices which will essentially reduce profits; and the fall of profits will diminish both the power and the will to save. Under these circumstances the accumulation of capital will be slow, and the demand for labour proportionably slow, till it comes nearly to a stand; while, perhaps, the new competitors, either by raising their own raw materials or by some other advantages, may still be increasing their capitals and population with some degree of rapidity.

But, secondly, even if it were possible for a considerable time to exclude any formidable foreign competition, it is found that domestic competition produces almost unavoidably the same effects. If a machine be invented in a particular country, by the aid of which one man can do the work of ten, the possessors of it will of course at first make very unusual profits; but, as soon as the invention is generally known, so much capital and industry will be brought into this new and profitable employment, as to make its products greatly exceed both the foreign and domestic demand at the old prices. These prices, therefore, will continue to fall, till the stock and labour employed in this direction cease to yield unusual profits. . . .

This country, from the extent of its lands, and its rich colonial possessions, has a large *arena* for the employment of an increasing capital; and the general rate of its profits is not, as it appears, very easily and rapidly reduced by accumulation. But a country . . . engaged principally in manufactures, and unable to direct its industry to the same variety of pursuits, would sooner find its rate of profits diminished by an increase of capital, and no ingenuity of machinery which was not continually progressive could save it, after a certain period, from low profits and low wages, and their natural consequences, a check to population. [II, pp. 79–81]

A country which raises its own food cannot by any sort of foreign competition be reduced at once to a necessarily declining population.

If the exports of a merely commercial country be essentially diminished by foreign competition, it may lose, in a very short time, its power of supporting the same number of people; but if the exports of a country which has resources in land be diminished, it will merely lose some of its foreign conveniences and luxuries. . . . It may indeed be checked in the rate of its progress for a time by the want of the same stimulus; but there is no reason for its becoming retrograde; and there is no doubt that the capital thrown out of employment by the loss of foreign trade will not lie idle. It will find some channel in which it can be employed with advantage, though not with the same advantage as before; and will be able to maintain an increasing population, though not increasing at the same rate as under the stimulus of a prosperous foreign trade. . . .

We must not, however, imagine that there is no limit to this progress though it is distant, and has certainly not been attained by any large landed nation yet known.

We have already seen that the limit to the population of commercial nations is the period when, from the actual state of foreign markets, they are unable regularly to import an increasing quantity of food. And the limit to the population of a nation which raises the whole of its food on its own territory is, when the land has been so fully occupied and worked, that the employment of another labourer on it will not, on an average, raise an additional quantity of food sufficient to support a family of such a size as will admit of an increase of population.

This is evidently the extreme practical limit to the progress of population. . . .

It is also of great importance to recollect that, long before this practical limit is attained in any country, the rate of the increase of population will gradually diminish. When the capital of a country becomes stationary from bad government, indolence, extravagance, or a sudden shock to commerce, it is just possible that the check to population may . . . be sudden, though, in that case, it cannot take place without a considerable convulsion. But when the capital of a country comes to a stop from the continued progress of accumulation and the exhaustion of the cultivable land, both the profits of stock and the wages of labour must have been gradually diminishing for a long period, till they are both ultimately so low as to afford no further encouragement to an increase of stock, and no further means for the support of an increasing population. If we could suppose that the capital employed upon the land was, at all times, as great as could possibly be applied with the same profit, and there were no agricultural improvements to save labour, it is obvious that, as accumulation proceeded, profits and wages would regularly fall, and the diminished rate in the progress of population would be quite regular. But practically this can never happen; and various causes, both natural and artificial, will concur to prevent this regularity, and occasion great variations at different times in the rate at which the population proceeds towards its final limit.

In the first place, land is practically almost always understocked with capital. . . .

Secondly; improvements in agriculture. If new and superior modes of cultivation be invented, by which not only the land is better managed, but is worked with less labour, it is obvious that inferior land may be cultivated at higher profits than could be obtained from richer land before; and an improved system of culture, with the use of better instruments, may, for a long period, more than counterbalance the tendency of an extended cultivation and a great increase of capital to yield smaller proportionate returns.

Thirdly; improvements in manufactures. When by increased skill and the invention of improved machinery in manufactures one man becomes capable of doing as much as eight or ten could before, it is well known that, from the principle of home competition and the consequent great increase of quantity, the prices of such manufactures will greatly fall; and, as far as they include the necessaries and accustomed conveniences of labourers and farmers, they must tend to diminish that portion of the value of the whole produce which is consumed necessarily on the land, and leave a larger remainder. From this larger remainder may be drawn a higher rate of profits, notwithstanding the increase of capital and extension of cultivation.

Fourthly; the prosperity of foreign commerce. If from a prosperous foreign commerce our labour and domestic commodities rise considerably in price, while foreign commodities are advanced comparatively very little, an event which is very common, it is evident that the farmer or labourer will be able to obtain the tea, sugar . . . etc., which he stands in need of, for a smaller quantity of corn or labour than before; and this increased power of purchasing foreign commodities will have precisely the same effect, in allowing the means of an extended cultivation without a fall of profits, as the improvements in manufactures just referred to. . . .

Though it is unquestionably and necessarily true, therefore, that the *tendency* of a continually increasing capital and extending cultivation is to occasion a progressive fall both of profits and wages; yet the causes above enumerated are evidently sufficient to account for great and long irregularities in this progress. . . .

There is, however, a limit, which, if the capital and population of a country continue increasing, they must ultimately reach and cannot pass; and . . . this limit, upon the principle of private property, must be far short of the utmost power of the earth to produce food. [II, pp. 88–96]

An Essay on Population (2nd edn., 1803). 2 vols. Dent, Everyman's Library.

3 Overproduction and Underconsumption
SISMONDI

J.-C.-L. Simonde de Sismondi (1773–1842) was a Swiss historian, economist and publicist with strong radical leanings. His economic ideas derived from Smith; but observation of social conditions generally and of the economic crisis of 1819 in England convinced him that the equilibrium between production and consumption which Smith and Say assumed to be automatic was unreal. Sismondi maintained that capitalism was basically unstable because of the inability of the workers to consume the fruits of production: that collectively they were not paid enough to buy all they produced. Therefore periodical crises were bound to occur in which there was a general glut, and underconsumption would become general unless markets could be continuously expanded. His ideas were taken up by the German, Rodbertus; by some Marxists, such as Rosa Luxemburg; and by J. A. Hobson, who later produced a more sophisticated theory of underconsumption. This extract is from Nouveaux Principes d'économie politique, *which was first published in 1819, though the text used here is from a reprint of the revised edition of 1827.*

The rich man contributes to the welfare of the poor when he saves from his income to add to his capital. Because it is he who shares out the total product annually, he keeps for his own consumption whatever he designates as revenue; but what he calls capital he hands over to the poor man as his income. Yet the rich man, when he makes this division, must have one other consideration in mind: he must never encourage work for which there is no demand, for the product of work which he orders without good reason will either not sell or will sell at a bad price. Then the profits for which he was looking in the following year will either be reduced or may even be replaced by a loss; and, having brought into existence a population of working men who have only their hands with which to earn a living, he will deprive them of the livelihood which he had led them to expect in return for their work. [I, p. 105]

Every technical improvement which has been applied to the methods of industry, unless it was the result of a new demand and was followed by greater consumption, has had virtually the same effects. It has, though very indirectly, killed men who were once producers and who are ignored once dead. It has also enriched new producers near to the inventor who, because they do not know their victims, assumed that each discovery was a benefit for humanity. . . .

When the large unit of agriculture succeeded to the small, perhaps more capital was absorbed by the land and was returned by it; and more wealth could perhaps be divided between the total of those engaged in agriculture. But the consumption of a single family of rich farmers, added to that of fifty families of very poor day-labourers, is not worth as much to the nation as was previously that of fifty peasant families, none of whom was rich, but none of whom lacked reasonable comfort. The same is true of the towns. The amount consumed by a single factory-owning millionaire, who employs a thousand workers on a subsistence wage, is not worth as much to the nation as the consumption of a hundred much less wealthy craftsmen, none of whom employs more than ten workers but who are much less poor than the factory hands. . . .

If, under these conditions, there is to be no check to employment and no general hardship, it is essential that the single rich family, which has taken control of the income once divided between the hundred, accounts for all the consumption which ninety-nine can no longer afford between them. Doubtless this one family will maintain a number of domestic servants who will help them to consume the fruits of the earth. But it will be less the agriculture of their own country that will be stimulated by their way of living than that of the most distant climates. In the same way, the one rich family could never by itself use the quantity of clothing and furniture which cannot now be bought by the ninety-nine others. It will magnificently reward the work, the good taste and style of a single craftsman, but it will leave without work nine-tenths of those national manufactures to which the more comfortably-off families no longer give employment.

It is worth comment that, whereas the general effect of the increase of capital is to concentrate opportunities for work in large-scale manufactures, the effect of great riches is almost entirely to exclude the products of these large-scale manufactures from the range of things bought by the rich. Every time some object which was previously made by a craftsman becomes the product of some blind machine, it loses something of its perfection and so also its value in the eyes of the fashionable. . . .

In this way, then, as a result of the concentration of wealth in the hands of a few owners, the internal market becomes ever more restricted and industry is more and more forced to find its markets overseas, where yet greater dangers threaten it.

Every state whose production is greater than its consumption turns equally toward this overseas market; and, though its limits are unknown, its size may seem unlimited. Nonetheless, now that sea transport is perfected, the trade routes are open, and safety is more certain, it begins to be evident that the world market was after all as restricted as that of the nation previously; that the general belief among all producers that they could sell to foreigners had increased production beyond the demand; and that the great reduction of price which the producers of one country were offering to the consumers of another was at the same time a verdict of death for the producers of that country. The resistance offered to this commercial attack has been violent and immoderate, but almost always supported by the people of these countries, however much this may at first sight be contrary to the interest of the inhabitants of the country as a whole in their capacity as consumers.

Hence, what we have seen at the beginning of this chapter to be true of the internal market – that it could only be extended by general prosperity – is becoming true also of the world market for any country which sends its products overseas and which wants a worldwide trade: the extension of the world market can result only from world prosperity. There is no other way in which men can obtain more income, satisfy new needs and buy what we want to sell them.

In this way the market for manufactures can be extended, and this should be the noblest ambition of the statesman, through the progress of civilization, the increase of comfort, and the promotion of security and goodwill in barbarian nations. Europe has arrived at the point at which she has everywhere an industry and a quantity of manufactures greater than her needs; but, if an ill-judged policy on her part does not check the progress of civilization among her neighbours, the level of consumption in these different countries will increase fast enough to employ all the excess labour which Europe does not know how to use, and will end the hardship into which the poor are now plunged. [I, pp. 263, 270–2]

Provided that a nation finds at its doorstep a market large enough to absorb all it can produce quickly and profitably, each of these technical discoveries is an advantage, because, rather than diminish the number of workers, it increases the volume of work and its products. Any country which takes the initiative in making such discoveries will for a long time succeed in extending its market in proportion to the number of men which each new invention leaves unemployed. She can employ them immediately by increasing those products which her invention enables her to provide at a lower price. But there will eventually come the day when the whole civilized world forms a single market, and when it will no longer be possible to find new customers in any new country. The total demand of the world market will then be an exact quantity for which the various industrial countries will compete. If one gains an advantage it will be at the expense of another. The total market cannot then be increased except through the general increase of wealth, or because types of articles once reserved for the rich become available to the poor. [II, p. 211]

Nouveaux Principes d'économie politique (1819; 2nd edn 1827). 2 vols., Geneva, Paris, Jeheber, 1951, trans D. K. F.

4 Declining Profits and the Problem of Wages

DAVID RICARDO

David Ricardo (1772–1823), a stockbroker of Jewish origin, became interested in economics through his study of monetary and tax questions. His Principles of Political Economy and Taxation, *first published in 1817, derived from Adam Smith, but showed the influence of Malthus's ideas. This and other works by Ricardo became central to classical theories of economics, and also had great influence on other theorists such as Marx. In this extract Ricardo maintains that only a rise of wages could reduce the profits of capital; and that there could only be a surplus of capital if a reduction of profits made it unprofitable to invest at home.*

The natural tendency of profits . . . is to fall; for, in the progress of society and wealth, the additional quantity of food required is obtained by the sacrifice of more and more labour. This tendency, this gravitation as it were of profits, is happily checked at repeated intervals by the improvements in machinery connected with the production of necessaries, as well as by discoveries in the science of agriculture, which enable us to relinquish a portion of labour before required, and therefore to lower the price of the prime necessary of the labourer. The rise in the price of necessaries and in the wages of labour is, however, limited; for as soon as wages should be equal . . . to . . . the whole receipts of the farmer, there must be an end of accumulation; for no capital can then yield any profit whatever, and no additional labour can be demanded, and consequently population will have reached its highest point. Long, indeed, before this period, the very low rate of profits will have arrested all accumulation, and almost the whole produce of the country, after paying the labourers, will be the property of the owners of land and the receivers of tithes and taxes. [pp. 66–7]

There are two ways in which capital may be accumulated; it may be saved either in consequence of increased revenue, or of diminished consumption. . . .

If, by the introduction of machinery, the generality of the commodities on which revenue was expended fell 20 per cent in value, I should be enabled to save as effectually as if my revenue had been raised 20 per cent; but in one case the rate of profits is stationary, in the other it is raised 20 per cent. If, by the introduction of cheap foreign goods, I can save 20 per cent from my expenditure, the effect will be precisely the same as if machinery had lowered the expense of their production, but profits would not be raised.

It is not, therefore, in consequence of the extension of the market that the rate of profit is raised, although such extension may be equally efficacious in increasing the mass of commodities, and may thereby enable us to augment the funds destined for the maintenance of labour, and the materials on which labour may be employed. It is quite as important to the happiness of mankind, that our enjoyments should be increased by the better distribution of labour, by each country producing those commodities for which by its situation, its climate, and its other natural or artificial advantages, it is adapted, and by their exchanging them for the commodities of other countries, as that they should be augmented by a rise in the rate of profits.

It has been my endeavour to show throughout this work, that the rate of profits can never be increased but by a fall in wages, and that there can be no permanent fall of wages but in consequence of a fall of the necessaries on which wages are expended. If, therefore, by the extension of foreign trade, or by improvements in machinery, the food and necessaries of the labourer can be brought to market, at a reduced price, profits will rise. If, instead of growing our own corn, or manufacturing the clothing and other necessaries of the labourer, we discover a new market from which we can supply ourselves with these commodities at a cheaper price, wages will fall and profits rise; but if the commodities obtained at a cheaper rate, by the extension of foreign commerce, or by the improvement of machinery, be exclusively the commodities consumed by the rich, no alteration will take place in the rate of profits. The rate of wages would not be affected, although wine, velvets, silks, and other expensive commodities should fall 50 per cent, and consequently profits would continue unaltered.

Foreign trade, then, though highly beneficial to a country, as it increases the amount and variety of the objects on which revenue may be expended, and affords, by the abundance and cheapness of commodities, incentives to saving, and to the accumulation of capital, has no tendency to raise the profits of stock, unless the commodities imported be of that description on which the wages of labour are expended. . . .

The same rule which regulates the relative value of commodities in one country, does not regulate the relative value of commodities exchanged between two or more countries.

Under a system of perfectly free commerce, each country naturally devotes its capital and labour to such employments as are most beneficial to each. . . . It is this principle which determines that wine shall be made in France and Portugal, that corn shall be grown in America and Poland, and that hardware and other goods shall be manufactured in England.

In one and the same country, profits are, generally speaking, always on the same level; or differ only as the employment of capital may be more or less secure and agreeable. It is not so between different countries. If the profits of capital employed in Yorkshire, should exceed those of capital employed in London, capital would speedily move from London to Yorkshire, and an equality of profits would be effected; but if in consequence of the diminished rate of production in the lands of England, from the increase of capital and population, wages should rise, and profits fall, it would not follow that capital and population would necessarily move from England to Holland, or Spain, or Russia, where profits might be higher. . . .

Experience . . . shows, that the fancied or real insecurity of capital, when not under the immediate control of its owner, together with the natural disinclination which every man has to quit the country of his birth and connexions, and intrust himself, with all his habits fixed, to a strange government and new laws, check the emigration of capital. These feelings . . . induce most men of property to be satisfied with a low rate of profits in their own country, rather than seek a more advantageous employment for their wealth in foreign nations. [pp. 74–7]

From the account which has been given of the profits of stock, it will appear that no accumulation of capital will permanently lower profits, unless there be some permanent cause for the rise of wages. . . . Adam Smith, however, uniformly ascribes the fall of profits to the accumulation of capital, and to the competition which will result from it, without ever adverting to the increasing difficulty of providing food for the additional number of labourers which the additional capital will employ. . . . M. Say has, however, most satisfactorily shown, that there is no amount of capital which may not be employed in a country, because demand is only limited by production. No man produces but with a view to consume or sell, and he never sells but with an intention to purchase some other commodity, which may be immediately useful to him, or which may contribute to future production. By producing, then, he necessarily becomes either the consumer of his own goods, or the purchaser and consumer of the goods of some other person. It is not to be supposed that he should, for any length of time, be ill-informed of the commodities which he can most advantageously produce, to attain the object which he has in view, namely, the possession of other goods; and, therefore, it is not probable that he will continually produce a commodity for which there is no demand.

There cannot, then, be accumulated in a country any amount of capital which cannot be employed productively, until wages rise so high in consequence of the rise of necessaries, and so little consequently remains for the profits of stock, that the motive for accumulation ceases. While the profits of stock are high, men will have a motive to accumulate. Whilst a man has any wished-for gratification unsupplied, he will have a demand for more commodities; and it will be an effectual demand while he has any new value to offer in exchange for them. . . .

There is only one case, and that will be temporary, in which the accumulation of capital with a low price of food may be attended with a fall of profits; and that is, when the funds for the maintenance of labour increase much more rapidly than population; – wages will then be high, and profits low. If every man were to forego the use of luxuries, and be intent only on accumulation, a quantity of necessaries might be produced, for which there could not be any immediate consumption. Of commodities so limited in number, there might undoubtedly be a universal glut, and consequently there might neither be demand for an additional quantity of such commodities, nor profits on the employment of more capital. If men ceased to consume, they would cease to produce. This admission does not impugn the general principle. In such a country as England, for example, it is difficult to suppose that there can be any disposition to devote the whole capital and labour of the country to the production of necessaries only.

When merchants engage their capitals in foreign trade, or in the carrying trade, it is always from choice, and never from necessity: it is because in that trade their profits will be somewhat greater than in the home trade. . . .

Adam Smith, however, speaks of the carrying trade as one not of choice, but of necessity; as if the capital engaged in it would be inert if not so employed, as if the capital in the home trade could overflow, if not confined to a limited amount. . . .

But could not this portion of the productive labour of Great Britain be employed in preparing some other sort of goods, with which something more in demand at home might be purchased? And if it could not, might we not employ this productive labour, though with less advantage, in making those goods in demand at home, or at least some substitute for them? If we wanted velvets, might we not attempt to make velvets; and if we could not succeed, might we not make more cloth, or some other object desirable to us?·

We manufacture commodities, and with them buy goods abroad, because we can obtain a greater quantity than we could make at home. Deprive us of this trade, and we immediately manufacture again for ourselves. . . .

It follows, then, from these admissions, that there is no limit to demand – no limit to the employment of capital while it yields any profit, and that however abundant capital may become, there is no other adequate reason for a fall of profit but a rise of wages, and further, it may be added that the only adequate and permanent cause for the rise of wages is the increasing difficulty of providing food and necessaries for the increasing number of workmen. [pp. 174–8]

Principles of Political Economy and Taxation (1817); ed. J. R. McCulloch, John Murray, 1888.

5 Declining Productivity and Profits

T. R. MALTHUS

It has been stated in the preceding section, that the varying rate of profits depends upon the causes which alter the proportion between the value of the advances necessary to production, and the value of the produce obtained.

The two main causes which affect these proportions, are, the productiveness, or unproductiveness of the last capitals employed upon the land, by which a smaller, or a greater proportion of the value of the produce is capable of supporting the labourers employed. This may be called the *limiting* principle of profits. And, secondly, the varying value of the produce of the same quantity of labour occasioned by the accidental or ordinary state of the demand and supply, by which a greater or smaller proportion of that produce falls to the share of the labourers employed. This may be called the *regulating* principle of profits, this second cause is constantly modifying the first, but it will be desirable to consider them separately.

If then we suppose the first cause to operate singly, and the corn wages of the individual labourer to be always the same, the whole skill in agriculture remained unchanged, and there were no taxes nor any means of obtaining corn from foreign countries, the rate of profits must regularly fall, as the society advanced, and as it became necessary to resort to inferior machines which required more labour to put in action. . . .

It is evident that if the number of labourers necessary to obtain a given produce were continually increasing, and the corn wages of each labourer remained the same, the portion destined to the payment of labour would be continually encroaching upon the portion destined to the payment of profits; and the rate of profits would of course continue regularly diminishing till, from the want of power or will to save, the progress of accumulation had ceased.

In this case, and supposing an equal demand for all the parts of the same produce, it is obvious that the profits of capital in agriculture would be in proportion to the fertility of the last land taken into cultivation, or to the amount of the produce obtained by a given quantity of labour. And as profits in the same country tend to an equality, the general rate of profits would follow the same course. . . .

The second cause which affects profits, is the varying value of the produce of the same quantity of labour on the same value of capital, determined by the state of the demand and supply. This may be called the regulating principle of profits, as within the extreme limits prescribed by the state of the land, all the variations of profits, whether temporary or durable, are regulated by it.

Such variations in the value of produce are occasioned principally by the abundance or scantiness of capital, including the funds for the maintenance of labour, as compared with the labour which it employs.

This is obviously a cause which, by awarding a greater or a smaller *proportion* of the produce to the labourer, must have a powerful influence on profits; and if considerable variations were to take place in the supplies of capital and produce and the supplies of labour, in a rich and unexhausted soil, the same effects might be produced on profits as by the operation of the first cause, and in a much shorter time. . . .

So entirely, indeed, does the rate of profits depend on the division of the produce, occasioned by the state of the supply and the demand, that in comparing two countries together, the rate of profits will sometimes be found the lowest in that country, in which the productiveness of labour on the land is the greatest.

In Poland, and some other parts of Europe, where capital is scarce, profits are said to be higher than in America; yet it is probable that the last land taken into cultivation in America is much richer than the last land taken into cultivation in Poland. But in America the labourer earns perhaps the value of eighteen or twenty quarters of wheat in the year; in Poland only the value of eight or nine quarters of rye. This difference in the division of the produce, must make a great difference in the rate of profits; yet the causes which determine this division, far from being of so temporary a nature that they may be safely overlooked, might operate most powerfully for a great length of time. Such is the extent of America, that the corn wages of its labour may not essentially fall for a long term of years; and the effects of a scanty but stationary capital on an overflowing but stationary population might last for ever. . . .

When cultivation is pushed to its extreme practical limits, that is, when the labour of a man upon the last land taken into cultivation will scarcely do more than support such a family as is necessary to maintain a stationary population, it is evident that no other cause or causes can prevent profits from sinking to the lowest rate required to maintain the actual capital. But though this principle is finally of the very greatest power, yet its progress is extremely slow and gradual; and while it is proceeding with scarcely perceptible steps to its final destination, the second cause is producing effects which entirely overcome it, and often for twenty or thirty, or even 100 years together, make the rate of profits take a course absolutely different from what it ought to be according to the first cause. [pp. 271–82]

Those who reject mere population as an adequate stimulus to the increase of wealth, are generally disposed to make everything depend upon accumulation. It is certainly true that no permanent and continued increase of wealth can take place without a continued increase of capital. . . .

But we have yet to inquire what is the state of things which generally disposes a nation to accumulate; and further, what is the state of things which tends to make that accumulation the most effective and lead to a further and continued increase of capital and wealth.

It is undoubtedly possible by parsimony to devote at once a much larger share than usual of the produce of any country to the maintenance of productive labour; and suppose this to be done, it is quite true that the labourers so employed are consumers as well as those engaged in personal services, and that as far as the labourers are concerned, there would be no diminution of consumption or demand. But . . . the consumption and demand occasioned by the workmen employed in productive labour can never *alone* furnish a motive to the accumulation and employment of capital; and with regard to the capitalists themselves, together with the landlords and other rich persons, they have, by the supposition, agreed to be parsimonious, and by depriving themselves of their usual conveniences and luxuries to save from their revenue and add to their capital. Under these circumstances, it is impossible that the increased quantity of commodities, obtained by the increased number of productive labourers, should find purchasers, without such a fall of price as would probably sink their value below that of the outlay, or, at least, so reduce profits as very greatly to diminish both the power and the will to save.

It has been thought by some very able writers, that although there may easily be a glut of particular commodities, there cannot possibly be a glut of commodities in general; because, according to their view of the subject, commodities being always exchanged for commodities, one half will furnish a market for the other half, and production being thus the sole source of demand, an excess in the supply of one article merely proves a deficiency in the supply of some other, and a general excess is impossible. M. Say . . . has indeed gone so far as to state that the consumption of a commodity by taking it out of the market diminished demand, and the production of a commodity proportionably increases it.

This doctrine, however, as generally applied, appears to me to be utterly unfounded, and completely to contradict the great principles which regulate supply and demand.

It is by no means true, as a matter of fact, that commodities are always exchanged for commodities. An immense mass of commodities is exchanged directly, either for productive labour, or personal services: and it is quite obvious, that this mass of commodities, compared with the labour with which it is to be exchanged, may fall in value from a glut just as any one commodity falls in value from an excess of supply, compared either with labour or money.

In the case supposed there would evidently be an unusual quantity of commodities of all kinds in the market, owing to those who had been before engaged in personal services having been converted, by the accumulation of capital, into productive labourers; while the number of labourers altogether being the same, and the power and will to purchase for consumption among landlords and capitalists being by supposition diminished, commodities would necessarily fall in value compared with labour, so as very greatly to lower profits, and to check for a time further production. But this is precisely what is meant by the term glut, which, in this case, is evidently general not partial.

M. Say, Mr Mill, and Mr Ricardo, the principal authors of these new doctrines, appear to me to have fallen into some fundamental errors in the view which they have taken of this subject. . . . [pp. 314-16]

If one fourth of the capital of a country were suddenly destroyed, or entirely transferred to a different part of the world, without any other cause occurring of a diminished demand for commodities, this scantiness of capital would certainly occasion great inconvenience to consumers, and great distress among the working classes; but it would be attended with great advantages to the remaining capitalists. Commodities, in general, would be scarce, and bear a high price on account of the deficiency in the means of producing them. Nothing would be so easy as to find a profitable employment for capital; but it would by no means be easy to find capital for the number of employments in which it was deficient; and consequently the rate of profits would be very high. In this state of things there would be an immediate and pressing demand for capital, on account of there being an immediate and pressing demand for commodities; and the obvious remedy would be, the supply of the demand in the only way in which it could take place, namely, by saving from revenue to add to capital. This supply of capital would . . . take place just upon the same principle as a supply of population would follow a great destruction of people on the supposition of there being an immediate and pressing want of labour evinced by the high real wages given to the labourer.

On the other hand, if the capital of the country were diminished by the failure of demand in some large branches of trade, which had before been very prosperous, and absorbed a great quantity of stock; or even if, while capital were suddenly destroyed, the revenue of the landlords was diminished in a greater proportion owing to peculiar circumstances, the state of things, with the exception of the distresses of the poor, would be almost exactly reversed. The remaining capitalists would be in no respect benefited by events which had diminished demand in a still greater proportion than they had diminished the supply. Commodities would be everywhere cheap. Capital would be seeking employment, but would not easily find it; and the profits of stock would be low. There would be no pressing and immediate demand for capital, because there would be no pressing and immediate demand for commodities; and, under these circumstances, the saving from revenue to add to capital, instead of affording the remedy required, would only aggravate the distresses of the capitalists, and fill the stream of capital which was flowing out of the country. [pp. 414–15]

Principles of Political Economy (2nd edn. 1836); Blackwell, 1951.

6 A Theory of Economic Imperialism
E. G. WAKEFIELD

E. G. Wakefield (1796–1862) was a publicist of other men's ideas and a practical projector of new colonies rather than an economist; but his contemporary influence, notably on J. S. Mill, was considerable. The Art of Colonization, *published in 1849, represented his mature ideas on 'systematic colonization' which he first put forward in 1829 in his* Letter from Sydney. *In this extract he argues for colonization on the grounds put forward by Smith and without the refinements added by others. He also adopts Smith's explanation of the higher profitability of new land in colonies. His importance is that, by linking the two propositions, he contrived a theory that surplus capital could most profitably be invested in colonies, and so supplied a positive argument for colonization. In a crude form this approximated to a theory of capitalist imperialism.*

There is a general circumstance, comprising many particulars, by which Great Britain is at present distinguished from all other countries. That circumstance may be termed a want of room for people of all classes. The peculiarity consists, not in mere want of room, for that is felt by some classes in old countries generally, but in the extension of the want to all classes. . . .

By a want of room, I mean a want of the means of a comfortable subsistence according to the respective standards of living established among the classes, and obviously arising from the competition of the members of each class with one another. Whatever the fund for the maintenance of any of the classes, it is divided amongst too many people; there are too many competitors for a limited fund of enjoyment. . . .

The hurtful competition of labourers with each other is an old story . . .; that of the other classes had not been noticed till it was pointed out by the colonizing theorists of 1830. Indeed it was then a new circumstance in our political economy, having grown up from 1815, with the cessation of war, which promoted a rapid increase of capital; with the improvement and spread of education, which augmented the numbers of the educated classes; and with the diminution of public expenditure, which cut down the fund for the maintenance of the children of the gentry. Since 1830, this competition . . . has been continually on the increase. [pp. 65–6]

With regard to the competition of capital with capital, I would only explain further, that it appears to be the immediate cause of all the other competitions. Our power of increasing capital seems to be unlimited. If the continually-increasing capital of Great Britain could be continually invested so as to yield high profits, the labourers' competition would cease, because there would be ample employment at good wages for the whole class. . . . The one thing needful for all society is more room for the profitable employment of capital: it is in the excess of capital above the means of profitable investment, that this country differs injuriously from the United States. Do you adopt this proposition? if not, you will not go along with me in deeming colonization a suitable remedy for our social ills. So anxious am I for our agreement on this point, that I will trouble you with one more illustration of the superabundance of capital in Great Britain.

I allude to the necessity in this country of an occasional destruction of capital on the grandest scale. . . . The practice with us seems to be to hoard up capital till we know not what to do with it, and then to throw it away as rapidly as possible till the quantity for use is brought to a level with the field of investment. Thus one observes for a time a general care and prudence in the making of investments: mere speculation is almost unknown: everybody that saves, saves now. Presently, a decreasing rate of interest on good securities shows that a want of room for capital is growing; and the least prudent turn an eye to unsafe securities which yield a higher return: but the hoarding goes on. At length, interest on good securities is so low . . . that the annoyance of risking to lose becomes less than that of the certainty of not gaining: and all the world, everybody being afraid lest his neighbour should get before him, rushes headlong into speculation. Capital without end is thrown into operations from which large returns are expected, but which turn out more or less ruinous: a great amount of capital has disappeared. The ruin and misery thus brought upon individuals frighten the whole body of capitalists: and now another set of people are ruined by the difficulty or impossibility of obtaining capital for safe undertakings. By degrees the panic subsides; steady hoarding goes on again; and after a while the same process is repeated. . . .

Whilst it is the peculiar characteristic of Great Britain to exhibit a want of room for all classes, it is that of colonies or new countries to exhibit plenty of room. In colonies, the field of production is unlimited; and the use of it may be enlarged faster than capital and population can possibly increase. In colonies, therefore, the greatest increase of capital and people occasions no mischievous competition. Both profits and wages are always at the maximum. And this happens not only in spite of the greatest increase of capital and people in the colony, but also in spite of a further increase by means of the importation of capital and people. Do what we may in colonies, we cannot overcrowd the field of employment for capital and labour.

But this proposition must be qualified. There may be a temporary excess of capital and people in a colony; and this sometimes happens in small colonies. It happens when a sudden importation of capital, exceeding the actual supply of labour, or of labour exceeding the supply of capital, disturbs the ordinary state of things. . . . But . . . these disturbances of the ordinary state of things do not last. An excessive capital is soon wasted; an excess of labour is soon remedied by fresh importations of capital, or by the rapid increase of capital in the colony. . . . The general rule is a continual state of high profits and high wages.

But there is another case of exception from this general rule which must not be overlooked. In many colonies . . . neither capital nor labour has always obtained a high remuneration. . . . The cause of the mischief in such cases, is one that has at all time prevailed over the greatest portion of the world; it is insecurity of property. . . . Security of property depends wholly on government. . . . I lay it down as an axiom therefore, that tolerably good colonial government is an essential condition of that state of continual high profits and high wages, which moderately well-governed colonies exhibit. . . .

The normal state of high profits and wages, notwithstanding the utmost importation of capital and people . . . arises partly from the manner in which the produce of colonial industry is distributed; partly from the great productiveness of industry in a country where only the most fertile spots need to be cultivated. In colonies, as compared with old countries, the landlord and the tax-gatherer get but a small share of the produce of industry: the producer, therefore, whether capitalist or labourer, gets a large share: indeed, they get nearly the whole. . . . Both the labourer and the capitalist, therefore, get more than they consume. . . . Colonies, therefore, are . . . naturally exporting communities: they have a large produce for exportation.

Not only have they a large produce for exportation, but that produce is peculiarly suited for exchange with old countries. In consequence of the cheapness of land in colonies, the great majority of the people are owners or occupiers of land; and their industry is necessarily in great measure confined to the producing of what comes immediately from the soil; viz., food, and the raw materials of manufacture. In old countries, on the other hand . . . it may be said that manufactured goods are their natural production for export. These are what the colonists do not produce. The colony produces what the old country wants; the old country produces what the colony wants. The old country and the colony, therefore, are, naturally, each other's best customers.

But of such great surplus production in a colony as renders the colony a best-possible customer of its mother-country, there is an essential condition over and above good government. At least, I rather think so. I doubt whether the singular energy of British industry – that characteristic of our race, whether here or in America – is not necessary to the production of a very large surplus produce under any circumstances: and looking at the present state of what may be termed the colonial world, I think that this notion is borne out by facts. . . . The United States of America, which have been chiefly colonized by English blood, are the best customers that ever mother-country had; and secondly, of the whole produce exported from Canada to England . . . nineteenth-twentieths, I feel confident, are raised by the enterprise and energy of British, that is, of Scotch and English blood, although a good deal more than half the population of Canada consists of Celtic–French and Milesian–Irish blood. I speak of enterprise and energy only, not of mere labour for hire; for in Canada, labour, hired and guided by men of English and Lowland-Scotch extraction, is principally that of Canadians of French origin and Milesian–Irish emigrants. Mere labour, without the enterprise and energy required for rendering a wilderness productive, will not raise a large surplus produce from even the most fertile soils. In the business, therefore of creating customers by colonization, Great Britain, like the older States of the American Union, would create better customers than most other countries would. [pp. 75–85]

A View of the Art of Colonization, J. W. Parker, 1849.

7 Profits and Capital Exports

J. S. MILL

John Stuart Mill (1806–73) was the son of James Mill, friend of Bentham, and was therefore virtually born a Utilitarian and radical. Most of his many books were attempts to synthesize and publicize the basic tenets of the philosophical radicals and liberals; and he did not add any new concept to the theory of surplus capital. Yet, by ingeniously combining the ideas of Smith, Malthus, Ricardo and Wakefield, he presented the theory in as complete a form as was possible within the scope of classical economics. The argument presented in this extract from his Principles of Political Economy *(first published in 1848) links the need to export capital with the convenience of sending it to colonies. It suggests, moreover, that this was not merely a possibility, but that export of capital was already an essential feature of the British economy. In this form the argument was widely accepted: for example by such Frenchmen as Jules Ferry and Leroy-Beaulieu.*

There is at every time and place some particular rate of profit, which is the lowest that will induce the people of that country and time to accumulate savings, and to employ those savings productively. This minimum rate of profit varies according to circumstances. It depends on two elements. One is, the strength of the effective desire of accumulation; the comparative estimate, made by the people of that place and era, of future interests when weighed against present. This element chiefly affects the inclination to save. The other element, which affects not so much the willingness to save as the disposition to employ savings productively, is the degree of security of capital engaged in industrial operations. A state of general insecurity no doubt affects also the disposition to save. . . . But in employing any funds which a person may possess as capital on his own account, or in lending it to others to be so employed, there is always some additional risk, over and above that incurred by keeping it idle in his own custody. This extra risk is great in proportion as the general state of society is insecure: it may be equivalent to twenty, thirty, or fifty per cent, or to no more than one or two; something, however, it must always be: and for this, the expectation of profit must be sufficient to compensate. . . .

I have already observed that this minimum rate of profit, less than which is not consistent with the further increase of capital, is lower in some states of society than in others; and I may add, that the kind of social progress characteristic of our present civilization tends to diminish it. In the first place, one of the acknowledged effects of that progress is an increase of general security. . . . In the second place, it is also one of the consequences of civilization that mankind become less the slaves of the moment, and more habituated to carry their desires and purposes forward into a distant future. . . . For these two reasons . . . a profit or interest of three or four per cent is as sufficient a motive to the increase of capital in England at the present day, as thirty or forty per cent in the Burmese Empire, or in England at the time of King John. . . . But though the minimum rate of profit is thus liable to vary, and though to specify exactly what it is would at any given time be impossible, such a minimum always exists; and whether it be high or low, when once it is reached, no further increase of capital can for the present take place. The country has then attained what is known to political economists under the name of the stationary state.

We now arrive at the fundamental proposition which this chapter is intended to inculcate. When a country has long possessed a large production, and a large net income to make savings from, and when, therefore, the means have long existed of making a great annual addition to capital . . . it is one of the characteristics of such a country, that the rate of profit is habitually within, as it were, a hand's breadth of the minimum, and the country therefore on the very verge of the stationary state. By this I do not mean that this state is likely, in any of the great countries of Europe, to be soon actually reached, or that capital does not still yield a profit considerably greater than what is barely sufficient to induce the people of those countries to save and accumulate. My meaning is, that it would require but a short time to reduce profits to the minimum, if capital continued to increase at its present rate, and no circumstances having a tendency to raise the rate of profit occurred in the meantime. The expansion of capital would soon reach its ultimate boundary, if the boundary itself did not continually open and leave more space. . . .

Let us suppose that in England even so small a net profit as one per cent . . . would constitute a sufficient inducement to save, but that less than this would not be a sufficient inducement. I now say, that the mere continuance of the present annual increase of capital, if no circumstance occurred to counteract its effect, would suffice in a small number of years to reduce the rate of net profit to one per cent.

To fulfil the conditions of the hypothesis, we must suppose an entire cessation of the exportation of capital for foreign investment. No more capital sent abroad for railways or loans; no more emigrants taking capital with them, to the colonies, or to other countries; no fresh advances made, or credits given, by bankers or merchants to their foreign correspondents. We must also assume that there are no fresh loans for unproductive expenditure, by the government, or on mortgage, or otherwise; and none of the waste of capital which now takes place by the failure of undertakings which people are tempted to engage in by the hope of a better income than can be obtained in safe paths at the present habitually low rate of profit. We must suppose the entire savings of the community to be annually invested in really productive employment within the country itself; and no new channels opened by industrial inventions, or by a more extensive substitution of the best known processes for inferior ones.

Few persons would hesitate to say, that there would be great difficulty in finding remunerative employment every year for so much new capital, and most would conclude that there would be what used to be termed a general glut. . . . But . . . this is not the mode in which the inconvenience would be experienced. The difficulty would not consist in any want of a market. If the new capital were duly shared among many varieties of employment, it would raise up a demand for its own produce, and there would be no cause why any part of that produce should remain longer on hand than formerly. What would really be, not merely difficult, but impossible, would be to employ this capital without submitting to a rapid reduction of the rate of profit.

As capital increased, population either would also increase, or it would not. If it did not, wages would rise, and a greater capital would be distributed in wages among the same number of labourers. There being no more labour than before, and no improvements to render the labour more efficient, there would not be any increase of the produce; and as the capital . . . would only obtain the same gross return, the whole savings of each year would be exactly so much subtracted from the profits of the next and of every following year. It is hardly necessary to say that in such circumstances profits would very soon fall to the point at which further increase of capital would cease. An augmentation of capital, much more rapid than that of population, must soon reach its extreme limit, unless accompanied by increased efficiency of labour (through inventions and discoveries, or improved mental and physical education), or unless some of the idle people, or of the unproductive labourers, became productive.

If population did increase with the increase of capital and in proportion to it, the fall of profits would still be inevitable. Increased population implies increased demand for agricultural produce. In the absence of industrial improvements, this demand can only be supplied at an increased cost of production, either by cultivating worse land, or by a more elaborate and costly cultivation of the land already under tillage. The cost of the labourer's subsistence is therefore increased; and unless the labourer submits to a deterioration of his condition, profits must fall. . . . On the whole, therefore, we may assume that in such a country as England, if the present annual amount of savings were to continue, without any of the counteracting circumstances which now keep in check the natural influence of those savings in reducing profit, the rate of profit would speedily attain the minimum, and all further accumulation of capital would for the present cease.

What, then, are these counteracting circumstances . . .? The resisting agencies are of several kinds.

First among them, we may notice one which is so simple and so conspicuous, that some political economists, especially M. de Sismondi and Dr Chalmers, have attended to it almost to the exclusion of all others. This is, the waste of capital in periods of over-trading and rash speculation, and in the commercial revulsions by which such times are always followed. . . .

This, doubtless, is one considerable cause which arrests profits in their descent to the minimum, by sweeping away from time to time a part of the accumulated mass by which they are forced down. But this is not . . . the principal cause. If it were, the capital of the country would not increase; but in England it does increase greatly and rapidly. . . .

This brings us to the second of the counter-agencies, namely, improvements in production. These evidently have the effect of extending what Mr Wakefield terms the field of employment, that is, they enable a greater amount of capital to be accumulated and employed without depressing the rate of profit: provided always that they do not raise, to a proportional extent, the habits and requirements of the labourer. . . . All inventions which cheapen any of the things consumed by the labourers, unless their requirements are raised in an equivalent degree, in time lower money wages: and by doing so, enable a greater capital to be accumulated and employed, before profits fall back to what they were previously. . . .

Equivalent in effect to improvements in production, is the acquisition of any new power of obtaining cheap commodities from foreign countries. If necessaries are cheapened, whether they are so by improvements at home or importation from abroad, is exactly the same thing to wages and profits. . . .

This brings us to the last of the counter-forces which check the downward tendency of profits. . . . This is, the perpetual overflow of capital into colonies or foreign countries, to seek higher profits than can be obtained at home. I believe this to have been for many years one of the principal causes by which the decline of profits in England has been arrested. It has a twofold operation. In the first place, it does what a fire, or an inundation, or a commercial crisis would have done: it carries off a part of the increase of capital from which the reduction of profits proceeds. Secondly, the capital so carried off is not lost, but is chiefly employed either in founding colonies, which become large exporters of cheap agricultural produce, or in extending and perhaps improving the agriculture of older communities. It is to the emigration of English capital, that we have chiefly to look for keeping up a supply of cheap food and cheap materials of clothing, proportional to the increase of our population; thus enabling an increasing capital to find employment in the country, without reduction of profit, in producing manufactured articles with which to pay for this supply of raw produce. Thus, the exportation of capital is an agent of great efficacy in extending the field of employment for that which remains: and it may be said truly that, up to a certain point, the more capital we send away, the more we shall possess and be able to retain at home.

In countries which are further advanced in industry and population, and have therefore a lower rate of profit, than others, there is always, long before the actual minimum is reached, a practical minimum, viz., when profits have fallen so much below what they are elsewhere, that, were they to fall lower, all further accumulations would go abroad. In the present state of the industry of the world, when there is occasion, in any rich and improving country, to take the minimum of profits at all into consideration for practical purposes, it is only this practical minimum that needs be considered. As long as there are old countries where capital increases very rapidly, and new countries where profit is still high, profits in the old countries will not sink to the rate which would put a stop to accumulation; the fall is stopped at the point which sends capital abroad. It is only, however, by improvements in production, and even in the production of things consumed by labourers, that the capital of a country like England is prevented from speedily reaching that degree of lowness of profit, which would cause all further savings to be sent to find employment in the colonies, or in foreign countries. [pp. 728–39]

Principles of Political Economy (1848; 7th edn. 1871); ed. Sir W. J. Ashley, Longmans, 1936.

8 Accumulation and Declining Profits

KARL MARX

Karl Marx (1818–83), journalist, economist, historian and social revolutionary, derived many of his concepts from the classical economists, but altered and refined them fundamentally. He appears to have had no concept of capitalism as tending to colonization and imperialism; but he had to consider the two problems of the concentration of capital into ever fewer hands – leading to monopoly – and of the declining tendency of the rate of profit. He explained both these phenomena rather differently from the classical economists, but arrived at similar conclusions which later Marxists could use to provide an apparently Marxist Theory of Capitalist Imperialism. These extracts from Capital represent those aspects of Marx's theories on which writers such as Luxemburg, Hilferding and Lenin later based their own theories of imperialism.

The Concentration and Centralization of Capital

Every individual capital is a larger or smaller concentration of means of production, with a corresponding command over a larger or smaller labour-army. Every accumulation becomes the means of new accumulation. With the increasing mass of wealth which functions as capital, accumulation increases the concentration of that wealth in the hands of individual capitalists, and thereby widens the basis of production on a large scale and of the specific methods of capitalist production. The growth of social capital is effected by the growth of many individual capitals. . . . At the same time portions of the original capitals disengage themselves and function as new independent capitals. Besides other causes, the division of property, within capitalist families, plays a great part in this. With the accumulation of capital, therefore, the number of capitalists grows to a greater or less extent. . . .

This splitting-up of the total social capital into many individual capitals or the repulsion of its fractions one from another, is counteracted by their attraction. . . . Capital grows in one place to a huge mass in a single hand, because it has in another place been lost by many. This is centralization proper, as distinct from accumulation and concentration.

The laws of this centralization of capitals . . . cannot be developed here. A brief hint at a few facts must suffice. The battle of competition is fought by cheapening of commodities. The cheapness of commodities depends, *caeteris paribus*, on the productiveness of labour, and this again on the scale of production. Therefore the larger capitals beat the smaller. It will further be remembered that, with the development of the capitalist mode of production, there is an increase in the minimum amount of individual capital necessary to carry on a business under its normal conditions. The smaller capitals, therefore, crowd into spheres of production which Modern Industry has only sporadically or incompletely got hold of. Here competition rages in direct proportion to the number, and in inverse proportion to the magnitudes, of the antagonistic capitals. It always ends in the ruin of many small capitalists, whose capitals partly pass into the hand of their conquerors, partly vanish. Apart from this, with capitalist production an altogether new force comes into play – the credit system.

In its beginnings, the credit system sneaks in as a modest helper of accumulation and draws by invisible threads the money resources scattered all over the surface of society into the hands of individual or associated capitalists. But soon it becomes a new and formidable weapon in the competitive struggle, and finally it transforms itself into an immense social mechanism for the centralization of capitals. . . .

Centralization in a certain line of industry would have reached its extreme limit, if all the individual capitals invested in it would have been amalgamated into one single capital. [*Note by Engels in 4th German edition, 1890*: The latest English and American 'trusts' are aiming to accomplish this by trying to unite at least all the large establishments of a certain line of industry into one great stock company with a practical monopoly.]

Centralization supplements the work of accumulation, by enabling the industrial capitalists to expand the scale of their operations. . . .

It is evident . . . that accumulation, the gradual propagation of capital by a reproduction passing from a circular into a spiral form, is a very slow process as compared with centralization, which needs but to alter the quantitative grouping of the integral parts of social capital. The world would still be without railroads, if it had been obliged to wait until accumulation should have enabled a few individual capitals to undertake the construction of a railroad. Centralization, on the other hand, accomplished this by a turn of the hand through stock companies. Centralization, by thus accelerating and intensifying the effects of accumulation, extends and hastens at the same time the revolutions in the technical composition of capital, which increase its constant part at the expense of its variables part and thereby reduce the relative demand for labour.

The masses of capital amalgamated over night by centralization reproduce and augment themselves like the others, only faster, and thus become new and powerful levers of social accumulation. . . .
[I, pp. 685–9]

III. Formation of stock companies. By means of these:

1. An enormous expansion of the scale of production and enterprises, which were impossible for individual capitals. At the same time such enterprises as were formerly carried on by governments are socialized.

2. Capital, which rests on a socialized mode of production and presupposes a social concentration of means of production and labour-powers, is here directly endowed with the form of social capital (capital [of] directly associated individuals) as distinguished from private capital, and its enterprises assume the form of social enterprises as distinguished from individual enterprises. It is the abolition of capital as private property within the boundaries of capitalist production itself.

3. Transformation of the actually functioning capitalist into a mere manager, an administrator of other people's capital, and of the owners of capital into mere owners, mere money-capitalists. . . .

In the stock companies the function is separated from the ownership of capital, and labour, of course, is entirely separated from the ownership of means of production and of surplus-labour. This result of the highest development of capitalist production is a necessary transition to the reconversion of capital into the property of the producers, no longer as the private property of individual producers, but as the common property of associates, as social property outright. On the other hand it is a transition to the conversion of all functions in the process of reproduction, which still remain connected with capitalist private property, into mere functions of the associated producers, into social functions.

Before we proceed any further, we call attention to the following fact, which is economically important: Since profit here assumes purely the form of interest, enterprises of this sort may still be successful, if they yield only interest, and this is one of the causes, which stem the fall of the rate of profit, since these enterprises, in which the constant capital is so enormous compared to the variable, do not necessarily come under the regulation of the average rate of profit.

[Note by Engels. Since Marx wrote the above, new forms of industrial enterprises have developed, which represent the second and third degree of stock companies. The daily increasing speed, with which production may to-day be intensified on all fields of great industry, is offset on the other hand by the ever increasing slowness, with which the markets for these increased products expand. What the great industries turn out in a few months, can scarcely be absorbed by the markets in years. Add to this the system of protective tariffs, by which every industrial country shuts itself off from all' others, particularly from England, and which increases home production still more by artificial means. The results are a chronic overproduction, depressed prices, falling or disappearing profits; in short, the long cherished freedom of competition has reached the end of its tether and is compelled to announce its own palpable bankruptcy. This is shown by the fact, that the great captains of industry of a certain line meet for the joint regulation of production by means of a kartel. A committee determines the quantity to be produced by each establishment and distributes ultimately the incoming orders. In some cases even international kartels were formed temporarily, for instance, one uniting the English and German iron producers. But even this form of socialization did not suffice. The antagonism of interests between the individual firms broke through the agreement quite frequently and restored competition. This led in some lines, where the scale of production permitted it, to the concentration of the entire production of this line in one great stock company under one joint management. In America this has been accomplished several times; in Europe the greatest illustration is so far the United Alkali Trust, which has brought the entire Alkali production of the British into the hands of one single business firm. The former owners of the individual works, more than thirty, have received the tax value of their entire establishment in shares of stock, totalling about 5 million pounds sterling, which represent the fixed capital of the trust. The technical management remains in the same hands, but the business management is centralized in the hands of the general management. The floating capital, amounting to about one million pounds, was offered to the public for subscription. The total capital is, therefore, 6 million pounds sterling. In this way competition in this line, which forms the basis of the entire chemical industry, has been replaced in England by monopoly, and the future expropriation of this line by the whole of society, the nation, has been well prepared. – F. E.]

This is the abolition of the capitalist mode of production within capitalist production itself, a self-destructive contradiction, which represents on its face a mere phase of transition to a new form of production. It manifests its contradictory nature by its effects. It establishes a monopoly in certain spheres and thereby challenges the interference of the state. It reproduces a new aristocracy of finance, a new sort of parasites in the shape of promoters, speculators and merely nominal directors; a whole system of swindling and cheating by means of corporation juggling, stock jobbing, and stock speculation. It is private production without the control of private property. [III, pp. 516–19]

The Law of the Falling Tendency of the Rate of Profit, and its Counteracting Causes

The law of the falling tendency of the rate of profit . . . says in so many words: If you take any quantity of the average social capital, say a capital of 100, you will find that an ever larger portion of it is invested in means of production, and an ever smaller portion in living labour. Since, then, the aggregate mass of the living labour operating the means of production decreases in comparison to the value of these means of production, it follows that the unpaid labour, and that portion of value in which it is expressed, must decline as compared to the value of the advanced total capital. Or, an ever smaller aliquot part of the invested total capital is converted into living labour, and this capital absorbs in proportion to its magnitude less and less surplus-labour, although the proportion of the unpaid part of the employed labour may simultaneously grow as compared with the paid part. The relative decrease of the variable, and the relative increase of the constant, capital, while both parts may grow absolutely in magnitude, is but another expression for the increased productivity of labour. . . .

The law of the falling tendency of the rate of profit . . . does not argue in any way against the fact that the absolute mass of the employed and exploited labour set in motion by the social capital, and consequently the absolute mass of the surplus-labour appropriated by it, may grow. Nor does it argue against the fact that the capitals controlled by individual capitalists may dispose of a growing mass of labour and surplus-labour, even though the number of the labourers employed by them may not grow.

Take for illustration's sake a certain population of working people, for instance, two millions. Assume, furthermore, that the length and intensity of the average working day, and the level of wages, and thereby the proportion between necessary and surplus-labour, are given. In that case the aggregate labour of these two millions, and their surplus-labour expressed in surplus-value, represent always the same magnitude of values. But with the growth of the mass of the constant (fixed and circulating) capital, which this labour manipulates, the proportion of this produced quantity of values declines as compared to the value of this total capital. And the value of this capital grows with its mass, although not in the same proportion. This proportion, and consequently the rate of profit, falls in spite of the fact that the same mass of living labour is controlled as before, and the same amount of surplus-labour absorbed by the capital. This proportion changes, not because the mass of living labour decreases, but because the mass of the materialized labour set in motion by living labour increases. It is a relative decrease, not an absolute one, and has really nothing to do with the absolute magnitude of the labour and surplus-labour set in motion. The fall of the rate of profit is not due to an absolute, but only to a relative decrease of the variable part of the total capital, that is, its decrease as compared with the constant part. . . . [III, pp. 252–4]

If we consider the enormous development of the productive powers of labour, even comparing but the last thirty years with all former periods; if we consider in particular the enormous mass of fixed capital, aside from machinery in the strict meaning of the term, passing into the process of social production as a whole, then the difficulty . . . of finding an explanation for the falling rate of profit, gives way to its opposite, namely to the question; How is it that this fall is not greater and more rapid? There must be some counteracting influences at work, which thwart and annul the effects of this general law, leaving to it merely the character of a tendency. For this reason we have referred to the fall of the average rate of profit as a tendency to fall.

The following are the general counterbalancing causes:

I. *Raising the Intensity of Exploitation*

The rate at which labour is exploited, the appropriation of surplus-labour and surplus-value, is raised by a prolongation of the working day and an intensification of labour. . . .

II. *Depression of Wages Below their Value.* . . .

III. *Cheapening of the Elements of Constant Capital.* . . .

From the point of view of the total capital, the value of the constant capital does not increase in the same proportion as its material volume. For instance, the quantity of cotton, which a single European spinning operator works up in a modern factory, has grown in a colossal degree compared to the quantity formerly worked up by a European operator with a spinning wheel. But the value of the worked-up cotton has not grown in proportion to its mass. The same holds good of machinery and other fixed capital. In short, the same development, which increases the mass of the constant capital relatively over that of the variable, reduces the value of its elements as a result of the increased productivity of labour. In this way the value of the constant capital although continually increasing, is prevented from increasing at the same rate as its material volume, that is, the material volume of the means of production set in motion by the same amount of labour-power. In exceptional cases the mass of the elements of constant capital may even increase, while its value remains the same or even falls. . . .

IV. *Relative Overpopulation.* . . .

V. *Foreign Trade*

To the extent that foreign trade cheapens partly the elements of constant capital, partly the necessities of life for which the variable capital is exchanged, it tends to raise the rate of profit by raising the rate of surplus-value and lowering the value of the constant capital. It exerts itself generally in this direction by permitting an expansion of the scale of production. But by this means it hastens on one hand the process of accumulation, on the other the reduction of the variable as compared to the constant capital, and thus a fall in the rate of profit. In the same way the expansion of foreign trade, which is the basis of the capitalist mode of production in its stages of infancy, has become its own product in the further progress of capitalist development through its innate necessities, through its need of an ever expanding market. Here we see once more the dual nature of these effects. (Ricardo entirely overlooked this side of foreign trade.)

Another question, which by its special nature is really beyond the scope of our analysis, is the following: Is the average rate of profit raised by the higher rate of profit, which capital invested in foreign, and particularly in colonial trade, realizes?

Capitals invested in foreign trade are in a position to yield a higher rate of profit, because, in the first place, they come in competition with commodities produced in other countries with lesser facilities of production, so that an advanced country is enabled to sell its goods above their value even when it sells them cheaper than the competing countries. To the extent that the labour of the advanced countries is here exploited as a labour of a higher specific weight, the rate of profit rises, because labour which has not been paid as being of a higher quality is sold as such. The same condition may obtain in the relations with a certain country, into which commodities are exported and from which commodities are imported. This country may offer more materialized labour in goods than it receives, and yet it may receive in return commodities cheaper than it could produce them. In the same way a manufacturer, who exploits a new invention before it has become general, undersells his competitors and yet sells his commodities above their individual values, that is to say, he exploits the specifically higher productive power of the labour employed by him as surplus-value. By this means he secures a surplus-profit. On the other hand, capitals invested in colonies, etc., may yield a higher rate of profit for the simple reason that the rate of profit is higher there on account of the backward development, and for the added reason, that slaves, coolies, etc., permit a better exploitation of labour. We see no reason, why these higher rates of profit realized by capitals invested in certain lines and sent home by them should not enter as elements into the average rate of profit and tend to keep it up to that extent.[1] We see so much less reason for the contrary opinion, when it is assumed that such favoured lines of investment are subject to the laws of free competition. What Ricardo has in mind as objections, is mainly this: With the higher prices realized in foreign trade, commodities are bought abroad and sent home. These commodities are sold on the home market, and this can constitute at best but a temporary advantage of the favoured spheres of production over others. This aspect of the matter is changed, when we no longer look upon it from the point of view of money. The favoured country recovers more labour in exchange for less labour, although this difference, this surplus, is pocketed by a certain class, as it is in any exchange between labour and capital. So far as the rate of profit is higher, because it is generally higher in the colonial country, it may go hand in hand with a low level of prices, if the natural conditions are favourable. It is true that a compensation takes place, but it is not a compensation on the old level, as Ricardo thinks.

However, this same foreign trade develops the capitalist mode of production in the home country. And this implies the relative decrease of the variable as compared to the constant capital, while it produces,

---

[1] Adam Smith was right in this respect, contrary to Ricardo, who said: 'They contend the equality of profits will be brought about by the general rise of profits; and I am of opinion that the profits of the favoured trade will speedily submit to the general level.' (Works, MacCulloch ed., p. 73.)

on the other hand, an over-production for the foreign market, so that it has once more the opposite effect in its further course.

And so we have seen in a general way, that the same causes, which produce a falling tendency in the rate of profit, also call forth counter-effects, which check and partly paralyse this fall. This law is not suspended, but its effect is weakened. Otherwise it would not be the fall of the average rate of profit, which would be unintelligible, but rather the relative slowness of this fall. The law therefore shows itself only as a tendency, whose effects become clearly marked only under certain conditions and in the course of long periods. [III, pp. 272–80]

Capital, ed. F. Engels. Vol. I (1867), Vol. III (1894); Chicago, C. H. Kerr, 1912, 1909.

Part Two

ADAPTATION AND MODIFICATION

The Historicists

The main difference between the classical economists and the later contributors to the Theory of Capitalist Imperialism is that, whereas the first group mostly argued theoretically (not seeking to explain actual historical events but creating possible models to explain European economic development), the later writers applied their concepts to concrete events, and used them either to support colonizing projects desired on various grounds, or to explain previous historical events. Practical application of the Theory became more common as time went on, and these extracts illustrate some of its main trends. Leopold of Belgium and Jules Ferry of France stand apart as practical statesmen who took the lead in projecting or defending colonization on economic grounds – i.e. as a solution to the problems of capitalism in Europe. Engels, Loria and Robertson are quoted to show how tentative connections between capital accumulation, rates of profit and colonization were forged in the years before Hobson's *Imperialism* first gave general currency to the Theory in a sophisticated form in 1902. Hobson's own gradual movement to this position is illustrated by extracts from his *Evolution of Modern Capitalism* (1894) and *The War in South Africa* (1900), which show how he fused the principle of underconsumption (derived from Sismondi) with a pragmatic interpretation of recent historical events. Leroy-Beaulieu, who had been supporting Mill's theory of capital export since 1874 in his influential books on colonization and economics, is quoted from the 1908 edition of his *Colonization* to show how in this edition he too adopted the new theory and differentiated for the first time between the advantages of investing capital in colonies and in other places overseas. Finally (excluding Brailsford, who restated Hobson's theory in 1914, primarily with reference to the warlike tendencies of modern states) we see the construction of a specifically Marxist Theory. This was difficult to achieve, since, as has been seen, Marx provided few definite leads. Rosa Luxemburg suggested one Marxist approach, based on the trading needs of Europe; but this was too vulnerable for general adoption. The vital step was taken by Hilferding, who, by suggesting that capitalism had changed its character at the end of the nineteenth century and become 'finance capitalism', provided a reasonable explanation for the sudden burst of imperialist activity after about 1870. This principle was gratefully adopted by most orthodox Marxists, and was woven into a remarkably logical theory of Imperialism by Bukharin and Lenin. Lenin's short book, written primarily as a demonstration that the First World War was the eve of the socialist revolution, became the standard Marxist and Communist explanation of Imperialism and remains virtually accepted doctrine in the Communist world.

9 Tropical Colonization, 1863
LEOPOLD, DUKE OF BRABANT

Leopold (1835–1909) became King of the Belgians in 1865. His importance for a study of Imperialism is that in the 1870s and 1880s he was one of the very few European statesmen who really believed in the economic value of acquiring tropical colonies; and his acquisition of the Congo Free State in 1885 began a new phase in the exploitation of tropical dependencies. His ideas were, however, formed much earlier, from a systematic study of colonial history; and this extract from a memorandum of 1863 on the possible advantages of colonization for Belgium, shows his belief in the investment opportunities tropical colonies offered an industrialized European country with no colonial empire.

There are three types of colony:

1. Slave colonies – Cuba;
2. Colonies inhabited by a numerous native race, which have been made a dependency of some European state – Java, the Philippines, Cochin China, India;

3. Colonies established by white emigration – America, Australia, Natal (temperate climates).

Since no one would think of founding slave colonies, we must be concerned with the two other methods of exploiting distant provinces.

Second Category

Natives subordinated to a European people.

Such countries are not real colonies but external possessions which are very productive if well chosen. Java is immensely rewarding, and your documents show that, over the centuries, the profits exceed the costs.

At Java there exists a type of forced labour which is the only way of civilizing and imposing moral standards on these lazy and corrupt peoples of the Far East. The day will come when this obligation can be abolished without danger to public security and without loss to the metropolis. Cultivators, made rich by the *corvée*, will one day be able to buy back their liberty from the state and become landowners. Taxes will replace labour obligations. . . .

Everyone knows the advantages Holland obtains from Java. One might say that this property is a very good field for the investment of Dutch capital, without taking any account of the political advantages it offers and the opportunities which more than 30,000 Dutchmen, living there over the centuries, have found for investment, careers and work.

The army, the navy, and the government of the Indies, which offer three vast openings to young Netherlanders, add nothing to the budget of the mother country; or, to be more exact, support her with an annual bonus of 75 million francs.

For a country whose working class will not emigrate, but whose middle class lack opportunities, such possessions are precious.

British India

British India, for long the possession of the Company, has never cost the mother country a penny. The last war in India, a great struggle which was maintained by the energy of all the British nation and inscribed with its most precious blood, proves how highly the British value their possession of India.

In India British capital is invested at 20, 30 and 40 per cent.

In India every British family has one or two of their children living

47

there and these children seek and find their fortunes there. These fortunes are sent back to London, and this capital city, like a beehive in which the bees, having sucked the finest flowers, return to store their honey, is one of the richest cities in the world.

India, *a British colony*, is the only part of Asia which is furrowed with railways, for which every piece of equipment naturally comes from London. . . .

India and Java are inexhaustible mines of wealth. The question can be summed up thus: is it advantageous to possess gold mines? . . .

Colonies or external possessions are, for states and their peoples, vast new fields for work which increase the resources of those who really want to undertake it. . . .

With the strong support of the lessons of history, and taking our stand on statistics and evidence, we are trying to show that:

1. Wherever and so long as there have been states, overseas provinces have been wanted and have been very useful to the motherland. . . .
3. Overseas provinces have brought back to the mother country far more in hard cash than they have cost, and that such possessions are excellent fields for the investment of capital for such states. . . .
4. Despite free trade, and the opening of all the colonies belonging to different peoples to the trade of all, it remains more advantageous to possess one's own external dependencies. We would be happy to see Belgians operating in and using colonies in general, but we think that it is in the interests of the country that it should have its own overseas possessions. In such places we see a way to increase our importance in the world, new careers open to our citizens, a new source of revenue to use which, as in Java, would constitute a free gift, a field for investing our capital, under the rule of our own laws, far more profitably than in the metal industry or even in railways which give only 3 or $3\frac{1}{2}$ per cent.

Belgium does not make use of the world: it is an instinct we must cause to be born in her. . . .

These facts being demonstrated and accepted, we will propose that the Chambers should pass laws for the extension of the fatherland by honest and lawful methods which are worthy of our age and by means which would advance civilization by our new establishments rather than check its movement by undertaking ambitious projects at the expense of our neighbours.

We propose that this extension of the country, a luxury to match our wonderful independence, should be made possible in the following way:

A sum, to be fixed later, should be taken from the surplus on the public revenues. This sum should be placed in an account called 'overseas'. This account will also be open to receive gifts and legacies. As soon as a certain amount has been amassed, we would undertake the development of some worthwhile country, following the best known methods.

This Belgian possession would have its separate revenues and budgets. Since we would be starting in a small way, whether in China, Japan, Borneo, Central America or the coast of Africa, we should never commit more than the funds available in the overseas account.

Letter on the Advantages of Colonization, 26 July 1863, in *Documents d'histoire précoloniale belge (1861–65)* ed. L. Le Febve De Vivy. Académie royale des Sciences coloniales, Brussels, 1955, pp. 19–23; trans. D. K. F.

10 Stock Exchange Influence, 1883 and 1894

F. ENGELS

Friedrich Engels (1820–95) a German journalist and businessman with strong radical and social beliefs, first collaborated with Marx in organizing revolutionary movements in Germany in 1844. He came of a wealthy family, and from 1850 to 1869 ran his own business in England. This enabled him to help to support Marx while he worked on his great projects at the same time as he collaborated with him. Engels wrote a number of books and pamphlets on his own account, but is best known for having edited the manuscripts left by Marx and publishing them as the second and third volumes of Capital. *In the years after Marx died in 1883 Engels believed that he could see in contemporary trends proof of some of Marx's ideas. In these extracts Engels suggests that new colonization was largely the product of the growth of the Stock*

Exchange and joint stock companies: and the same argument is put forward in his addition to volume III of Capital which is printed above (pp. 38–9). This belief became integral with the later Theory of Capitalist Imperialism, and Engels's comments may be seen as a link between Marx's ideas on concentration of capital and Hilferding's theory of finance capital.

Engels to K. Kautsky, London, 18 September, 1883

. . . I thought the article on colonization very good. It is a pity that you make use chiefly of the German material, which is dull as usual and lacking the most vivid aspects of tropical colonization, and its latest form; I mean colonization in the interests of stock exchange swindles, such as is now being enacted in Tunisia and Tonkin by France openly and frankly.

Supplement to Capital, Vol. III 1894

II. *The Stock Exchange* (excerpt)

7. Then colonization. Today this is purely a subsidiary of the stock exchange, in whose interests the European powers divided Africa a few years ago, and the French conquered Tunis and Tonkin. Africa leased directly to companies (Niger, South Africa, German South-West and German East Africa), and Mashonaland and Natal seized by Rhodes for the stock exchange.

K. Marx and F. Engels on Colonialism. Moscow, Foreign Languages Publishing House, 1960; Lawrence and Wishart.

11 Economic Colonization, 1885 and 1890

JULES FERRY

Jules Ferry (1832–93) was a leading figure in French politics during the first twenty years of the Third Republic, and was Prime Minister in 1879–81 and 1883–85. He showed little interest in colonization until 1883 and was not interested in economic theory: but he was a strong nationalist and was determined that France should take a major part in the general tendency towards colonial expansion of the 1880s. He did not formulate a general theory of colonization until 1885, when, after his fall from office, he defended his 'forward' policies in Tonkin and elsewhere to the Chamber. These arguments, amplified in his book on Tonkin which was published in 1890, are mainly interesting as showing how a clever politician could contrive an economic theory of colonization from ideas then current. Whether or not Ferry really believed what he said, his argument had considerable influence and was regarded by many as a general theory of economic imperialism.

It is, in fact, obvious that a country which allows a great wave of emigration to leave it is neither a happy nor a rich country; and it is not a reproach to France nor a disgrace to say of her that she has less emigrants than any other country in Europe. But this is not the only important aspect of colonization. To rich countries colonies offer the most profitable field for the investment of capital. The famous Stuart Mill devoted a chapter of his work to demonstrate this, and he summarizes it thus: 'For old and rich countries colonization is one of the most profitable enterprises to indulge in.' . . . France, which has always had a surplus of capital and has exported considerable quantities of it to foreign states – in fact, the export of capital made by this great and rich country must be counted in milliards of francs – I say that France has an interest in considering this side of the colonial question.

But, gentlemen, there is another and more important side of this question, which is far more important than what I have just been discussing. The colonial question is, for countries like ours which are, by the very character of their industry, tied to large exports, vital to the question of markets. . . . From this point of view . . . the foundation of a colony is the creation of a market. . . . In fact it has been stated, and there are many examples to be found in the economic history of modern peoples, that it is sufficient for the colonial link to exist between the mother country which produces and the colonies which she has founded for economic predominance to accompany and, in some degree, to depend on, political predominance.

In *Discours et Opinions de Jules Ferry*, ed. P. Roubiquet. 7 vols. Paris, Armand Colin, 1896–7, Vol. V, p. 194 f.; trans. D. K. F.

From Tonkin et la Mère-Patrie

Colonial policy is the daughter of industrialization. For rich states, where capital abounds and accumulates rapidly, where the industrial system is continually growing and where it attracts, if not the majority, at least the most alert and ambitious section of the labouring class; where even the cultivation of the land must become industrialized to survive, exports are essential to political good health; and the field open for the employment of capital, like the demand for labour, is controlled by the extent of the foreign market. If Europe had been able to establish something like a division of industrial labour between the manufacturing countries, based on the natural and social aptitudes and economic conditions of the different countries, securing cotton manufacturing and metallurgy in one place, reserving alcohol and sugar for one country, woollens and silks for another, Europe would not have had to look outside its own boundaries for markets for what it produced. The treaties of 1860 aimed at this ideal. But today everyone wants to spin and weave, to forge and distil. All Europe makes as much sugar as possible and tries to export it. The entry of the latest countries to develop large-scale industry – the United States and Germany – the arrival in all forms of industry of little states whose peoples were asleep or exhausted – a regenerated Italy, Spain enriched by French capital, Switzerland with so much enterprise and wisdom – these events have placed the whole of the west, while it waits for Russia who is learning and growing, on a slope which it cannot climb.

On the other side of the Vosges, and across the Atlantic, the protective system has increased the number of manufactures, closed previous markets, and brought strong competition into the markets of Europe. It is something to defend oneself in turn by raising barriers, but by itself it is not enough. In his fine book on the colonization of Australia Mr Torrens has clearly shown that an increase of manufacturing capital, unless it is accompanied by a proportionate increase of foreign markets, tends to produce a general lowering of prices, profits and salaries simply as a result of domestic competition.

The protective system is a steam engine without a safety-valve unless it is balanced and supported by a sensible and serious colonial policy. Surplus capital engaged in industry not only tends to diminish the profits of capital but also to check the rise of wages, though this is the natural and desirable tendency of all modern societies. Moreover, this is not an abstract tendency, but a reality made of flesh and bone, of passion and will, which becomes restless, complains and defends itself. The economic crisis which has pressed so hard on the European worker since 1876 or 1877, the industrial sickness which followed it, whose most depressing symptom consists in strikes – long, often unwise but always formidable – these have coincided in France, Germany and even in England with a significant and persistent decline in the volume of exports. Europe can perhaps be thought of as a business concern which sees the volume of its business declining over a certain number of years. Europe's consumption is saturated: it is essential to discover new seams of consumers in other parts of the world. The alternative is to place modern society in bankruptcy and to prepare for the dawn of the twentieth century a cataclysmic social liquidation whose consequences cannot be calculated.

It is because she was the first to foresee these distant horizons that England took the lead in the modern industrial movement. It is because she saw the potential danger to her hegemony which might, following the secession of the United States of North America, result from the separation of Australia and India that she laid siege to Africa on four fronts: in the south, by the plateau of the Cape and Bechuanaland; in the west, by the Niger and the Congo; in the north-east, by the valley of the Nile; in the east by Suakim, the Somali coast and the basin of the great equatorial lakes. It is to prevent British enterprise from obtaining for its sole profit the new markets which are opening up to the products of the west that Germany meets England with her inconvenient and unexpected rivalry in all parts of the globe. Colonial policy is an international expression of the eternal laws of competition.

A policy which sacrifices present and necessary acquisitions to the demands of the future is a policy of deceit and improvidence. It is appropriate to an impetuous people, eager to play the highest role, not to France, who is peaceful and deliberate, and who has not ceased to believe in the essential justice of things, but who can and must wait until the hour sounds the call to her destiny. We can only be certain that France will not willingly precipitate that moment. Nevertheless, the outside world marches on; interests change, positions alter, new groupings of forces prepare and organize. Must we, in the name of the highest form of nationalism and by taking a short view, place French policy in a dead end and, with our eyes fixed on the blue line of the Vosges, leave everything to be done, to be pledged, and to be resolved without us and around us? A policy of clean hands would, on all the evidence, have meant Italy in Tunis, we taking second place, Germany in Cochin China, England in Tonkin, both in Madagascar as in New Guinea; in a word, the bankruptcy of our rights and our hopes, a new treaty of 1763, without the excuse of Rosbach and the Pompadour.

Tonkin et la Mère-Patrie (Paris 1890–9); *Discours*, V, pp. 557–9, 562; trans. D. K. F.

12 The Theory of Underconsumption, 1894
J. A. HOBSON

J. A. Hobson (1858–1940) was an English journalist and amateur econo-mist. At heart a liberal, he was strongly influenced by Marxist ideas and played an important role in the development of the Labour Party. As a writer on economics he formulated his theory that underconsumption was the basis of unemployment and social hardship as early as 1889, and then ex-panded it in The Evolution of Modern Capitalism *in 1894. His interest in colonies came later, and began as a typical Liberal's distaste for the cost and brutality involved in annexing tropical dependencies. By 1900 others had linked the economic problems of capitalism with colonization, but Hobson's experience in South Africa during the Boer War convinced him that im-perialism was the direct product of capitalism. In 1900 he described this con-nection, with heavy emphasis on the Jewish character of international capital-ism, in* The War in South Africa: *two years later his book,* Imperialism: a Study *provided a convincing general statement of the theory that under-consumption in capitalist Europe forced the powers to acquire colonies. This book has remained the best known non-Marxist exposition of the Theory of Capitalist Imperialism.*

In considering the effect of modern machine-production upon the Business, the most obvious external change is a great increase in size. The typical unit of production is no longer a single family or a small group of persons working with a few cheap simple tools upon small quantities of material, but a compact and closely organized mass of labour composed of hundreds or thousands of individuals, co-operating with large quantities of expensive and intricate machinery, through which passes a continuous and mighty volume of raw material on its journey to the hands of the consuming public. . . .

While the mass of capital and labour which constitutes a business is growing, the latter grows less rapidly than the former. That is to say, capital is in point of size becoming more and more the dominant factor in the business. . . .

In addition to increased size we find increased and ever-increasing complexity of structure in the business-unit. This has proceeded in two directions, horizontally and laterally – that is to say, by subdivision and accession of processes on the one hand, and by an increased variety of products, and therefore of processes, upon the other hand. [pp. 88, 92–3]

Modern machinery has in almost all cases raised the size of the market. The space-area of competition has been immensely widened, especially for the more durable classes of goods. It is machinery of transport . . . that is chiefly responsible for this expansion. Cheaper, quicker, safer, and more calculable journeys have shrunk space for competing purposes. Improved means of rapid and reliable information about methods of production, markets, changes in price and trade have practically annihilated the element of distance. [p. 99]

The establishment of a world-market for a larger and larger number of commodities is transforming with marvellous rapidity the industrial face of the globe. This does not now appear so plainly in the more highly-developed countries of Europe, which, under the influence of half a century's moderately free competition for a European market, have already established themselves in tolerably settled conditions of specialized industry. But in the new world, and in those older countries which are now fast yielding to the incursions of manufacturing and transport machinery, the specializing process is making rapid strides. . . .

As large areas of Asia, South and Central Africa, Australia, and South America fall under the control of European commercial nations, are opened up by steamships, railways, telegraphs, and are made free receptacles for the increased quantity of capital which is unable to find a safe remunerative investment nearer home, we are brought nearer to a condition in which the whole surface of the world will be disposed for industrial purposes by these same forces which have long been confined in their direct and potent influence to a small portion of Western Europe and America. [pp. 107–8]

To keen-eyed business men engaged in the thick of large-scale competition it becomes increasingly clear that good profits can only be obtained in one of two ways. A successful firm must either be in possession of some trade secret, patent, special market, or such other private economy as places it in a position of monopoly in certain places or in certain lines of goods, or else it must make some arrangement with competing firms whereby they shall consent to abate the intensity or limit the scope of their competition. It will commonly be found that both these conditions are present where a modern firm of manufacturers or merchants succeeds in maintaining during a long period of time a prosperous or paying business. [p. 122]

It is commonly said by English writers upon economics that the state of over-production, the redundancy of capital and labour, though found in one or two or several trades at the same time, cannot be of general application. If too much capital and labour is engaged in one industry there is, they argue, too little in another, there cannot be at the same time a general state of over-production. Now if by general over-production is meant not that every single industry is supplied with an excess of capital, but that there exists a net over-supply, taking into account the plethora in some trades and the deficiency in others, this assertion of English economists is not in accordance with ascertained facts or with the authority of economists outside of England.

If a depression of trade signified a misapplication of capital and labour, so that too much was applied in some industries, too little in others, there would be a rise of prices in as many cases as there was a fall of prices, and the admitted symptom of depression, the simultaneous fall of price in all or nearly all the staple industries, would not occur. The most careful students of the phenomena of depressed trade agree in describing the condition as one of general or net excess of the forms of capital. They are also agreed in regarding the enormous growth of modern machinery as the embodiment of a general excess of producing power over that required to maintain current consumption. [pp. 169–70]

The general relation of modern Machinery to Commercial Depression is found to be as follows: Improved machinery of manufacture and transport enables larger and larger quantities of raw material to pass more quickly and more cheaply through the several processes of production. Consumers do not, in fact, increase their consumption as quickly and to an equal extent. Hence the onward flow of productive goods is checked in one or more of the manufacturing stages, or in the hands of the merchant, or even in the retail shop. This congestion of the channels of production automatically checks production, depriving of all use a large quantity of the machinery, and a large quantity of labour. The general fall of money income which has necessarily followed from a fall of prices, uncompensated by a corresponding expansion of sales, induces a shrinkage of consumption. . . .

This is an accurate account of the larger phenomena visible in the commercial world in a period of disturbance. When the disease is at its worst, the activity of producer and consumer at its lowest, we have the functional condition of under-production due to the pressure of a quantity of over-supply, and we have a corresponding state of under-consumption.

Machinery thus figures as the efficient cause of industrial disease, but the real responsibility does not rest on the shoulders of the inventor of new machinery, or of the manufacturer, but of the consumer.

The root-evil of depressed trade is under-consumption. If a quantity of capital and labour is standing idle at the same time, in all or in the generality of trades, the only possible reason why they remain unemployed is that there is no present demand for the goods which by co-operation they are able to produce. . . .

Since all commerce is ultimately resolvable into exchange of commodities for commodities, it is obvious that every increase of production signifies a corresponding increase of power to consume. Since there exists in every society a host of unsatisfied wants, it is equally certain that there exists a desire to consume everything that can be produced. But the fallacy involved in the supposition that over-supply is impossible consists in assuming that the power to consume and the desire to consume necessarily co-exist in the same persons. . . .

There are, in fact, two distinct motives which induce individuals to continue to produce, one is the desire to consume, the other the desire to save – *i.e.*, to postpone consumption. It is true that the latter may be said also to involve a desire to consume, the results of the savings at some indefinitely future time, but the motive of their production at present is a desire to reduce the quantity of the present

consumption of the community, and to increase the quantity of postponed consumption. . . .

But if saving means postponed consumption, and the desire to save,
as well as the desire to consume, is a *vera causa* in production, then the
fact of continued production affords no proof that such production
must be required to supply articles which are desired for consumption.
Ultimately a belief that some one will consent to consume what is produced underlies the continued production of a 'saving person', but . . .
the belief of a competing producer that he can get a market for his
goods, even when justified by events, is no guarantee against excessive
production in the whole trade.

If, then, those who have the power to consume in the present desire
to postpone their consumption they will refuse to demand consumptive
goods, and will instead bring into existence an excess of productive
goods. . . .

It is not therefore correct to say that the rate of production determines the rate of consumption just as much as the rate of consumption
determines the rate of production. The current productive power
of capital and labour places a maximum limit upon current consumption, but an increase of productive power exercises no sufficient
force to bring about a corresponding rise in consumption. . . . Nor
is there any *a priori* reason why there should not be from time to
time such general maladjustment. If ignorance and miscalculation leads
to the investment of too much capital in, say, the cotton and iron
industries, it is not unreasonable to suppose that in a complex industrial
society there should be such general miscalculation of the right proportion between saving and spending that too much should be saved
at certain periods. . . .

Machinery has intensified the malady of under-consumption or
over-saving, because it has increased the opportunities of conflict
between the interests of individuals and those of the community.
With the quickening of competition in machine industries the opportunities to individuals of making good their new 'savings' by cancelling
out the old 'savings' of others continually grow in number, and as an
ever larger proportion of the total industry falls under the dominion
of machinery, more and more of this dislocation is likely to arise. . . .

It must be clearly recognized that the trouble is due to a genuine
clash of individual interests in a competitive industrial society, where
the frequent, large, and quite incalculable effects of improved machinery and methods of production give now to this, now to that group

of competitors a temporary advantage in the struggle. It was formerly believed that this bracing competition, this free clash of individual interest, was able to strike out harmony. . . .

It now appears that this is not the case, and that the failure cannot in the main be attributed to an imperfect understanding by individuals of the means by which their several interests may be best subserved, but is due to the power vested in individuals or groups of individuals to secure for themselves advantages arising from improved methods of production without regard for the vested interests of other individuals or of society as a whole. [pp. 179–209]

We have seen that the possession of an excessive proportion of 'power to consume' by classes who, because their normal healthy wants are already fully satisfied, refuse to exert this power, and insist upon storing it in unneeded forms of capital, is directly responsible for the slack employment of capital and labour. If the operation of industrial forces throw an increased proportion of the 'power to consume' into the hands of the working classes, who will use it not to postpone consumption but to raise their standard of material and intellectual comfort, a fuller and more regular employment of labour and capital must follow. . . . If the power of purchase now 'saved' by the wealthier classes passed into the hands of the workers in higher money wages, and was not spent by them in raising their standard of comfort, but was 'invested' in various forms of capital, no stimulus to industry would be afforded; the 'savings' of one class would have fallen into the hands of another class, and their excess would operate to restrict industry precisely as it now operates. . . . From the standpoint of the community nothing else than a rise in the average standard of current consumption can stimulate industry. [pp. 282–3]

The Evolution of Modern Capitalism, Walter Scott, 1894; (later editions, 1906, 1919).

13 Wars for Colonies, 1898

A. LORIA

A. Loria (1857–1943) was an Italian academic economist of some distinction, and also a supporter of social reform through the redistribution of income. The Economic Foundations of Society, first published in a different form in 1885, and re-issued in Italian in 1898, is an attempt to show how all political and social institutions are moulded by the distribution of wealth between different sections of society. This extract is printed to show how capitalism and colonization were being linked in the twenty years before 1900. Hobson may have been influenced by Loria's argument, for he quoted part of this extract in his Imperialism.

The moment political power is conquered by profits, and when accumulation becomes accordingly the normal function of property, the proprietors find active employment for their energies in capitalization and the direction of industrial enterprise. Thus they have neither the means nor the desires to fritter away their forces in useless wars. Henceforth militant politics are practically put aside. . . . As a result, war is only resorted to under the wage system as a subsidiary method of furthering the expansion of accumulation and rounding out capitalistic revenues after other more pacific and economic means have been tried without success. One consequence of this change is, therefore, the declining frequency of warfare in modern times. . . .

Another consequence flowing from the transition to the wage economy is the essentially commercial character of modern warfare that looks only to the advantage of the bourgeois class which furnishes the means and manufactures the necessary instruments. . . .

It was the desire for commercial expansion that led to the celebrated opium war between England and China, which was terminated by the peace of Nankin and resulted in the opening up of several Chinese ports to the Europeans. . . . And why, indeed, are wars undertaken if not to conquer colonies which permit the employment of fresh capital, to acquire commercial monopolies, or to obtain the exclusive use of certain highways of commerce? The wage society cannot comprehend why a crusade should have been undertaken to redeem the Holy Sepulchre, but it would readily understand a movement in this direction if it were a question of preserving the neutrality of the isthmus of Suez. [pp. 264–7]

When a country which has contracted a debt is unable . . . to offer sufficient guarantee for the punctual payment of interest, what happens? Sometimes an out and out conquest of the debtor country follows. Thus France's attempted conquest of Mexico during the second empire was undertaken solely with the view of guaranteeing the interest of French citizens holding Mexican securities. But more frequently the insufficient guarantee of an international loan gives rise to the appointment of a financial commission by the creditor countries in order to protect their rights and guard the fate of their invested capital. The appointment of such a commission usually amounts, in the end, however, to a veritable conquest. We have examples of this in Egypt, which has to all practical purposes become a British province, and in Tunis, which has in like manner become a dependency of France, who supplied the greater part of the loan. The Egyptian revolt against foreign domination resulting from the debt came to nothing, as it met with invincible opposition from capitalistic combinations, and Tel-el-Kebir's success, bought with money, was the most brilliant victory wealth has ever obtained on the field of battle. [p. 273]

The Economic Foundations of Society (first edition, 1885; second completely revised edition in Italian, 1898); English translation, Swan Sonnenschein, 1899.

14 A Liberal View, 1899

J. M. ROBERTSON

J. M. Robertson (1856–1933) was a Scottish writer, rationalist and politician, who combined strong free-trading beliefs with socialist ideas on a planned economy. Among his many other interests were sociology and mythology. This extract from Patriotism and Empire, *published in 1899, is important because it contains most of the arguments used at greater length by Hobson in 1902. What it lacks is a theoretical basis, deriving imperialism not merely from evidence of speculation and the pressures of sectional interests but from the fundamental features of modern capitalism.*

Shortly put, the imperialist's case is that expansion of 'the empire' is necessary—

1. To provide openings for the emigration of our superfluous population; and
2. To 'open up fresh markets'.

When answered that we need not own our markets, and that trade normally goes on between different States, he answers

3. That 'trade follows the flag'. . . .

And first as to the formula about scope for emigration. Only actual observation could convince one that this plea is ever used in good faith, so nakedly does it collide with the notorious statistical facts. A glance at the Registrar-General's statistics shows us that year by year from two to six times as many British emigrants pass to the United States as to all the colonies together. . . . Furthermore, the regions in which alone there is any ostensible prospect of 'expansion' in the near future are precisely those which offer least outlet for genuine emigration: to wit, China, uncolonized Africa, and parts of South America. . . .

Putting aside, then, the 'pasteboard portico' of the pseudo-Malthusian theory, we come to the real motives: (1) The primary desire of the speculative commercial class for new grounds in which to buy cheap and sell dear; (2) the suffusive instinct of spoliation and dominion which, on the part of the 'services' and the general public, backs them up; and (3) the sinister interest of those industrial sections which thrive on the production of war material. It would be hard to conceive a more mindless system of social evolution than that presupposed by the resort, at this time of day, to the early ideal that trade is best to be pushed by barter with semi-barbarians. . . . The true problem, then, is not to induce more uncivilized people to buy our products and pay for them with theirs, but to increase the consuming power of the producing masses already interchanging. A raising of the standard of comfort among our own mass, a substitution of decent conditions for hideous misery among the lower strata of the imperial State, would at once widen markets in an indefinitely progressive degree; while no amount of expansion in Asia and Africa, as things now go, can conceivably lessen our own normal rate of pauperism. [pp. 173–7]

The relevant sense, then, in which trade 'follows the flag' is this: that the flag is the means by which the gamblers of trade can best find their way to new grounds of exploitation, leaving the seat of 'empire' at home to sink, it may be, like a derelict ship. Doubtless there is a temporary alternative. Denuded of productive industries, and therefore of industrial population, England may for a time remain a seat of empire as did Italy until the transference of the Roman centre to Constantinople. Her soil would be owned and divided as pleasure-ground among an aristocracy of capitalists, who would employ simply the labour needed for their own service, their incomes being drawn from investments or industries in other regions. . . . No empire can long subsist as such when the sources of its wealth are outside of its proper soil. . . . The one decisive difference of conditions between the British Empire and those of Rome and Spain is the possession of an adequate source of real wealth and power in its home industry. Once that is gone, decadence must follow in the one case as in the others. . . .

English life for a generation back has become in every decade more thoroughly leavened with the spirit of gambling; and that spirit normally tends to cast out the methods of scrupulous industry. More and more, for twenty years back, has stock-jobbing enterprise run either to semi-fraudulent domestic undertakings or to foreign mining adventures, which proceed upon no proved knowledge and cater for no sound demand. And so far as is yet seen, the exploitation of South Africa, which is for the present the chief theatre of imperialist instincts and interests, is doing no more for human needs than the gold-mining of the past in California, where one of the permanent results was the destruction of great areas of cultivable land. . . .

We come back, then, to the vital aspect of imperialism for the mass of the working population. The only interests really furthered by fresh expansion are those of the speculative trading class, the speculative capitalist class, the military and naval services, the industrial class which supplies war material, and generally those who look to an imperial civil service as a means of employment for themselves and their kin. . . .

As against all the sophistries we have passed under review, the central truth falls to be stated thus: imperial expansion is substantially a device on the part of the moneyed class, primarily to further its own chances, secondarily to put off the day of reckoning as between capital and labour. . . . While imperialism prospers, there will be no vital social reform; and reactionary Ministers have begun to see that by playing the game of militarist imperialism they can safely push aside the appeal for such reform. One of the first sequelae of the triumph of Omdurman was the definite repudiation of Ministerial promises in the direction of Old Age Pensions. [pp. 181-8]

Patriotism and Empire (1899), 3rd edn. Grant Richards, 1900.

15 South African Imperialists, 1900

J. A. HOBSON

It is difficult to state the truth about our doings in South Africa without seeming to appeal to the ignominious passion of Judenhetze. Nevertheless a plain account of the personal and economic forces operative in the Transvaal is essential to an understanding of the issue, and must not be shirked. A few of the financial pioneers in South Africa have been Englishmen, like Messrs Rhodes and Rudd; but recent developments of Transvaal gold-mining have thrown the economic resources of the country more and more into the hands of a small group of international financiers, chiefly German in origin and Jewish in race. By superior ability, enterprise, and organization these men, out-competing the slower-witted Briton, have attained a practical supremacy which no one who has visited Johannesburg is likely to question.

It should be distinctly understood that the stress which my analysis lays upon the Jew has reference to the class of financial capitalists of which the foreign Jew must be taken as the leading type.

Before I went there, the names of Beit, Eckstein, Barnato, &c., were of course not unknown to me; the very ship in which I crossed bore many scores of Jewish women and children. But until I came to examine closely the structure of industry and society upon the Rand I had no conception of their number or their power. I thus discovered that not Hamburg, not Vienna, not Frankfort, but Johannesburg is the New Jerusalem. . . .

It thus appears that the industrial and agricultural future of the Transvaal is already hypothecated to this small ring of financial foreigners, who not merely own or control the present values, but have, by buying up mining properties and claims of a contingent future value, secured an even more complete supremacy over the economic future. . . .

Put in a concise form, it may be said that this war is being waged in order to secure for the mines a cheap adequate supply of labour. . . . For this reason our international capitalists are expanders of the British Empire.

The War in South Africa, Nisbet, 1900, pp. 189–94, 231, 233.

16 'Imperialism: a Study' 1902

J. A. HOBSON

Quibbles about the modern meaning of the term Imperialism are best resolved by reference to concrete facts in the history of the last thirty years. During that period a number of European nations, Great Britain being first and foremost, have annexed or otherwise asserted political sway over vast portions of Africa and Asia, and over numerous islands in the Pacific and elsewhere. The extent to which this policy of expansion has been carried on, and in particular the enormous size and the peculiar character of the British acquisitions, are not adequately realized even by those who pay some attention to Imperial politics. [p. 15]

Taking the growth of Imperialism as illustrated in the recent expansion of Great Britain and of the chief continental Powers, we find the distinction between Imperialism and colonization . . . closely borne out by facts and figures, and warranting the following general judgements:

First – Almost the whole of recent imperial expansion is occupied with the political absorption of tropical or sub-tropical lands in which white men will not settle with their families.

Second – Nearly all the lands are thickly peopled by 'lower races'.

Thus this recent imperial expansion stands entirely distinct from the colonization of sparsely peopled lands in temperate zones, where white colonists carry with them the modes of government, the industrial and other arts of the civilization of the mother country. The 'occupation' of these new territories is comprised in the presence of a small minority of white men, officials, traders, and industrial organizers, exercising political and economic sway over great hordes of population regarded as inferior and as incapable of exercising any considerable rights of self-government, in politics or industry. (pp. 25–6)

Next, let us inquire whether the vast outlay of energy and money upon imperial expansion is attended by a growing trade within the Empire as compared with foreign trade. In other words, does the policy tend to make us more and more an economically self-sufficing Empire? Does trade follow the flag? . . . Taking under survey our whole Empire, we reach the conclusion that, excluding our commerce with India, the smallest, least valuable, and most uncertain trade is that done with our tropical possessions, and in particular with those which have come under imperial control since 1870. The only considerable increase of our import trade since 1884 is from our genuine colonies in Australasia, North America, and Cape Colony; the trade with India has been stagnant, while that with our tropical colonies in Africa and the West Indies has been in most cases irregular and dwindling. Our export trade exhibits the same general character, save that Australia and Canada show a growing resolution to release themselves from dependence upon British manufactures; the trade with the tropical colonies, though exhibiting some increase, is very small and very fluctuating.

As for the territories acquired under the new Imperialism, except in one instance, no serious attempt to regard them as satisfactory business assets is possible. Egypt alone yields a trade of some magnitude; of the other possessions, three only – Lagos, Niger Coast Protectorate, and North Borneo – are proved to do a trade with Great Britain exceeding one million pounds in value. . . . Apart from its quantity, the quality of the new tropical export trade is of the lowest, consisting for the most part . . . of the cheapest textile goods of Lancashire, the cheapest metal goods of Birmingham and Sheffield, and large quantities of gun-powder, spirits, and tobacco.

Such evidence leads to the following conclusions bearing upon the economics of the new Imperialism. First, the external trade of Great Britain bears a small and diminishing proportion to its internal industry and trade. Secondly, of the external trade, that with British possessions bear a diminishing proportion to that with foreign countries. Thirdly, of the trade with British possessions, the tropical trade, and in particular the trade with the new tropical possessions, is the smallest, least progressive, and most fluctuating in quantity, while it is lowest in the character of the goods which it embraces. [pp. 34, 42–4]

Seeing that the Imperialism of the last three decades is clearly condemned as a business policy, in that at enormous expense it has procured a small, bad, unsafe increase of markets, and has jeopardized the entire wealth of the nation in rousing the strong resentment of other nations, we may ask, 'How is the British nation induced to embark upon such unsound business?' The only possible answer is that the business interests of the nation as a whole are subordinated to those of certain sectional interests that usurp control of the national resources and use them for their private gain. . . .

Although the new Imperialism has been bad business for the nation, it has been good business for certain classes and certain trades within the nation. The vast expenditure on armaments, the costly wars, the grave risks and embarrassments of foreign policy, the stoppage of political and social reforms within Great Britain, though fraught with great injury to the nation, have served well the present business interests of certain industries and professions. . . .

In order to explain Imperialism on this hypothesis we have to answer two questions. Do we find in Great Britain to-day any well-organized group of special commercial and social interests which stand to gain by aggressive Imperialism and the militarism it involves? If such a combination of interests exists, has it the power to work its will in the arena of politics?

What is the direct economic outcome of Imperialism? A great expenditure of public money upon ships, guns, military and naval equipment and stores, growing and productive of enormous profits when a war, or an alarm of war, occurs; new public loans and important fluctuations in the home and foreign Bourses; more posts for soldiers and sailors and in the diplomatic and consular services;

improvement of foreign investments by the substitution of the British flag for a foreign flag; acquisition of markets for certain classes of exports, and some protection and assistance for trades representing British houses in these manufactures; employment for engineers, missionaries, speculative miners, ranchers and other emigrants.

Certain definite business and professional interests feeding upon imperialistic expenditure, or upon the results of that expenditure, are thus set up in opposition to the common good, and, instinctively feeling their way to one another, are found united in strong sympathy to support every new imperialist exploit. . . .

By far the most important factor in Imperialism is the influence relating to investments. The growing cosmopolitanism of capital is the greatest economic change of this generation. Every advanced industrial nation is tending to place a larger share of its capital outside the limits of its own political area, in foreign countries, or in colonies, and to draw a growing income from this source. . . .

Mr Mulhall gives the following estimate of the size and growth of our foreign and colonial investments since 1862:

Year	Amount	Annual Increase
	£	Per cent
1862 . . .	144,000,000	...
1872 . . .	600,000,000	45·6
1882 . . .	875,000,000	27·5
1893 . . .	1,698,000,000	74·8

This last amount is of especial interest, because it represents the most thorough investigation made by a most competent economist for the *Dictionary of Political Economy*. The investments included under this figure may be classified under the following general heads:

Loans	Million £	Railways	Million £	Sundries	Million £
Foreign .	525	U.S.A. .	120	Banks . .	50
Colonial .	225	Colonial .	140	Lands . .	100
Municipal .	20	Various .	128	Mines, &c.	390
	770		388		540

In other words, in 1893 the British capital invested abroad represented about 15 per cent of the total wealth of the United Kingdom: nearly one-half of this capital was in the form of loans to foreign and colonial Governments; of the rest a large proportion was invested in railways, banks, telegraphs, and other public services, owned, controlled, or vitally affected by Governments, while most of the remainder was placed in lands and mines, or in industries directly dependent on land values. . . .

Now, without placing any undue reliance upon these estimates, we cannot fail to recognize that in dealing with these foreign investments we are facing by far the most important factor in the economics of Imperialism. Whatever figures we take, two facts are evident. First, that the income derived as interest upon foreign investments enormously exceeds that derived as profits upon ordinary export and import trade. Secondly, that while our foreign and colonial trade, and presumably the income from it, are growing but slowly, the share of our import values representing income from foreign investments is growing very rapidly.

In a former chapter I pointed out how small a proportion of our national income appeared to be derived as profits from external trade. It seemed unintelligible that the enormous costs and risks of the new Imperialism should be undertaken for such small results in the shape of increase to external trade. . . . The statistics of foreign investments, however, shed clear light upon the economic forces which are dominating our policy. While the manufacturing and trading classes make little out of their new markets . . . it is quite otherwise with the investor.

It is not too much to say that the modern foreign policy of Great Britain is primarily a struggle for profitable markets of investment. . . .

Aggressive Imperialism, which costs the tax-payer so dear, which is of so little value to the manufacturer and trader, which is fraught with such grave incalculable peril to the citizen, is a source of great gain to the investor who cannot find at home the profitable use he seeks for his capital, and insists that his Government should help him to profitable and secure investments abroad.

If, contemplating the enormous expenditure on armaments, the ruinous wars, the diplomatic audacity of knavery by which modern Governments seek to extend their territorial power, we put the plain, practical question, *Cui bono?* the first and most obvious answer is, The investor. . . .

Investors who have put their money in foreign lands, upon terms which take full account of risks connected with the political conditions of the country, desire to use the resources of their Government to minimize these risks, and so to enhance the capital value and the interest of their private investments. The investing and speculative classes in general also desire that Great Britain should take other foreign areas under her flag in order to secure new areas for profitable investment and speculation. [pp. 51–63]

If the special interest of the investor is liable to clash with the public interest and to induce a wrecking policy, still more dangerous is the special interest of the financier, the general dealer in investments. In large measure the rank and file of the investors are, both for business and for politics, the cat's-paws of the great financial houses, who use stocks and shares not so much as investments to yield them interest, but as material for speculation in the money market. . . . No great quick direction of capital is possible save by their consent and through their agency. Does any one seriously suppose that a great war could be undertaken by any European State, or a great State loan subscribed, if the house of Rothschild and its connections set their face against it?

Every great political act involving a new flow of capital, or a large fluctuation in the values of existing investments, must receive the sanction and the practical aid of this little group of financial kings. These men, holding their realized wealth and their business capital, as they must, chiefly in stocks and bonds, have a double stake, first as investors, but secondly and chiefly as financial dealers. As investors, their political influence does not differ essentially from that of the smaller investors, except that they usually possess a practical control of the businesses in which they invest. As speculators or financial dealers they constitute, however, the gravest single factor in the economics of Imperialism. . . .

In view of the part which the non-economic factors of patriotism, adventure, military enterprise, political ambition, and philanthropy play in imperial expansion, it may appear that to impute to financiers so much power is to take a too narrowly economic view of history. And it is true that the motor-power of Imperialism is not chiefly financial: finance is rather the governor of the imperial engine, directing the energy and determining its work: it does not constitute the fuel of the engine, nor does it directly generate the power. Finance manipulates the patriotic forces which politicians, soldiers, philanthropists, and traders generate; the enthusiasm for expansion which issues from these sources, though strong and genuine, is irregular and blind; the financial interest has those qualities of concentration and clear-sighted calculation which are needed to set Imperialism to work. An ambitious statesman, a frontier soldier, an over-zealous missionary, a pushing trader, may suggest or even initiate a step of imperial expansion, may assist in educating patriotic public opinion to the urgent need of some fresh advance, but the final determination rests with the financial power. The direct influence exercised by great financial houses in 'high politics' is supported by the control which they exercise over the body of public opinion through the Press, which, in every 'civilized' country, is becoming more and more their obedient instrument. . . .

Such is the array of distinctively economic forces making for imperialism, a large loose group of trades and professions seeking profitable business and lucrative employment from the expansion of military and civil services, from the expenditure on military operations, the opening up of new tracts of territory and trade with the same, and the provision of new capital which these operations require, all these finding their central guiding and directing force in the power of the general financier. . . . [pp. 63–8]

American Imperialism is the natural product of the economic pressure of a sudden advance of capitalism which cannot find occupation at home and needs foreign markets for goods and for investments.

The same needs exist in European countries, and, as is admitted, drive Governments along the same path. Over-production in the sense of an excessive manufacturing plant, and surplus capital which cannot find sound investments within the country, force Great Britain, Germany, Holland, France to place larger and larger portions of their economic resources outside the area of their present political domain, and then stimulate a policy of political expansion so as to take in the new areas. The economic sources of this movement are laid bare by periodic trade-depressions due to an inability of producers to find adequate and profitable markets for what they can produce. . . .

Every improvement of methods of production, every concentration of ownership and control, seems to accentuate the tendency. As one nation after another enters the machine economy and adopts advanced industrial methods, it becomes more difficult for its manufacturers, merchants, and financiers to dispose profitably of their economic resources, and they are tempted more and more to use their Governments in order to secure for their particular use some distant undeveloped country by annexation and protection. . . .

It is this economic condition of affairs that forms the taproot of Imperialism. If the consuming public in this country raised its standard of consumption to keep pace with every rise of productive powers, there could be no excess of goods or capital clamorous to use Imperialism in order to find markets: foreign trade would indeed exist, but there would be no difficulty in exchanging a small surplus of our manufactures for the food and raw material we annually absorbed, and all the savings that we made could find employment, if we chose, in home industries. . . .

The root questions underlying the phenomena are clearly these: 'Why is it that consumption fails to keep pace automatically in a community with power of production?' 'Why does under-consumption or over-saving occur?' . . . [pp. 85–7]

[*Hobson's answer consists of the argument he used in* The Evolution of Modern Capitalism *printed above, pp. 54–9.*]

The fallacy of the supposed inevitability of imperial expansion as a necessary outlet for progressive industry is now manifest. It is not industrial progress that demands the opening up of new markets and areas of investment, but mal-distribution of consuming power which prevents the absorption of commodities and capital within the country. The over-saving which is the economic root of Imperialism is found by analysis to consist of rents, monopoly profits, and other unearned or excessive elements of income, which, not being earned by labour of head or hand, have no legitimate *raison d'être*. Having no natural relation to effort of production, they impel their recipients to no corresponding satisfaction of consumption: they form a surplus wealth, which, having no proper place in the normal economy of production and consumption, tends to accumulate as excessive savings. Let any turn in the tide of politico-economic forces divert from these owners their excess of income and make it flow, either to the workers in higher wages, or to the community in taxes, so that it will be spent instead of being saved, serving in either of these ways to swell the tide of consumption – there will be no need to fight for foreign markets or foreign areas of investment. . . . It is idle to attack Imperialism or Militarism as political expedients or policies unless the axe is laid at the economic root of the tree, and the classes for whose interest Imperialism works are shorn of the surplus revenues which seek this outlet. [pp. 91, 99]

Imperialism: a Study, Nisbet, 1902.

17 Colonial Investments, 1908

P. LEROY-BEAULIEU

Leroy-Beaulieu (1843–1916) was a leading French economist and journalist, though a publicist rather than an original thinker. He was a liberal of the same type as J. S. Mill, and adopted Mill's version of the theory of capital exports as a means of preventing the declining rate of profit which he incorporated in his Essai sur la répartition des richesses *(1st edn., 1880) and also in his more famous,* De la colonisation chez les peuples modernes, *first published in 1874. In earlier editions of* Colonisation *no special distinction was made between the advantages of exporting capital to colonies and elsewhere. Possibly as a result of the work of Hobson and others, the 1908 edition contained this passage; though Leroy-Beaulieu still maintained a favourable attitude to capital exports and colonization.*

A careful reader might, however, object that the export of capital could proceed without colonization. That is true. Yet, other things being equal, it is more worth while to export capital to one's own colonies than to totally foreign countries. In the former one is more certain to find a sound administration, impartial justice, a favourable welcome and fair treatment both by the public and the government. Many countries have an inclination to treat foreign capital roughly when they think they can do without it in the future. From this point of view, capitalists run lower risks in the colonies, which are in some sense an extension of the metropolis. Again, from a moral point of view, there is great pleasure to be had in thinking that one's wealth has contributed to creating distant societies which increase the greatness of the nation, and which preserve and honour the language, customs and spirit of the mother country.

De la colonisation chez les peuples modernes. 6th edn., Paris, Félix Alcan, 1908; p. 487, trans. D. K. F.

18 Finance Capitalism, 1910

R. HILFERDING

Rudolf Hilferding (1877–1941) was a leading Viennese intellectual and Social Democrat before 1914 who founded the Independent Socialist Party. After 1918 he went to Germany and played a leading part in politics there, becoming Finance Minister in 1923 and 1928. He took refuge in Paris on Hitler's accession to power in 1933, and was caught there in 1940. He died in 1941 when imprisoned by the Secret Police, allegedly by suicide. Finance Capital, published in 1910, was a major contribution to the Theory of Capitalist Imperialism because it provided a coherent Marxist explanation of why capitalism should become imperialist. Its argument, deriving from Engels's additions to Marx and reflecting extended debate on the question in Vienna, was adopted by Bukharin and Lenin and so became integral with the final Marxist dogma.

The development of capitalist industry develops concentration of the banking system. The concentrated banking system is in itself an important force making for the highest degree of capitalistic concentration in cartels and trusts. How do these in turn affect the banking system? The cartel or the trust is an enterprise representing capital at its most powerful. In the mutual dependence of capitalistic enterprises it is the amount of capital which in the first place determines which enterprise will be dependent on the other. Advanced cartelization causes the banks to unite and expand in order not to become dependent on the cartel or trust. Cartelization promotes amalgamation of the banks just as, conversely, bank amalgamation stimulates cartelization. A large number of banks, for instance, are interested in a steel works merger; they work together towards this end, even against the will of individual industrialists. It is, on the other hand, possible that community of interests established by the industrialists may conversely cause two banks, hitherto rivals, to develop common interests and to begin to act jointly in a certain sphere of business. Industrial combinations have a similar effect on the expansion of the industrial interests of a bank which, previously interested merely in the raw material sector, is now forced, as a result of these combinations, to expand its activity to the processing industries also.

A precondition for a cartel is a big banking house in a position to supply at any given moment the enormous credits needed for payment and production for a whole industrial sector.

We have seen that, at the beginning of capitalistic production, the money used by the banks originated from two sources: first, from the money of the non-productive class, and, second, from the reserve capital of the industrial and commercial capitalists. We have also seen how the development of credit is directed towards placing the entire reserve capital of the capitalist class, as well as the greatest part of the money belonging to the non-producing classes, at the disposal of industry. In other words, contemporary industry operates with a capital which is far greater than the total capital possessed by the industrial capitalists themselves. As capitalism develops, the amount of money which the non-productive class puts at the disposal of the banks, and through them at the disposal of the industrialist, is steadily increasing. The banks thus control these sums of money which are indispensable to industry. With the development of capitalism and its credit organizations, industry becomes more and more dependent on the banks. On the other hand the banks can only attract the money of the non-producing classes and keep the ever-growing original deposits at their disposal if they pay interest on this money. They could do this, so long as these funds were not too vast, by using them as credits for speculation and circulating credit. With the increase of these funds, however, and with the diminishing importance of speculation and commerce, it was necessary to transfer them more and more into industrial capital. Without the ever-growing expansion of credit for production the usefulness of the deposits, and also the interest on bank deposits, would have sunk far lower long ago. Indeed, to some extent, this actually happened in England, where only the deposit banks negotiate circulating credit; with the result that the interest on deposits is minimal. This causes a steady flow of these deposits into industrial investments through the purchase of shares. The public thus does directly what the bank also does in forming a connection between industry and the banks of deposit. The result for the public is the same, as it has in any case no share in the promoter's profit. But, for industry, it means less dependence on bank capital in England as compared with Germany.

The dependence of industry on the banks is thus the result of property relationships. A steadily increasing proportion of industrial capital does not belong to the industrialists who use it. They can dispose of the capital only through the bank, which represents the owners of the money to them. On the other hand, the bank must place a steadily increasing part of its capital in industry. In this way the bank itself is growing, to an ever increasing extent, an industrial capitalist itself. I call this *bank capital, that is capital in the form of money which in this way is in fact transformed into industrial capital, finance capital*. This always represents money to its owners; it is invested by its owners in the form of money capital which bears interest and can be withdrawn at any time as money. But in reality most of this money deposited with the banks is transformed into industrial productive capital (capital goods and working capacity) and is thus fixed as part of the process of production. A steadily growing part of the money used by industry is finance capital, capital at the disposal of the banks and used by the industrialists.

This finance capital grows with the development of joint stock companies and reaches its climax with the monopolizing of industry. Industrial profit gains a more secure and stable character, and the investment opportunities open to bank capital in industry also expand steadily. But the bank disposes of the bank capital and the bank itself is controlled by those who hold a majority of its shares. It is thus clear that, with growing concentration of property, the owners of the fictitious capital which gives control over the banks and of the capital which gives power over industry, become more and more identical; and this all the more so because of the way we have seen the big bank gaining more and more the power of disposing of fictitious capital.

We have seen how industry becomes increasingly dependent on bank capital; but this does not mean that the industrial magnates also become dependent on banking magnates. Just as capital in its highest form is transformed into finance capital, so the great capitalist – the finance capitalist – more and more consolidates his disposal of the entire capital of the nation by means of controlling bank capital. Here the union of functions in the same persons plays an important role.

Through the creation of cartels and trusts finance capital obtains its highest level of power. . . . [pp. 280–4]

The protective tariff . . . grants the cartel a profit over and above that reached through cartelization and gives it the power of levying to some extent an indirect tax on the people at home. . . .

The increase in price on the home market tends, however, to decrease the sale of cartelized products and in that way comes into conflict with the tendency to reduce production costs by extending the scale of production. The existence of the cartels may be endangered wherever they have not yet attained a firm footing. The largest and best equipped undertakings which find the reduction of their sales through the cartel policy unbearable, reopen the competitive struggle in order to destroy the weaker undertakings and, when the struggle has ceased, a stronger cartel on a new basis may very well come into existence. Should the cartel be on a firm footing it will try to make up for the restrictions on the home market by increasing exports so as to maintain former production and where possible increase it. The cartel must, of course, sell on the world market at the world market price. Should the cartel be at all efficient and capable of export (which is the case according to our hypothesis) its actual price will correspond to the world market price. The cartel, however, is also in a position to sell at less than its production price, since it has gained a certain extra profit, determined by the amount of the duty, on home sales. It is, therefore, in a position to utilize a part of this extra profit in extending its sales areas abroad by undercutting its competitors. Should this succeed it can increase its production in the long run, reduce production costs and obtain a new extra profit as the price on the home market remains the same. The cartel achieves the same result by paying its home customers export premiums from its extra profits when they export its products. . . .

Free trade was by no means considered by its protagonists as something to be exclusively applied to England. Industrial circles in that country were far more concerned with spreading the doctrine of free trade throughout the world as this would secure for them a monopoly of the world's markets. Restrictive tariffs by other states meant a corresponding restriction of outlets for British goods. A change has, however, taken place today in the sense of capital's being able to surmount this hurdle. The introduction or increase of customs duties in another country still means a reduction of sales outlets for those trying to export there, that is to say a hindrance to their industrial development. A protective tariff nonetheless means extra profits and thus provides a spur to others to produce the goods in the foreign country itself instead of sending them in. While capitalism was at an undeveloped stage this possibility was relatively small, partly because local legislation intervened to prevent such a contingency and partly because the economic premises for capitalist production did not yet exist to a sufficient degree. There was a lack of state security, a lack of labour, especially skilled labour: barriers which had to be gradually overcome and which made the transfer of capital extraordinarily difficult. But these hindrances have been disposed of for the most part today. And it is thus possible for the capital of a developed country to overcome the injurious results of the protective tariff system with regard to the rate of profit by means of capital exports.

While the general application of the protective tariff system aims at dividing up the world market into an ever greater number of economic areas on state lines, the development of finance capital increases the importance of the size of the economic area itself. . . .

Two opposed tendencies have thus become apparent. The protective tariff becomes an offensive weapon for trade rivalry in the hands of the cartels by means of which the price war is intensified together with national power and diplomatic interventions simultaneously employed to strengthen their position in the competitive struggle. The protective tariff, on the other hand, stabilizes the national cartels thus promoting the formation of inter-cartel structures. The result of these tendencies is that these international agreements represent a truce rather than a continuing community of interests since every shift in the protective tariff armament and every change in the market conditions of the state alter the basis of the agreements and make new contracts necessary. The only cases where more lasting structures arise are those where free trade more or less gets rid of the national barriers or where the cartel is not based on the protective tariff but exists thanks to a natural monopoly as is the case, for example, with petroleum.

Cartelization, at the same time, extraordinarily increases the direct importance of the size of the economic areas as far as the amount of profit is concerned. We have seen that the protective tariff provides extra profit for the capitalist monopoly for sales on the home market. The larger the economic area, the greater the home sales (recall the proportion of production reaching the export markets from the steel mills of the United States on the one hand and from those of Belgium on the other) and the greater the cartel profits. The greater the latter the higher the export premiums and the stronger the ability to compete successfully on the world market. The more active intervention in world politics caused by the 'colonial passion' was accompanied by the effort to make the economic area as extensive as possible by means of the protective tariff wall.

In cases where the effects of the protective tariff unfavourably influence the rate of profit the cartel reacts with means placed at its disposal by the protective system itself. The development of export premiums which follow in the train of protective tariffs makes it possible to break (at least partially) foreign protective tariff walls and thus obviates to a certain degree the restriction of production. . . . Industrial circles threatened by the protective tariff of foreign countries make use of this very protective tariff by transferring a part of their production abroad. Even if this makes the extension of the parent business impossible and if increased profits accruing from production cost reduction are lost, compensation is afforded by the increased profit on goods produced abroad for the same capital owners. Capital exports, therefore, which, in another form, receive a mighty impetus through the protective tariff of their own country, are similarly spurred on by the foreign country and contribute at the same time to spreading the capitalist system throughout the world and to the internationalization of capital itself. . . .

If modern protective tariff policy strengthens capital's ever present urge to extend continually the frontiers of its domination, the concentration of all unused financial capital in the hand of the banks leads to the planned organization of capital exports. The close connection of the banks with industry permits them to attach the condition that money capital granted will be used for the benefit of industry. The furtherance of capital export is thus expedited to an extraordinary degree in all its forms.

By capital export we understand the export of value intended to produce added value abroad. It is an essential part of this process that the added value remains at the disposal of the home capital. If, for example, a German capitalist emigrates to Canada, sets up in business there and does not return home, this is a loss for German capital; the capital is, so to speak, denationalized. This is not capital export, it is transfer of capital. This transfer of capital amounts to a deduction from the home and a growth of the foreign capital. One can only speak of capital export if the capital used abroad remains at the disposal of the home country and the added value created by the home capitalists may be readily disposed of. . . .

With the development of finance capital in Europe, European capital as such frequently finds its way abroad. One of the large German banks establishes a branch in a foreign country; this bank negotiates a loan, whose proceeds are used to build an electrical plant; the development of the branch is handed over to an electricity company, which remains in connection with the bank in the homeland. Or the whole process is even more simplified. The foreign branch of the bank establishes an industrial enterprise, issues shares in the homeland, and sends the produce back again to those enterprises which are connected with the head office of the bank. This transaction occurs on the largest scale when the loan transactions between the two states are used for the purpose of procuring industrial deliveries. It is the close connection between bank and industry which expedites this growth of capital export.

A condition for the export of capital is the differential between rates of profit. Capital export is instrumental in levelling out national profit rates. The level of profit depends on the organic components of the capital, that is, on the level which capitalist development has reached. The more advanced this is, the lower the general rate of profit will be. This general condition does not have to be considered here, since it relates to goods on the world market whose price is determined by the most highly developed methods of production. But there are other special points which have to be considered. The rate of interest is much higher in countries with a low capitalistic development and which are for the first time accepting credit and banking organizations than in developed capitalistic states. Added to this is the fact that parts of the wages or the profit of the employer are contained in the interest. The high rate of interest acts as an immediate stimulus for the export of loan capital. The profits of the capitalist are higher because labour is extraordinarily cheap and because the lower quality of the labour is balanced by excessively long working hours. Ground rents are low or nominal, as there is ample land available, either naturally, or by forcible expropriation of the natives. The low price of land thus lowers the costs of production. In such places there also occurs an increase of profits as the result of privileges and monopolies. Should it be a case of products whose outlet is the new market itself high extra profits will result, as in this case capitalistically produced goods compete with goods produced by artisans.

In whatever way the export of capital occurs, the absorption capacity of the foreign market will always increase. The limited capacity of foreign markets to absorb the products of European industry was the old barrier to the export of goods. The capacity of these markets to consume was limited by the disposition to overproduction resulting from their natural economic or in other ways undeveloped methods of production, whose productivity could not be increased quickly and which were even less likely to be changed into production for the market in a short time. . . .

The export of capital as loan capital increases the consumer capacity of the new market to an extraordinary degree. Suppose a newly established market to be capable of exporting goods to the value of a million pounds, its capacity to absorb goods in exchange (assuming exchange at the same values) is one million pounds also. If this value is exported into the foreign country not as goods but as loan capital; for instance in the form of a state loan; the value of one million pounds which is at the disposal of the new market through the export of its surplus of goods serves not as a means to the exchange of goods but as a means of paying interest on the loan capital. Now it is possible to export into this country goods to the value not of one but, say, of ten million pounds, provided this value of goods is sent as capital with an interest rate of 10 per cent; and to the value of 20 millions if the interest rate sinks to 5 per cent. At the same time, this demonstrates the great significance of the drop in the rate of interest for the capacity of the market to expand. The sharp competition of foreign loan capital has the effect of lowering the rate of interest quickly in backward countries also, and thus again increases the possibility of capital export. But far more important than the export of loan capital is the effect of the export of capital in the form of industrial capital, and this is the reason why the export of industrial capital becomes increasingly important. For the transfer of capitalistic production to the foreign market frees the latter completely from the limitations imposed by its own consumer capacity. The return from this new production ensures the realization of the capital. This newly established market is not, however, valuable merely because of the sales made to it. Capital invested in these new territories itself turns to forms of production whose sales are safe in the world market. The capitalization of South Africa, for example, is completely detached from the absorption capacity of South Africa, since the main sphere of production – mining for gold – has unlimited consumer capacity. Capitalization is here dependent only on the natural capacity of the mine workings to expand and the presence of an adequate labour force. A similar example may be seen in the copper mines, which are also independent of the consumer capacity of the colony; while those industries really producing consumption goods have to rely mainly on the new market for demand for their goods and very soon come up against the difficulty of the limit of consumption capacity.

Thus the export of capital pushes back the limits imposed by the consumer capacity of the new market. At the same time the introduction of capitalistic methods of transport and production into the foreign country also generates rapid economic development: the establishment of a larger internal market through the destruction of the pattern of natural economy; the expansion of production for the market and hence the increase of those products which will be exported and which will, in this way, produce new interest on the newly imported capital. The establishment of colonies and new markets once used to imply the establishment of new consumer products; but today new investment of capital is primarily directed toward places which deliver raw material for industry. Simultaneously with the expansion of home industry which serves the needs of capital export, the exported capital turns to the production of raw material for those industries. In this way the products of the exported capital find an opening in the homeland, and the narrow circle in which production in England moves gains an extraordinary extension through the mutual stimulus of home industry and the products of the exported capital.

But we know also that the opening up of new markets is an important factor in ending an industrial depression, in extending periods of prosperity and in reducing the consequences of crises. Capital export speeds up the opening of foreign countries and develops their productive capacity to the highest degree. At the same time production at home will be increased, as this has to produce those goods which are sent abroad as capital. Thus capital export is a mighty stimulus to capitalistic production, which, once capital export becomes general, enters a new *Sturm und Drang* period, during which the cycle of prosperity and depression and crises appears to be shortened. The quick increase of production creates an increase in demand for labour, which strengthens the trade unions; the tendency to create poverty, immanent in capitalism, seems to be overcome in countries which had long been capitalist. The rapid rise of production does not bring home to people the evil effects of capitalist society and creates an optimistic assessment of its vitality.

Whether colonies and new markets are now developed more or less fast will now essentially depend on their capacity to serve as places' for capital investment. The richer the colony is in those products which can be capitalistically produced, which have a sure sale in the world market and which are important for home industry, the greater this capacity will be. The rapid expansion of capitalism since 1895 has produced an increase of prices, especially of metals and cotton, and has thus made it necessary to open up new sources of these very important raw materials. Capital awaiting export is therefore always looking for territories which can produce these goods and goes to these places: mines, especially, will be worked by the most advanced· capitalistic methods immediately. This production again creates a greater surplus which the colony can export, and this makes fresh capital investment possible. In this way the capitalization of new markets will be enormously speeded up. The obstacle to the opening up of a new market is not the lack of capital there, for capital export solves this. In most cases another disturbing factor comes more and more to the fore – the lack of 'free' labour, which means paid labour. . . .

As always, when capitalism is confronted for the first time with conditions which obstruct the realization of its aims, and which could be overcome by purely economic methods only gradually and far too slowly, it appeals to the supreme power of the state and makes it the means of expropriation by force. By such means it creates the necessary free wage-labour proletariat, whether, as in the first period of capital's history, this process relates to the European peasant, the Mexican or Peruvian Indians; or, as today, the African Negro. Violent methods are a natural part of colonial policy, which would lose its capitalistic character without it. They form an integral part of it, just as the existence of a destitute proletariat is a necessary pre-condition of capitalism. The possibility of pursuing a colonial policy and also abolishing its violent methods is an illusion which cannot be taken seriously, any more than the possibility of abolishing the proletariat but at the same time maintaining capitalism. . . . [pp. 386–401]

The desire for an expansionist policy revolutionizes the entire view of life held by the bourgeoisie. They are no longer peace-loving and humanitarian. The old free-traders did not look on free trade as being merely the best economic policy but as a starting point for an era of peace. Finance capital lost this belief a long time ago. It does not believe in the harmony of capitalistic interests, but recognizes that competition develops more and more into a political struggle for power. The ideal of peace fades away, and the ideal of the greatness and power of the state replaces the humanitarian ideal. The modern state came into existence as the realization of the struggle of the nation for unity. The idea of the nation (which found its natural limit in forming a nation as the basis for the state, and therefore recognized the right of all other nations to form their own states and regarded the state as the natural limit of the nation), is now transformed into belief in the exaltation of one nation over other nations. The ideal is now to secure for one's own nation supremacy over the whole world, an ambition which is as unlimited as the struggle of capitalism for profits. Capital is now the conqueror of the world, and every new country it conquers represents a new boundary which it has to cross. This struggle is going to be an economic necessity, for to lag behind lowers the profits of finance capital, reduces its ability to compete and, in the end, could make the smaller economic unit a tributary to the larger. It is at root an economic phenomenon; but it is justified on ideological grounds through that peculiar transformation of the idea of the nation, which no longer recognizes the right of every nation to political self-government and independence, and which no longer expresses the democratic principle of the equality of all human beings at the national level. On the contrary, the attitude characteristic of monopoly in the field of economics is again reflected in the superior status which is thought due to one's own nation. This status seems to be above all others. Because the subjugation of foreign nations is carried out by force (that means, in a very natural way), the ruling nation appears to owe this domination to its special natural characteristics—i.e. to the character of its race. Thus, in the ideology of race, there develops disguised as natural science, the reality of finance capital's striving for power, which in this way can prove that its actions depend on and are made necessary by nature and science.

The principle of oligarchic authority replaces that of democratic equality. This principle apparently captivates the whole nation in its attitude to foreign policy; but, in the sphere of domestic policy, it changes to an emphasis on the power of the ruling class over the working class. At the same time the rising power of the workers invigorates the attempts of capitalism to strengthen the power of the state as a safeguard against proletarian demands. Thus originates the ideology of Imperialism as a means of overcoming the old liberal ideals. It scoffs at their naïvety. What an illusion to believe in a harmony of interests in a world of capitalist competition where the superiority of weapons alone is decisive! What an illusion to wait for the reign of eternal peace and to preach the rights of nations, when power alone decides their fate! What folly to wish to carry the settlement of legal relationships within a state outside its borders; what an irresponsible intrusion into the world of business are these humanitarian activities, which made the workers into a movement, which invented the idea of social reform at home, which wants to abolish contract slavery – the only method of exploitation in the colonies! Eternal justice is a beautiful dream, but one cannot even build railways at home with moral principles. How can we conquer the the world if we wait for our rivals to be converted to our principles? [pp. 426–8]

Finanzkapital (1910). *Marx-Studien,* Vol. III. Vienna, Verlag der Wiener Volksfuchhandlung, 1923; trans. E. Bass and D. Adam.

19 A Rival Marxist Theory, 1913

ROSA LUXEMBURG

Rosa Luxemburg (1870–1919) was a Polish nationalist and socialist who settled in Germany in 1896 and thereafter played a leading part in Social Democratic arguments and politics. As a devout Marxist she upheld the principle that capitalism must inevitably break down under its own defects against the 'revisionists' led by Bernstein. At the same time she maintained, like Lenin, that the workers should seize power by revolution without waiting for the eventual collapse. The Accumulation of Capital *was primarily an attempt to rout the revisionists by extending and modifying some of Marx's principles. Her explanation of imperialism, however, owes more to earlier writers such as Sismondi, and, by contrast with Hilferding's argument, regards imperialism as characteristic of capitalism at all stages of its development. Because of its logical defects the argument failed to become standard Marxist theory, but remains an ingenious and in many ways convincing explanation of the relationship between capitalism, overseas trade, capital exports and colonization.*

Marx's diagram of enlarged reproduction cannot explain the actual and historical process of accumulation. And why? Because of the very premises of the diagram. The diagram sets out to describe the accumulative process on the assumption that the capitalists and workers are the sole agents of capitalist consumption. We have seen that Marx consistently and deliberately assumes the universal and exclusive domination of the capitalist mode of production as a theoretical premise of his analysis in all three volumes of *Capital*. Under these conditions, there can admittedly be no other classes of society than capitalists and workers; as the diagram has it, all 'third persons' of capitalist society – civil servants, the liberal professions, the clergy, etc. – must, as consumers, be counted in with these two classes, and preferably with the capitalist class. This axiom, however, is a theoretical contrivance – real life has never known a self-sufficient capitalist society under the exclusive domination of the capitalist mode of production. . . .

The problem amounts to this: If an increasing part of the surplus value is not consumed by the capitalists but employed in the expansion of production, what, then, are the forms of social reproduction? . . . The workers and capitalists themselves cannot possibly realize that part of the surplus value which is to be capitalized. Therefore, the realization of the surplus value for the purposes of accumulations is an impossible task for a society which consists solely of workers and capitalists. . . .

Realization of the surplus value is doubtless a vital question of capitalist accumulation. It requires as its prime condition . . . that there should be a strata of buyers outside capitalist society. Buyers, it should be noted, not consumers, since the material form of the surplus value is quite irrelevant to its realization. The decisive fact is that the surplus value cannot be realized by sale either to workers or to capitalists, but only if it is sold to such social organizations or strata whose own mode of production is not capitalistic. Here we can conceive of two different cases:

1. Capitalist production supplies consumer goods over and above its own requirements, the demand of its workers and capitalists, which are bought by non-capitalist strata and countries. The English cotton industry, for instance, during the first two-thirds of the nineteenth century, and to some extent even now, has been supplying cotton textiles to the peasants and petty-bourgeois townspeople of the European continent, and to the peasants of India, America, Africa and so on. The enormous expansion of the English cotton industry was thus founded on consumption by non-capitalist strata and countries. . . .

2. Conversely, capitalist production supplies means of production in excess of its own demand and finds buyers in non-capitalist countries. English industry, for instance, in the first half of the nineteenth century supplied materials for the construction of railroads in the American and Australian states. . . . Another example would be the German chemical industry which supplies means of production such as dyes in great quantities to Asiatic, African and other countries whose own production is not capitalistic. . . .

In addition, there is no obvious reason why means of production and consumer goods should be produced by capitalist methods alone. . . . How much capitalist accumulation depends upon means of production which are not produced by capitalist methods is shown for example by the cotton crisis in England during the American War of Secession, when the cultivation of the plantations came to a standstill, or by the crisis of European linen-weaving during the war in the East, when flax could not be imported from serf-owning Russia. We need only recall that imports of corn raised by peasants – i.e. not produced by capitalist methods – played a vital part in the feeding of industrial labour, as an element, that is to say, of variable capital, for a further illustration of the close ties between non-capitalist strata and the material elements necessary to the accumulation of capital.

Moreover, capitalist production, by its very nature, cannot be restricted to such means of production as are produced by capitalist methods. Cheap elements of constant capital are essential to the individual capitalist who strives to increase his rate of profit. In addition, the very condition of continuous improvements in labour productivity as the most important method of increasing the rate of surplus value, is unrestricted utilization of all substances and facilities afforded by nature and soil. To tolerate any restriction in this respect would be contrary to the very essence of capital, its whole mode of existence. After many centuries of development, the capitalist mode of production still constitutes only a fragment of total world production. . . . If it were dependent exclusively on elements of production obtainable within such narrow limits, its present level and indeed its development in general would have been impossible. From the very beginning, the forms and laws of capitalist production aim to comprise the entire globe as a store of productive forces. Capital, impelled to appropriate productive forces for purposes of exploitation, ransacks the whole world, it procures its means of production from all corners of the earth, seizing them, if necessary by force, from all levels of civilization and from all forms of society. The problem of the material elements of capitalist accumulation, far from being solved by the material form of the surplus value that has been produced, takes on quite a different aspect. It becomes necessary for capital progressively to dispose ever more fully of the whole globe, to acquire an unlimited choice of means of production, with regard to both quality and quantity, so as to find productive employment for the surplus value it has realized. . . .

Between the production of surplus value, then, and the subsequent period of accumulation, two separate transactions take place – that of realizing the surplus value, i.e. of converting it into pure value, and that of transforming this pure value into productive capital. They are both dealings between capitalist production and the surrounding non-capitalist world. From the aspect both of realizing the surplus value and of procuring the material elements of constant capital, international trade is a prime necessity for the historical existence of capitalism – an international trade which under actual conditions is essentially an exchange between capitalistic and non-capitalistic modes of production.

Hitherto we have considered accumulation solely with regard to surplus value and constant capital. The third element of accumulation is variable capital which increases with progressive accumulation. . . . One of the fundamental conditions of accumulation is therefore a supply of living labour which can be mobilized by capital to meet its demands. This supply can be increased under favourable conditions – but only up to a certain point – by longer hours and more intensive work. Both these methods of increasing the supply, however, do not enlarge the variable capital, or do so only to a small extent (e.g. payments for overtime). Moreover, they are confined to definite and rather narrow limits which they cannot exceed owing to both natural and social causes. The increasing growth of variable capital which accompanies accumulation must therefore become manifest in ever greater numbers of employed labour. Where can this additional labour be found? . . .

Since capitalist production can develop fully only with complete access to all territories and climes, it can no more confine iself to the natural resources and productive forces of the temperate zone than it can manage with white labour alone. Capital needs other races to exploit territories where the white man cannot work. It must be able to mobilize world labour power without restriction in order to utilize all productive forces of the globe – up to the limits imposed by a system of producing surplus value. This labour power, however, is in most cases rigidly bound by the traditional pre-capitalist organization of production. It must first be 'set free' in order to be enrolled in the active army of capital. The emancipation of labour power from primitive social conditions and its absorption by the capitalist wage system is one of the indispensable historical bases of capitalism. . . . Obtaining the necessary labour power from non-capitalist societies, the so-called 'labour-problem', is ever more important for capital in the colonies. All possible methods of 'gentle compulsion' are applied to solving this problem, to transfer labour from former social systems to the command of capital. This endeavour leads to the most peculiar combinations between the modern wage system and primitive authority in the colonial countries. This is a concrete example of the fact that capitalist production cannot manage without labour power from other social organizations. [pp. 348–64]

Imperialism is the political expression of the accumulation of capital in its competitive struggle for what remains still open of the non-capitalist environment. Still the largest part of the world in terms of geography, this remaining field for the expansion of capital is yet insignificant as against the high level of development already attained by the productive forces of capital; witness the immense masses of capital accumulated in the old countries which seek an outlet for their surplus product and strive to capitalize their surplus value, and the rapid change-over to capitalism of the pre-capitalist civilizations. On the international stage, then, capital must take appropriate measures. With the high development of the capitalist countries and their increasingly severe competition in acquiring non-capitalist areas, imperialism grows in lawlessness and violence, both in aggression against the non-capitalist world and in ever more serious conflicts among the competing capitalist countries. But the more violently, ruthlessly and thoroughly imperialism brings about the decline of non-capitalist civilizations, the more rapidly it cuts the very ground from under the feet of capitalist accumulation. Though imperialism is the historical method for prolonging the career of capitalism, it is also a sure means of bringing it to a swift conclusion. This is not to say that capitalist development must be actually driven to this extreme: the mere tendency towards imperialism of itself takes forms which make the final phase of capitalism a period of catastrophe. [p. 446]

Thus capitalist accumulation as a whole, as an actual historical process, has two different aspects. One concerns the commodity market and the place where surplus value is produced – the factory, the mine, the agricultural estate. Regarded in this light, accumulation is a purely economic process, with its most important phase a transaction between the capitalist and wage labourer. . . .

The other aspect of the accumulation of capital concerns the relations between capitalism and the non-capitalist modes of production which start making their appearance on the international stage. Its predominant methods are colonial policy, an international loan system – a policy of spheres of interest – and war. Force, fraud, oppression, looting are openly displayed without any attempt at concealment, and it requires an effort to discover within this tangle of political violence and contests of power the stern laws of the economic process. . . .

In reality, political power is nothing but a vehicle for the economic process. The conditions for the reproduction of capital provide the organic link between these two aspects of the accumulation of capital. The historical career of capitalism can only be appreciated by taking them together. 'Sweating blood and filth with every pore from head to toe' characterizes not only the birth of capital but also its progress in the world at every step, and thus capitalism prepares its own downfall under ever more violent contortions and convulsions. [pp. 452–3]

The more ruthlessly capital sets about the destruction of non-capitalist strata at home and in the outside world, the more it lowers the standard of living for the workers as a whole, the greater also is the change in the day-to-day history of capital. It becomes a string of political and social disasters and convulsions, and under these conditions, punctuated by periodical economic catastrophes or crises, accumulation can go on no longer.

But even before this natural economic impasse of capital's own creating is properly reached it becomes a necessity for the international working class to revolt against the rule of capital.

Capitalism is the first mode of economy with the weapon of propaganda, a mode which tends to engulf the entire globe and to stamp out all other economies, tolerating no rival at its side. Yet at the same time it is also the first mode of economy which is unable to exist by itself, which needs other economic systems as a medium and soil. Although it strives to become universal, and, indeed, on account of this its tendency, it must break down – because it is immanently incapable of becoming a universal form of production. In its living history it is a contradiction in itself, and its movement of accumulation provides a solution to the conflict and aggravates it at the same time. At a certain stage of development there will be no other way out than the application of socialist principles. The aim of socialism is not accumulation but the satisfaction of toiling humanity's wants by developing the productive forces of the entire globe. And so we find that socialism is by its very nature an harmonious and universal system of economy. [pp. 466–7]

The Accumulation of Capital (1913); Routledge and Kegan Paul, 1951.

20 The Liberal View Restated, 1914

H. N. BRAILSFORD

H. N. Brailsford (1873–1958) belonged to much the same generation of educated Liberals with strong socialist leanings and pacifist beliefs as Hobson. As an internationalist, and one of those who later put forward the concept of a League of Nations in 1917, he approached imperialism from the standpoint of its effects on international relations. This extract from The War of Steel and Gold *(1914) is included because it shows the joint influence of Hobson's arguments and those emphasizing monopolistic capitalism as the root of imperialism. It also illustrates the marked anti-semitic streak found in most early critics of 'capitalist imperialism'.*

There can be no science of foreign politics so long as foreign affairs are in the hands of small cliques, among whom personal caprice is liable at any moment to upset calculations of national interest. What, moreover, are national interests? There is no calculus by which their relative importance is assessed, nor is there any recognized standard by which even democratic states measure the point at which a vast private interest assumes the standing of a national stake. . . . The real difficulty of distinguishing between a private and a national interest begins when we consider the duty of our diplomacy to 'protect' our subjects abroad. . . . The word bore its simple meaning in the eighteenth century, when we went to war with Spain because Spanish officials in the West Indies had cut off Captain Jenkins' ear. Modern Imperialism is concerned with a Jenkins whose ears are seldom in danger. It is for his investments that he demands protection. The modern extension of the principle was first enunciated by Palmerston in an historic speech in 1850. It seems to hold that a subject residing or trading abroad is entitled to call upon the whole resources of diplomacy, backed if necessary by arms, to defend not only his personal safety but his material interests, if these are threatened by the people or government of the country in which he resides or trades. . . .

Palmerston's doctrine, looked at askance in his own day, has become the unchallenged dogma not only of our own, but of every other Great Power. In the heroic age Helen's was the face that launched a thousand ships. In our golden age the face wears more often the shrewd features of some Hebrew financier. [pp. 52–4]

The hunting of concessions abroad and the exploitation of the potential riches of weak states and dying empires is fast becoming an official enterprise, a national business. We are engaged in Imperial trading, with the flag as its indispensable asset, but the profits go exclusively into private pockets.

This Imperial trading has its questionable aspects from the standpoints of the British public and also of the nation with which our diplomacy deals. But it has another consequence which is no less serious. It brings us continually into conflict with the diplomacy of other Powers which are engaged in competing for the same concessions on behalf of their own financiers. It is not the rivalry of merchants engaged in selling goods which makes ill-feeling between nations. The merchant rarely invokes diplomatic aid to enable him to keep or secure a customer. The trouble arises only over concessions, loans and monopolies which bring the European financier into relations with a foreign Government. . . .

Diplomacy in these rivalries becomes the tool of the vast aggregations of modern capital in oil trusts, steel trusts and money trusts, and wherever rival combinations of capital are competing, as British and American oil companies compete in Central America, the reaction will be felt in the relations of their Governments. The struggle for a balance of power is in effect a struggle to map out these exclusive areas of financial penetration. To this end are the working classes in all countries taxed and regimented in conscript armies; for armies and fleets are the material arguments behind this financial diplomacy. [pp. 61–3]

Here at length we have discovered the stake which an armed Imperialism watches and seeks to enlarge. . . . Imperialism is simply the political manifestation of the growing tendency of capital accumulated in the more civilized industrial countries to export itself to the less civilized and the less settled. To secure itself, it seeks to subdue or to 'civilize' its new fields of investment – as it understands 'civilization'. In crossing the seas and entering new lands, it must take with it the machinery which renders the process of capitalist exploitation profitable and secure – its laws of debtor and creditor, its police for the protection of property, its armaments and its administrators.

Why, then, is it that capital seeks to export itself? There are many cogent reasons abroad. At home the fundamental fact is the rapid accumulation of surplus capital. It grows in the hands of trust magnates, bankers, and ground landlords more rapidly than the demand for it at home. It tries continually to get itself employed at home, and the result is that periodic over-production, which shows itself in a 'slump' of trade and a crisis of unemployment. Capital, like labour, has its periods of unemployment, and its favourite method of meeting them is emigration. When rates of interest fall at home, it begins to look abroad for something at once remunerative, and not too risky, and it is to diplomacy that it turns to protect it from risks. If, further, we go on to ask why capital cannot get itself profitably employed at home as fast as it is accumulated, the answer is briefly that its too rapid accumulation has stood in the way of a simultaneous development of the consumers who might have given it employment. Had a little more of the profits of the trade 'boom' gone to labour, and a little less to capital, it is manifest that labour would have had more money to spend, and the new surplus capital – less considerable in amount – might have been employed in meeting this new demand. . . . The reason for the too rapid export of capital abroad is, in short, the bad division of wealth at home. . . .

The other reason which is most potent in inducing capital to flow abroad is the elementary fact that coloured labour can be more ruthlessly exploited than white, that the supposed risks of a foreign investment enable him to charge usurious interest, and that on both grounds the profits to be made abroad are greater than the profits to be made at home. . . .

To complete our survey of the motives of 'real politics', it is necessary to glance at two powerful but secondary interests which Imperialism calls into action as it develops. There is first of all the social pressure due to the fact that Imperialism makes careers for 'younger sons'. . . . There must be tens of thousands of families, all relatively wealthy, influential and well educated, to whom the sudden ending of the Empire would mean financial ruin and social extinction. The larger the Empire grows, the more numerous are the posts which it has to offer.

The influence of another powerful economic factor upon the growth of imperialism has always been suspected. . . . A spirited or apprehensive foreign policy . . . involves an increase of armaments; this increase creates a great industry, which naturally uses the whole of its influence, in the press, in society and in Parliament, to stimulate the demand for further armaments. . . .

All over the world these forces, concentrated, resolute and intelligent, are ceaselessly at work to defeat the more diffused and less easily directed forces which make for disarmament and peace. The number of persons who have anything to gain by armaments and war is relatively small. . . . But their individual stake is larger, and they work in alliance with Society, which regards Empire as a field for the careers of its sons, and with finance, which treats it as a field for investment. Instinctively and by habit they support each others' claims, and the governing class opposes to the half-conscious and badly-led democracy the solid phalanx of interest and ambition. . . . The idealists in modern politics are a volunteer band, without a trained staff, unpaid, and above all undisciplined, pitted against a regular army of mercenary troops which follows skilled generals and acknowledges the duty of solidarity and obedience. [pp. 78–94]

The War of Steel and Gold, G. Bell, 1914.

21 Marxist Theory Matures, 1915

N. I. BUKHARIN

Bukharin (1888–1938) was one of the young intellectuals who founded the Social Democratic Party in Russia in 1906. He spent much of the next ten years abroad publishing socialist propaganda, and became joint editor of Pravda. *In 1917 he was on the Central Committee of the Communist Party and was a close colleague of Lenin. He was expelled from the party in 1929 as a left-wing Bolshevik, was later reinstated, but was finally expelled and executed in 1938. This extract from* Imperialism and World Economy *(written in 1915) is included because it shows how far Hilferding's ideas had been adopted by then, and in particular the fact that imperialism was seen not as an option for capitalists but a necessary feature of capitalism in an advanced stage of development. In fact it includes most of the elements which comprise Lenin's more famous theory.*

We have laid bare three fundamental motives for the conquest policies of modern capitalist states: increased competition in the sales markets, in the markets of raw materials, and for the spheres of capital investment. This is what the modern development of capitalism and its transformation into finance capitalism has brought about.

Those three roots of the policy of finance capitalism, however, represent in substance only three facets of the same phenomenon, namely of the conflict between the growth of productive forces on the one hand, and the 'national' limits of the production organization on the other.

Indeed, overproduction of manufactured goods is at the same time underproduction of agricultural products. Underproduction of agricultural products is in this case important for us in so far as the demand on the part of industry is excessively large, i.e., in so far as there are large volumes of manufactured goods which cannot be exchanged for agricultural products; in so far as the ratio between those two branches of production has been (and is more and more) disturbed. This is why growing industry seeks for an agrarian 'economic supplement' which, within the framework of capitalism, particularly its monopoly form, i.e., finance capital, inevitably expresses itself in the form of subjugating agrarian countries by force of arms. . . .

But even aside from simply 'relieving the congestion' by exporting capital in commodity form, there is also a further connection between capital export and the decrease in the overproduction of commodities. Otto Bauer has very well formulated this connection.

Thus (he says) the exploitation of economically backward countries by the capitalists of a European country has two series of consequences; directly, it creates new spheres of investment for capital in the colonial country, and at the same time more selling opportunities for the industry of the dominating power; indirectly, it creates new spheres for the application of capital also inside of the dominating country, and increases the sale of the products of all its industries. . . .[1] [pp. 104–6]

To sum up: the development of the productive forces of world capitalism has made gigantic strides in the last decades. The upper hand in the competitive struggle has everywhere been gained by large-scale production; it has consolidated the 'magnates of capital' into an ironclad organization, which has taken possession of the entire economic life. State power has become the domain of a financial oligarchy; the latter manages production which is tied up by the banks into one knot. This process of the organization of production has proceeded from below; it has fortified itself within the framework of modern states, which have become an exact expression of the interests of finance capital. Every one of the capitalistically advanced 'national economies' has turned into some kind of a 'national' trust. This process of the organization of the economically advanced sections of world economy, on the other hand, has been accompanied by an extraordinary sharpening of their mutual competition. The overproduction of commodities, which is connected with the growth of large enterprises; the export policy of the cartels, and the narrowing of the sales markets in connection with the colonial and tariff policy of the capitalist powers; the growing disproportion between tremendously developed industry and backward agriculture; the gigantic growth of capital export and the economic subjugation of entire regions by 'national' banking combines – all this has thrown into the sharpest possible relief the clash of interests between the 'national' groups of capital. Those groups find their final argument in the force and power of the state organization, first of all in its army and navy. A mighty state military power is the last trump in the struggle of the powers. The fighting

[1] Otto Bauer: *Die Nationälitatenfrage und die Sozialdemokratie*, Vienna, 1907, p. 464.

force in the world market thus depends upon the power and consolidation of the 'nation', upon its financial and military resources. A self-sufficient national state, and an economic unit limitlessly expending its great power until it becomes a world kingdom – a world-wide empire – such is the ideal built up by finance capital. [pp. 108–9]

Imperialism is a policy of conquest. But not every policy of conquest is imperialism. Finance capital cannot pursue any other policy. This is why, when we speak of imperialism as the policy of finance capital, its conquest character is self-understood; at the same time, however, we point out what production relations are being reproduced by this policy of conquest. Moreover, this definition also includes a whole series of other historic trends and characteristics. Indeed, when we speak of finance capital, we imply highly developed economic organisms and, consequently, a certain scope and intensity of world relations; in a word, we imply the existence of a developed world economy; by the same token we imply a certain state of production relations, of organizational forms of the economic life, a certain interrelation of classes, and also a certain *future* of economic relations, etc., etc. Even the form and the means of struggle, the organization of state power, the military technique, etc., are taken to be a more or less definite entity, whereas the formula 'policy of conquest' is good for pirates, for caravan trade, and also for imperialism. In other words, the formula 'policy of conquest' defines nothing, whereas the formula 'policy of conquest of finance capital', characterizes imperialism as a definite historical entity.

From the fact that the epoch of finance capitalism is an historically limited phenomenon, it does not follow, of course, that it has stepped into the light of day like *Deus ex machina*. In reality it is an historic continuation of the epoch of industrial capitalism, just as the latter was a continuation of the phase of commercial capitalism. This is why the fundamental contradictions of capitalism which, in the course of its development, are continually being reproduced on a wider scale, find their sharpest expression in our own epoch. The same is true of the anarchic structure of capitalism, which finds its expression in competition. The anarchic character of capitalist society is expressed in the fact that social economy is not an organized collective body guided by a single will, but a system of economies interconnected through exchange, each of which produces at its own risk, never being in a position to adapt itself more or less to the volume of social demand and to the production carried on in other individual economies. This calls forth a struggle of the economies against each other, a war of capitalist competition. The forms of this competition can be widely different. The imperialist policy in particular is one of the forms of the competitive struggle. . . . [pp. 114–5]

If we now approach the question of the necessity of imperialism (the impossibility of overcoming it), we realize at once that there is no ground whatever to treat its necessity in this sense. On the contrary, imperialism is the policy of finance capitalism, i.e., a highly developed capitalism implying a considerable ripeness of the organization of production; in other words, imperialist policies by their very existence bespeak the ripeness of the objective conditions for a new socioeconomic form; consequently, all talk about the 'necessity' of imperialism as a limit to action is liberalism, is in itself semi-imperialism. The further existence of capitalism and imperialism becomes nothing more nor less than a question of the interrelation between mutually struggling class forces. [p. 133]

The entire structure of world economy in our times forces the bourgeoisie to pursue an imperialist policy. As the colonial policy is inevitably connected with violent methods, so every capitalist expansion leads sooner or later to a bloody climax. . . .

The same thing may be said about imperialism. It is an integral element of finance capitalism without which the latter would lose its capitalist meaning. To imagine that the trusts, this embodiment of monopoly, have become the bearers of the free trade policy, of peaceful expansion, is a deeply harmful Utopian fantasy.

But is not the epoch of 'ultra-imperialism' a real possibility after all, can it not be affected [sic] by the centralization process? Will not the state capitalist trusts devour one another gradually until there comes into existence an all-embracing power which has conquered all the others? This possibility would be thinkable if we were to look at the social process as a purely mechanical one, without counting the forces that are hostile to the policy of imperialism. In reality, however, the wars that will follow each other on an ever larger scale must inevitably result in a shifting of the social forces. The centralization process, looked at from the capitalist angle, will inevitably clash with a sociopolitical tendency that is antagonistic to the former. Therefore it can by no means reach its logical end; it suffers collapse and achieves completion only in a new, purified, non-capitalist form. It is for this reason that Kautsky's theory is by no means realizable. It looks upon imperialism not as an inevitable accompaniment of capitalist development, but as upon one of the 'dark sides' of capitalist development. . . . His concept implies a slurring over of the gigantic contradictions which rend asunder modern society, and in this respect it is a reformist concept. It is a characteristic feature of theorizing reformism that it takes pains to point out all the elements of capitalism's adaptation to conditions without seeing its contradictions. For a consistent Marxist, the entire development of capitalism is nothing but a process of a continuous reproduction of the contradictions of capitalism on an ever wider scale. The future of world economy, as far as it is a capitalist economy, will not overcome its inherent lack of adaptation; on the contrary, it will keep on reproducing this lack of adaptation on an ever wider scale. These contradictions are actually harmonized in another production structure of the social organism – through a well-planned Socialist organization of economic activities. [pp. 141–3]

Imperialism and World Economy (1917); New York, International Publishers, 1929.

22 The Mature Marxist Theory, 1916

V. I. LENIN

Lenin (1870–1924) was a leading Marxist and revolutionary in Russia before 1914, and was exiled to Siberia from 1895 to 1900. Like Bukharin he spent much of the next seventeen years abroad, organizing the Russian socialist movement which he led to success in 1917. Imperialism was written in 1915–16 when Lenin was in Switzerland. Its primary aim was to prove that the First World War was a struggle for the redivision of the world between the imperialist powers, and that its effect would be so to weaken capitalism in Russia and other European countries that the proletariat could stage successful revolutions. Partly because of its comprehensive treatment this short book became the accepted Marxist expression of the Theory of Capitalist Imperialism and remains so in the 1960s. Yet virtually nothing in this book was new, and Lenin's debt to Hilferding and Hobson is particularly obvious.

The enormous growth of industry and the remarkably rapid process of concentration of production in ever-larger enterprises represent one of the most characteristic features of capitalism. Modern censuses of production give very complete and exact data on this process.

In Germany, for example, for every 1,000 industrial enterprises, large enterprises, i.e., those employing more than 50 workers, numbered three in 1882, six in 1895 and nine in 1907; and out of every 100 workers employed, this group of enterprises employed 22, 30 and 37 respectively. Concentration of production, however, is much more intense than the concentration of workers, since labour in the large enterprise is much more productive. [p. 21]

Fifty years ago, when Marx was writing *Capital*, free competition appeared to most economists to be a 'natural law'. Official science tried, by a conspiracy of silence, to kill the works of Marx, which by a theoretical and historical analysis of capitalism showed that free competition gives rise to the concentration of production, which, in turn, at a certain stage of development, leads to monopoly. Today, monopoly has become a fact. . . .

For Europe, the time when the new capitalism *definitely* superseded the old can be established with fair precision: it was the beginning of the twentieth century. [p. 26]

The principal stages in the history of monopolies are the following: (1) 1860–70, the highest stage, the apex of development of free competition; monopoly is in the barely discernible, embryonic stage. (2) After the crisis of 1873, a wide zone of development of cartels; but they are still the exception. They are not yet durable. They are still a transitory phenomenon. (3) The boom at the end of the nineteenth century and the crisis of 1900–3. Cartels become one of the foundations of the whole of economic life. Capitalism has been transformed into imperialism. [p. 28]

Monopoly! This is the last word in the 'latest phase of capitalist development'. But we shall only have a very insufficient, incomplete, and poor notion of the real power and the significance of modern monopolies if we do not take into consideration the part played by the banks.

The principal and primary function of banks is to serve as an intermediary in the making of payments. In doing so they transform inactive money capital into active capital, that is, into capital producing a profit; they collect all kinds of money revenues and place them at the disposal of the capitalist class.

As banking develops and becomes concentrated in a small number of establishments the banks become transformed, and instead of being modest intermediaries they become powerful monopolies having at their command almost the whole of the money capital of all the capitalists and small businessmen and also a large part of the means of production and of the sources of raw materials of the given country and in a number of countries. The transformation of numerous modest intermediaries into a handful of monopolists represents one of the fundamental processes in the transformation of capitalism into capitalist imperialism. . . .

When carrying the current accounts of a few capitalists, the banks, as it were, transact a purely technical and exclusively auxiliary operation. When, however, those operations grow to enormous dimensions we find that a handful of monopolists control all the operations, both commercial and industrial, of the whole of capitalist society. They can, by means of their banking connections, by running current accounts and transacting other financial operations, first *ascertain exactly* the position of the various capitalists, then *control* them, influence them by restricting or enlarging, facilitating or hindering their credits, and finally they can *entirely determine* their fate, determine their income, deprive them of capital, or, on the other hand, permit them to increase their capital rapidly and to enormous dimensions, etc. . . . [pp. 38–44]

At the same time a very close personal union is established between the banks and the biggest industrial and commercial enterprises, the merging of one with another through the acquisition of shares, through the appointment of bank directors to the Supervisory Boards (or Boards of Directors) of industrial and commercial enterprises, and *vice versa*. . . .

The 'personal union' between the banks and industry is completed by the 'personal union' between both and the state.

'Seats on the Supervisory Board,' writes Jeidels, 'are freely offered to persons of title, also to ex-civil servants, who are able to do a great deal to facilitate' (!!) 'relations with the authorities. . . . Usually, on the Supervisory Board of a big bank, there is a member of parliament or a Berlin city councillor.'

The building, so to speak, of the great capitalist monopolies is therefore going on full steam ahead in all 'natural' and 'supernatural' ways. A sort of division of labour amongst some hundreds of kings of finance who reign over modern capitalist society is being systematically developed. . . .

At precisely what period were the 'new activities' of the big banks finally established? Jeidels gives us a fairly exact answer to this important question:

'The ties between the banks and industrial enterprises . . . were scarcely a characteristic economic phenomenon before the 'nineties; in one sense, indeed this initial date may be advanced to the year 1897, when the important "mergers" took place and when, for the first time, the new form of decentralized organization was introduced to suit the industrial policy of the banks. This starting point could perhaps be placed at an even later date, for it was the crisis (of 1900) that enormously accelerated and intensified the process of concentration of industry and banking, consolidated that process, for the first time transformed the connection with industry into the monopoly of the big banks, and made this connection much closer and more active.'

Thus, the beginning of the twentieth century marks the turning point from the old capitalism to the new, from the domination of capital in general to the domination of finance capital. . . .

We now have to describe how, under the general conditions of commodity production and private property, the 'domination' of capitalist monopolies inevitably becomes the domination of financial oligarchy. . . .

The 'holding system', to which we have already briefly referred above, should be considered the cornerstone. . . . Experience shows that it is sufficient to own 40 per cent of the shares of a company in order to direct its affairs, since a certain number of small, scattered shareholders find it impossible, in practice, to attend general meetings, etc. The 'democratization' of the ownership of shares . . . is, in fact, one of the ways of increasing the power of the financial oligarchy. . . .

Finance capital, concentrated in a few hands and exercising a virtual monopoly, exacts enormous and ever-increasing profits from the floating of companies, issue of stock, state loans, etc., tightens the grip of financial oligarchies and levies tribute upon the whole of society for the benefit of monopolists. [pp. 51–66]

It is characteristic of capitalism in general that the ownership of capital is separated from the application of capital to production, that money capital is separated from industrial or productive capital, and that the rentier who lives entirely on income obtained from money capital, is separated from the entrepreneur and from all who are directly concerned in the management of capital. Imperialism, or the domination of finance capital, is that highest stage of capitalism in which this separation reaches vast proportions. The supremacy of finance capital over all other forms of capital means the predominance of the rentier and of the financial oligarchy; it means the crystallization of a small number of financially 'powerful' states from among all the rest. . . .

Under the old capitalism, when free competition prevailed, the export of *goods* was the most typical feature. Under modern capitalism, when monopolies prevail, the export of *capital* has become the typical feature. . . .

England became a capitalist country before any other, and by the middle of the nineteenth century, having adopted free trade, claimed to be the 'workshop of the world', the great purveyor of manufactured goods to all countries, which in exchange were to keep her supplied with raw materials. But in the last quarter of the nineteenth century, *this* monopoly was already undermined. Other countries, protecting themselves by tariff walls, had developed into independent capitalist states. On the threshold of the twentieth century, we see a new type of monopoly coming into existence. Firstly, there are monopolist capitalist combines in all advanced capitalist countries; secondly, a few rich countries, in which the accumulation of capital reaches gigantic proportions, occupy a monopolist position. An enormous 'super-abundance of capital' has accumulated in the advanced countries.

It goes without saying that if capitalism could develop agriculture, which today lags far behind industry everywhere, if it could raise the standard of living of the masses, who are everywhere still poverty-stricken and underfed, in spite of the amazing advance in technical knowledge, there could be no talk of a superabundance of capital. This 'argument' the petty-bourgeois critics of capitalism advance on every occasion. But if capitalism did these things it would not be capitalism; for uneven development and wretched conditions of the masses are fundamental and inevitable conditions and premises of this mode of production. As long as capitalism remains what it is, surplus capital will never be utilized for the purpose of raising the standard of living of the masses in a given country, for this would mean a decline in profits for the capitalists; it will be used for the purpose of increasing those profits by exporting capital abroad to the backward countries. In these backward countries profits are usually high, for capital is scarce, the price of land is relatively low, wages are low, raw materials are cheap. The possibility of exporting capital is created by the fact that numerous backward countries have been drawn into international capitalist intercourse; main railways have either been built or are being built there; the elementary conditions for industrial development have been created, etc. The necessity for exporting capital arises from the fact that in a few countries capitalism has become 'over-ripe' and (owing to the backward state of agriculture and the impoverished state of the masses) capital cannot find 'profitable' investment.

Here are approximate figures showing the amount of capital invested abroad by the three principal countries:

CAPITAL INVESTED ABROAD
(In billions of francs)

Year	Great Britain	France	Germany
1862	3·6	—	—
1872	15·0	10 (1869)	—
1882	22·0	15 (1880)	?
1893	42·0	20 (1890)	?
1902	62·0	27–37	12·5
1914	75–100·0	60	44·0

This table shows that the export of capital reached formidable dimensions only in the beginning of the twentieth century. Before the war the capital invested abroad by the three principal countries amounted to between 175,000,000,000 and 200,000,000,000 francs. At the modest rate of 5 per cent, this sum should have brought in from 8 to 10 billions a year. This provided a solid basis for imperialist oppression and the exploitation of most of the countries and nations of the world; a solid basis for the capitalist parasitism of a handful of wealthy states!

How is this capital invested abroad distributed among the various countries? *Where* does it go? Only an approximate answer can be given to this question, but sufficient to throw light on certain general relations and ties of modern imperialism.

APPROXIMATE DISTRIBUTION OF FOREIGN CAPITAL
(ABOUT 1910)

(In billions of marks)

Continent	Gr. Britain	France	Germany	Total
Europe. . . .	4	23	18	45
America	37	4	10	51
Asia, Africa and Australia . . .	29	8	7	44
Total . . .	70	35	35	140

The principal spheres of investment of British capital are the British colonies, which are very large also in America (for example, Canada) not to mention Asia, etc. In this case, enormous exports of capital are bound up with the possession of enormous colonies, of the importance of which for imperialism we shall speak later. In regard to France, the situation is quite different. French capital exports are invested mainly in Europe, particularly in Russia (at least ten billion francs). This is mainly *loan* capital, in the form of government loans and not investments in industrial undertakings. Unlike British colonial imperialism, French imperialism might be termed usury imperialism. In regard to Germany, we have a third type; the German colonies are inconsiderable, and German capital invested abroad is divided fairly evenly between Europe and America.

The export of capital greatly affects and accelerates the development of capitalism in those countries to which it is exported. While, therefore, the export of capital may tend to a certain extent to arrest development in the countries exporting capital, it can only do so by expanding and deepening the further development of capitalism throughout the world. . . .

The capital exporting countries have divided the world among themselves in the figurative sense of the term. But finance capital has also led to the *actual* division of the world.

Monopolist capitalist combines – cartels, syndicates, trusts – divide among themselves, first of all, the whole internal market of a country, and impose their control, more or less completely, upon the industry of that country. But under capitalism the home market is inevitably bound up with the foreign market. Capitalism long ago created a world market. As the export of capital increased, and as the foreign and colonial relations and the 'spheres of influence' of the big monopolist

combines expanded, things 'naturally' gravitated towards the formation of international cartels.

This is a new stage of world concentration of capital and production, incomparably higher than the preceding stages. . . . The capitalists divide the world, not out of any particular malice, but because the
degree of concentration which has been reached forces them to adopt
this method in order to get profits. And they divide it in proportion to
'capital', in proportion to 'strength', because there cannot be any other
system of division under commodity production and capitalism. . . .

The epoch of modern capitalism shows us that certain relations are
established between capitalist alliances, *based* on the economic division
of the world; while parallel with this fact and in connection with it,
certain relations are established between political alliances, between
states, on the basis of the territorial division of the world, of the
struggle for colonies, of the 'struggle for economic territory'.

In his book, *The Territorial Development of the European Colonies*, A.
Supan,[1] the geographer, gives the following brief summary of this
development at the end of the nineteenth century:

PERCENTAGE OF TERRITORIES BELONGING
TO THE EUROPEAN COLONIAL POWERS
(Including United States)

	1876	1900	Increase or Decrease
Africa	10·8	90·4	+79·6
Polynesia . . .	56·8	98·9	+42·1
Asia.	51·5	56·6	+ 5·1
Australia . . .	100·0	100·0	—
America . . .	27·5	27·2	— 0·3

'The characteristic feature of this period,' he concludes, 'is, therefore,
the division of Africa and Polynesia.'

As there are no unoccupied territories – that is, territories that do not
belong to any state – in Asia and America, Mr Supan's conclusion must
be carried further, and we must say that the characteristic feature of this
period is the final partition of the globe – not in the sense that a *new
partition* is impossible – on the contrary, new partitions are possible
and inevitable – but in the sense that the colonial policy of the capitalist
countries has *completed* the seizure of the unoccupied territories on our

[1] A. Supan, *Die territoriale Entwicklung der europäischen Kolonien*, Gotha, 1906,
p. 254.

planet. For the first time the world is completely divided up, so that in the future *only* redivision is possible; territories can only pass from one 'owner' to another, instead of passing as unowned territory to an 'owner'.

Hence, we are passing through a peculiar period of world colonial policy, which is closely associated with the 'latest stage in the development of capitalism', with finance capital. . . .

Colonial policy and imperialism existed before this latest stage of capitalism, and even before capitalism. Rome, founded on slavery, pursued a colonial policy and achieved imperialism. But 'general' arguments about imperialism, which ignore, or put into the background the fundamental difference of social-economic systems, inevitably degenerate into absolutely empty banalities, or into grandiloquent comparisons like: 'Greater Rome and Greater Britain'. Even the colonial policy of capitalism in its *previous* stages is essentially different from the colonial policy of finance capital.

The principal feature of modern capitalism is the domination of monopolist combines of the big capitalists. These monopolies are most firmly established when *all* the sources of raw materials are controlled by the one group. And we have seen with what zeal the international capitalist combines exert every effort to make it impossible for their rivals to compete with them; for example, by buying up mineral lands, oil fields, etc. Colonial possession alone gives complete guarantee of success to the monopolies against all the risks of the struggle with competitors, including the risk that the latter will defend themselves by means of a law establishing a state monopoly. The more capitalism is developed, the more the need for raw materials is felt, the more bitter competition becomes, and the more feverishly the hunt for raw materials proceeds throughout the whole world, the more desperate becomes the struggle for the acquisition of colonies. . . .

Finance capital is not only interested in the already known sources of raw materials; it is also interested in potential sources of raw materials, because present-day technical development is extremely rapid, and because land which is useless today may be made fertile tomorrow if new methods are applied (to devise these new methods a big bank can equip a whole expedition of engineers, agricultural experts, etc.), and large amounts of capital are invested. This also applies to prospecting for minerals, to new methods of working up and utilizing raw materials, etc., etc. Hence, the inevitable striving of finance capital to extend its economic territory and even its territory in general. In the same way that the trusts capitalize their property by estimating it at two or three times its value, taking into account its 'potential' (and not present) returns, and the further results of monopoly, so finance capital strives to seize the largest possible amount of land of all kinds and in any place it can, and by any means, counting on the possibilities of finding raw materials there, and fearing to be left behind in the insensate struggle for the last available scraps of undivided territory, or for the repartition of that which has been already divided. . . . [pp. 76–102]

We must now try to sum up and put together what has been said above on the subject of imperialism. Imperialism emerged as the development and direct continuation of the fundamental attributes of capitalism in general. But capitalism only became capitalist imperialism at a definite and very high stage of its development, when certain of its fundamental attributes began to be transformed into their opposites, when the features of a period of transition from capitalism to a higher social and economic system began to take shape and reveal themselves all along the line. Economically, the main thing in this process is the substitution of capitalist monopolies for capitalist free competition. Free competition is the fundamental attribute of capitalism, and of commodity production generally. Monopoly is exactly the opposite of free competition; but we have seen the latter being transformed into monopoly before our eyes, creating large-scale industry and eliminating small industry, replacing large-scale industry by still larger-scale industry, finally leading to such a concentration of production and capital that monopoly has been and is the result: cartels, syndicates and trusts, and merging with them, the capital of a dozen or so banks manipulating thousands of millions. At the same time monopoly, which has grown out of free competition, does not abolish the latter, but exists over it and alongside of it, and thereby gives rise to a number of very acute, intense antagonisms, friction and conflicts. Monopoly is the transition from capitalism to a higher system.

If it were necessary to give the briefest possible definition of imperialism we should have to say that imperialism is the monopoly stage of capitalism. Such a definition would include what is most important, for, on the one hand, finance capital is the bank capital of a few big monopolist banks, merged with the capital of the monopolist combines of manufacturers; and, on the other hand, the division of the world is the transition from a colonial policy which has extended without hindrance to territories unoccupied by any capitalist power, to a colonial policy of monopolistic possession of the territory of the world which has been completely divided up.

But very brief definitions, although convenient, for they sum up the main points, are nevertheless inadequate, because very important features of the phenomenon that has to be defined have to be especially deduced. And so, without forgetting the conditional and relative value of all definitions, which can never include all the concatenations of a phenomenon in its complete development, we must give a definition of imperialism that will embrace the following five essential features:

1. The concentration of production and capital developed to such a high stage that it created monopolies which play a decisive role in economic life.
2. The merging of bank capital with industrial capital, and the creation, on the basis of this 'finance capital', of a financial oligarchy.
3. The export of capital, which has become extremely important, as distinguished from the export of commodities.
4. The formation of international capitalist monopolies which share the world among themselves.
5. The territorial division of the whole world among the greatest capitalist powers is completed.

Imperialism is capitalism in that stage of development in which the dominance of monopolies and finance capital has established itself; in which the export of capital has acquired pronounced importance; in which the division of the world among the international trusts has begun; in which the division of all territories of the globe among the great capitalist powers has been completed. [pp. 107–9]

Imperialism, The Highest Stage of Capitalism (1916); Moscow, Foreign Languages Publishing House, 1947.

Part Three

DISSECTION AND EVALUATION

The Critics

There are various ways in which a complex theory of this type can be evaluated. One method is to examine its internal premises and logic to see if it makes sense simply as a theoretical model. Another is to apply it to the historical facts which it claims to explain to see if it fits. Again, it is possible to take the same historical facts – in this case the export of capital and the acquisition of colonies – and to consider whether alternative explanations are more convincing. The following extracts illustrate these different techniques as applied to Marx (as the authority claimed by most neo-Marxist theorists), Hobson and the neo-Marxists. The verdicts given are all, in varying ways, adverse. This is not to imply that there is not a vast literature supporting these theories. Examples are not included because most Marxist writers tend to explain or gloss the originals, adding little to the strength of the argument. Significantly, no satisfactory attempt has been made to demonstrate in detail that the facts of colonial expansion support the Theory of Capitalist Imperialism.

I

Marx as Originator

23 Marx and Neo-Marxism

E. M. WINSLOW

E. M. Winslow (1896–). American Economist and Writer.

We shall look in vain in the writings of Karl Marx for a theory of modern imperialism as such. Yet Marx is the father of the idea that capitalism is responsible in modern times for the creation of surplus products for which it must find ever-expanding markets or die, and in seeking them fight to the death. It makes little difference whether he called this out-thrust of the national capitalist systems 'imperialism' or not. 'Capitalism' was the all-embracing term to Marx, and he had no need for any other concept. . . . [p. 116]

Foreign Trade and the Problem of Capitalist Expansion

Any economic argument involving modern capitalism in imperialistic expansion obviously must say something regarding foreign trade and finance. Likewise, any theory of capitalist development which excludes the foreign trade and financial aspect leaves no room for a capitalistic theory of imperialism; in fact such treatment would establish the basis for denying that capitalism has any economically necessary connection with imperialism.

Both types of treatment are to be found in Marx, and from this curious lack of consistency has sprung the confusion of method among Marx's followers . . . in handling the theory of imperialism. In saying that both types of treatment are to be found in Marx, it must be emphasized that he had no theory of foreign trade, but only some scattered remarks about it. In some places he stresses the dependence of capitalism on foreign trade, and in others he rejects the relevancy of foreign trade to his analysis of capitalism. The confusion goes back to his failure to develop a consistent theory of capitalist development.

Marx's failure to develop a consistent theory of capitalism is in part due to basic errors in his assumptions and analysis, and partly to the fact that he did not live to round out his theory and settle upon some one of the various hypotheses which he considered.

We shall in particular examine two lines of argument bearing on foreign trade. First, Marx's theory of the falling tendency of the rate of profit, in which foreign countries become important to the capitalist economy as a source of cheap raw materials and foodstuffs. Second, his theory of underconsumption, with its implication (to some of Marx's followers rather than to Marx) that foreign markets for exports are essential as a means of disposing of goods for which no market can be found at home. On either of these hypotheses a theory of capitalist imperialism might be based, but not on both at once, because they are mutually contradictory. Actually, neither, without considerable qualification, has been acceptable to Marx's followers as a basis for a theory of imperialism.

Then there is an entirely different line of thought in Marx which appears to deny that foreign trade is essential to capitalism. This is particularly significant, because it leaves no room for a theory of imperialism, and the cogency of the argument has led certain socialists to regard imperialism as a policy of capitalism rather than an absolute essential. And what is more significant, perhaps, it has been used by these same socialists to show, on Marxian grounds, that capitalism need not collapse, but can go on indefinitely as a self-contained and self-equilibrating system, provided the correct proportions are maintained between the industries producing consumers' goods and those producing producers' goods. This, however, is regarded as theoretically possible only, since Marx makes it clear that capitalism lacks a plan for controlling investment and production. Such equilibrium as may appear is due to an accident, in which newly mined gold plays the central part as the accidental equilibrating factor.

In those parts of his theory which bear most heavily upon profits, Marx undertook to show that the rate of profit has a continuous tendency to decline.[1] Obviously, if it should fall to zero there no longer would be any motive for the profit-seeking capitalist to produce, and capitalism would die. But it does not have to fall to zero in order to injure capitalism; Marx is clear that it merely has to fall below the level to which capitalists are accustomed, or to the point where it no longer pays them to remain in business. For capitalism as a whole this tendency

[1] *Capital*, Vol. III, Part III.

means that the source of savings, or capital accumulation, dries up, causing the system to stagnate from lack of capital for expansion.

In the face of what actually went on in the capitalist world, Marx could not say that the rate of profit showed any imminent signs of falling to zero. In fact it held up so well, and even showed such a strong tendency to rise, that he was obliged to explain both why there should be a declining tendency and what circumstances were always arising to offset this tendency. The rate of profit tends to fall, he explained, because capitalists, each acting independently in his own interests, substitute labor-saving devices, or machines, for labor, thus causing the organic composition of capital, or the amount of capital per man, to rise. This in turn means spreading the resulting surplus value, derived alone from the men employed, over a widening capital base, causing the ratio of income to capital to fall. If capitalists were all banded together in a common purpose they would not do this, because according to Marx only labor is the source of the surplus value from which profits arise, and the common capitalist purpose could be served only by preserving for their constant use the source of surplus value, which is also the source of profit. But each one alone, faced with rising wage rates, can reap a temporary advantage over his competitors by expanding his production through the use of machines. When all do the same thing independently at once, however, the total result is overproduction – a greater output of consumer goods than can be taken off the market at the 'profitable' price, inasmuch as the wage earners fail to receive the necessary purchasing power in the form of wages, while the capitalists who thus receive this foregone purchasing power do not spend it all on consumer goods, but save it for further investment. The result is a crisis of overproduction; values – from the capitalists' point of view – have to be destroyed because the surplus goods have to be sold for less than their value. They cost the equivalent of a certain amount of labor power, but must be sold for less.

Marx failed to show that the destruction of capital depends on the falling rate of profit, because he assumed an unchanging rate of exploitation, which in turn requires that wage rates rise as productivity increases. Such an outcome, however, was entirely out of harmony with Marx's whole system of thought. Modern economists, by ascribing productivity to capital as well as to labor and by bringing the discussion of profit in line with the problem of effective demand, do not emerge with a unique law of profits, but relate profits as well as wages to the total productivity of society under given conditions. By this sort of analysis it can be explained how both wages and profits can rise with productivity. But Marx, faced with this fact, was forced to turn to the underconsumption theory to explain the destruction of capitalism – a matter which we shall discuss presently. To explain the fact most glaringly contradicting his theory of declining profits, namely, that profits actually rise, he was obliged to resort to a set of 'counteracting causes' which should have been taken into account in the first place. Having already committed himself, he could patch up his mistake by belatedly recognizing the facts. Thus, he proceeds to list six counteracting factors which intervene to keep the rate of profit up.[1] Only one of these, however, namely, 'foreign trade', has any claim to being a connecting link between a capitalism in distress from falling profits and its attempt to solve its problem by 'imperialistic' methods.

In the same way that capitalists find it profitable to invest in cheap labor or in cheap substitutes for labor in the form of machines, they also find it to their advantage to invest in the cheapest possible raw materials. Anything that results in 'cheapening the elements of constant capital' (which is Marx's expression for everything except labor, which he calls 'variable capital') raises the rate of profit. Foreign trade has this result because it brings into the country both cheaper raw materials and cheaper foodstuffs, thus lowering costs. Therefore, whenever capitalists have an opportunity to import raw materials and foodstuffs which are cheaper than those obtainable at home, they do so; and a capitalist country – which to Marx always means a country dominated by profit-seekers – will seek out and exploit foreign sources of supply even if it has to conquer them by forceful methods.

However, there is a flaw in this argument which has forced Marx's followers to seek the cause of imperialism in other aspects of international relations. The question is: How can a capitalist country exchange goods containing a given amount of surplus value for goods containing a greater amount?

It is implicit in Marx's theory of value that it is impossible within a country for one capitalist to gain in this way at the expense of another, assuming the complete mobility of labor, because goods produced under such conditions must exchange at their full value, and their full value must represent the same amount of labor for all producers who

---

[1] They are (1) raising the intensity of exploitation; (2) depression of wages below their value; (3) cheapening the elements of constant capital (raw materials, etc.); (4) relative overpopulation; (5) foreign trade; and (6) increasing stock capital. – *Capital*, III, 272–82.

are drawing upon the same homogeneous and mobile labor supply. Assuming the same conditions to prevail between countries as within countries not only would [this] mean that international trade merely gives the interrelationships a wider sphere and a 'greater latitude', but it would also mean that the whole world is considered as one unit, no different except in size from any component part. In other words, there is no unique gain from foreign trade.

On the other hand, if there is not complete mobility of labor between countries, it follows that commodities can be produced in one country with a high composition of capital (that is, more capital per man, as in highly industrialized countries) and in another with a lower composition. It would therefore be to the advantage of the highly developed country, which produces less value and reaps less profit because it uses relatively less labor, to exchange its products for those of a country which produces more value because it uses relatively more labor. But since it is obvious that it would be equally to the disadvantage of the latter to make the exchange, the presumption must be that there is no basis for a free and mutual exchange under such terms and that it would not take place. If, however, the highly developed country owns the less developed, or if capitalists in the one have investments in the other, it is clear that the exchange might be forced. Therefore, on Marx's general assumptions, there must be an export of capital before there can be any basis for foreign trade. But this Marx did not see, and it has escaped some of his followers, who even thought that Marx provided the proof that trade will naturally and automatically take place between highly developed and less developed countries. It will take place, of course, but not on the conditions set up by Marx. Foreign trade as a counteracting cause to the falling rate of profit turns out to be a delusion.

Since Marx failed to make it clear that his assumptions require an export of capital before there can be any gain from imports of raw materials and foodstuffs, he left no basis for imperialism in his analysis of the declining rate of profit. Certain of his followers were to elevate the international 'finance-capitalists' to the role of empire builders, but they had to support their theory on better grounds than they could find in Marx and to make a special point of the fact that the international movement of capital creates ties which the trade in goods cannot possibly create.

In the underconsumption theory of crises, which develops in Marx as a rival of the theory of the falling tendency of the rate of profit, there is even less on which to base a theory of imperialism. Rosa Luxemburg and other neo-Marxists made underconsumption the cornerstone of capitalism's need of imperialism, but they did so only by adding ideas which Marx never worked out and perhaps never entertained. As thus developed, the thesis is that capitalists are constantly engaged in a struggle for foreign markets on which to dump that part of their product which the workers are unable to purchase and therefore unable to consume (hence 'underconsumption') because they always receive less than the value of the products which they create. They are chronically underpaid and perpetually unable to take off the domestic market all that is produced there. In other words, exports appear in this neo-Marxian theory as an offset to underconsumption at home.

So far as Marx's treatment is concerned, exports are never definitely presented as an offset to underconsumption in the way that imports were presented as an offset to declining profit rates. In fact, he presented no counteracting forces to underconsumption, emphatically denying the most obvious one, namely, the popular idea that underconsumption could be offset simply by the payment of higher wages.[1] Such action, said Marx, is entirely alien to the nature of capitalism, and impossible besides, so long as the competitive drive for profit constitutes the only economic motive. In the same vein, he undoubtedly would deny that exports can be a remedy for underconsumption. Such counteracting forces may be imagined, but they are not to be found in Marx.

It is true that Marx often speaks of the dependence of modern capitalism 'on the markets of the world' and states that 'except in periods of prosperity there rages between the capitalists the most furious combat for the share of each other in the markets', and he might have called this imperialism, with exports providing the connecting link. But the fact remains that exports are never given this important task. Indeed, Marx abstracts exports and foreign trade generally at the very points of his analysis where they might be expected to play a part.

Thus it becomes obvious that if imports cannot be regarded as an offset to the declining rate of profit which threatens capitalism, on the one hand, and if exports are no remedy for the underconsumption which threatens it, on the other, there is nothing left in Marx

[1] See *Capital*, II, 475–76. Marx's underconsumption thesis is well stated in *Capital*, III, 568.

on which to base a theory of capitalist imperialism. The spirit of such a theory undoubtedly exists in Marx, but not the body. What he said, in effect, was that capitalism is planless, and because it is planless there can be no remedy against falling profits, except in the most makeshift sense, and none at all against underconsumption, which springs from the wrong distribution of the product of industry between wages and profits. Because of their lack of planned co-ordination in production and distribution, capitalists invest too much in capital-goods industries and not enough in consumer-goods industries, thus creating a chronic state of 'disproportionality' which finds expression in such phenomena as underconsumption. Marx's central thesis was that only a planned economy, for which he used the word socialism, can maintain the correct proportions in industry and prevent underconsumption. In effect, therefore, he was saying that socialism is the antidote not only to capitalism but also to imperialism. [pp. 125–32]

Definite conclusions regarding any positive place for Marx in the theory of imperialism – even a socialist theory – are not easy to state. We are thrown off the track at the outset by his tendency to dismiss colonial expansion and exploitation as a pre-capitalist phenomenon, not a characteristic of highly developed industrial capitalism. Even in those parts of his general theory of capitalist development where he speaks of foreign trade, and even appears to emphasize its necessity, it was distinctly a side issue. He simply was not interested in this aspect of the problem. This is indicated by the way in which he excluded foreign trade in various important parts of his analysis, showing clearly that he regarded it merely as a complicating, not an essentially significant, factor. His portrayal of the capitalist world as a closed system, while no doubt never intended to be a picture of reality, could certainly be taken as evidence that he would not have held capitalism responsible for imperialism in the sense that the latter was absolutely necessary. This deduction is further strengthened by his construction of a new 'Say's Law' of markets, his appeal to newly mined gold as the balancing factor between supply and demand, and finally by the impression, which he succeeded in creating whether he intended to or not, that the only thing wrong with capitalism is not lack of foreign markets, or lack of consuming power, or even falling profits, but lack of any plan for maintaining the correct proportion between producers' goods and consumers' goods industries.

Marx's followers inherited all his great jumble of ideas and theories, and one by one they showed their ingenuity in picking out those parts which for one reason or another most appealed to them. This process of selection is most clearly seen in the development of the neo-Marxian theories of imperialism. [pp. 146–7]

The Pattern of Imperialism, Columbia University Press, 1948.

II

J. A. Hobson's *Imperialism*

24 Underconsumption Evaluated

E. E. NEMMERS

E. E. Nemmers (1916–   ). *Lawyer and Educator. Professor of Business Administration, Northwestern University, U.S.A.*

Hobson viewed his theory of imperialism as an application of his general theory of underconsumption. It is not easy to state this theory briefly. Late in his career, Hobson was content to stand by a rather naked statement of Say's law, recognizing only the aspect of mal-distribution of incomes in real terms and passing over a shift in liquidity preference schedules of all individuals as being a consequence of the crisis. Hobson never attached much importance to – and it can fairly be said that he never really recognized – the concept of liquidity preference, nor the role of the banking system in the trade cycle and the role of the rate of interest.[1] In short, Hobson's theory concentrates on maldistribution between saving and consumption arising from un-equal distribution of income in the traditional shares. He argues there is a tendency to save an increasing percentage of income the higher the individual's income and the more mature the economy. These ten-dencies, together with diminishing investment opportunities, create depression. In considering diminishing investment opportunities less emphasis is placed on the diminishing marginal efficiency of capital and more on the shrinking market resulting from over-saving.

The book of 386 pages constituting *Imperialism*, after an introductory

[1] Passages can be quoted from Hobson's works showing that he understood the credit-rationing effect of the banking system during the later stages of a boom in particular. And, understanding this, Hobson might be expected to develop insights with respect to the role of liquidity. He did not, however. Indeed, it can be argued that all Keynes did to the Hobsonian system was (1) increase the systematization, (2) integrate liquidity preference into the theory, (3) develop the theory of other parts of the cycle besides the crisis and (4) develop the role of the rate of interest.

chapter, is divided into two parts: (1) the first 97 pages on 'The Economics of Imperialism' and (2) the balance on 'The Politics of Imperialism'. Our brief statement is based on the 20-page Introduction which contains the complete logic.

Aside from the qualifications already pointed out in the preceding section upon Hobson's theory of underconsumption, there are questions about the premise that an economy chronically tends to over-save, i.e. to over-invest in productive facilities. For Hobson, saving and investment are the same thing, until after the crisis and with the exception of money saved by one person and lent to another for consumption purposes. Over-saving results in turning out more goods than the remaining (uninvested) income can consume at prices sufficient to enable the recovery of the investment. This premise Hobson rests on two propositions. The first is that there is a 'right' amount of saving out of a given income, which will maintain equilibrium in the economy. This ratio is fixed only when the rates of the usual parameters are fixed, e.g., population, technology, etc. The second is that almost all saving comes from rent, dividend and interest.

The logical difficulty with the first proposition is great. Hobson insists that this proposition is vital to his system. He does not recognize the possibilities of varying proportions of capital and labor, but operates with fixed production coefficients in mind. In fact he largely passes over the deepening of capital on grounds of rapidly changing technology and rapidly changing consumption patterns. He does not consider the possibility that the larger the saving (investment) from current income, the less the danger of ultimate glut of consumer goods because of the greater loss of capital due to an increased rate of technological change; in short, that technological change can act in the same capacity as war in destroying excessive saving.[1] He considers over-investment as primarily duplicative (widening of capital) rather than deepening.

[1] He gives passing recognition to this argument in *The Industrial System* (London: Longmans, 1909), p. 52: 'But while it thus might seem that the opportunities for useful saving were infinite, i.e., that any proportion of the current general income could serviceably be saved provided that at some distant time society increased correspondingly its rate of consumption, this is not truly the case . . .' because the changing arts (1) 'very soon result in promoting an increased flow of finished goods', and (2) 'the proportion of new saving which can be so applied to fructify at some far distant date is necessarily small, restricted principally by our inability to forecast far ahead either the needs of coming men or the most economical modes of providing for them'.

Hobson may be right in arguing that 'there must be a definite quantitative relation between the rate of production and the rate of consumption'[1] (abstracting for the moment from the serious problem of inventories, to which he directs no attention) but when he adds 'or in other words, between the quantity of employment of capital and labour and the quantity of commodities withdrawn from the productive stream within any given time' he illustrates the defects which we have just noted; namely, a broad *ceteris paribus* assumption which cannot be justified, particularly when the factors included in the assumption are liquidity preference, the interest rate and other matters already pointed out.

Thus, without altering the *practical* apparatus of the Hobsonian theory of imperialism, the order to causation may be reversed! Rather than pent-up savings and overrunning production at home seeking outlets abroad, the causation may be the superior investment opportunities abroad offering higher profits and increasing home consumption, thereby raising the home standard of living. Hobson recognizes this as partly true in *Imperialism* but considers it as subordinate – a by-product.

Similarly, the second proposition supporting the oversaving premise of Hobson's theory of imperialism – that the great bulk of saving comes from rent, dividends and interest – is suspect. Internal saving by business firms does not show as consumption potential in distributive shares. Large portions of saving are by shares which can hardly be classed as surplus. Events of the last fifty years have changed the traditional pattern of income distribution assumed by Hobson and the shift in standard of living has likewise enabled new classes to save to the point where the factual basis upon which Hobson rested his surplus argument is no longer so secure. His thesis, however, could be supported by arguing that the rate of saving has not changed though the composition of savers is different.

The question still remains whether as an economy grows more mature it does not over-save. Hobson correctly sees that the vital argument centers around the role of the rate of interest at this juncture. He rejects the classical argument that the rate of interest falls or rises to adjust the supply of saving to the demand for investment funds, claiming that savers will not stop as the interest rate falls. But even assuming inelastic supply of loanable funds, the greater part of the classical argument about the role of the rate of interest remains un-

[1] *The Industrial System*, p. 41.

answered. Without arguing that savers are discouraged, a fall in the rate of interest may make feasible a *large* increase in the amount of profitable investment – in short the question remains as one of the elasticity of the demand curve for money for investment. Hobson implies or assumes that it is quite inelastic.

We have not yet come to grips, however, with the basic tenet of the Hobsonian system. Hobson argues in his autobiography that his most significant contribution was the discovery of

> two salient truths: first, that in many markets the volume of supply was restricted, naturally or artificially, so as to give the sellers, as a body, a superior bargaining force for the sale of their goods, reflected in a higher price than was economically necessary to evoke their productive services. Secondly, the selling prices, even where 'free-bargaining' prevailed, were determined in accord with the relative importance to certain buyers or sellers of effecting a purchase or sale: these marginal buyers or sellers fixed the price at a point where it was just worth their while to buy or sell, the others buyers or sellers got from this price something more than would have been a sufficient inducement, i.e., a 'surplus' element.

While this is the fallacious[1] Böhm-Bawerk argument of marginal pairs, Hobson is drawing other social and welfare conclusions. From this basis Hobson argues:

> If a tendency to distribute income or consuming power according to needs were operative, it is evident that consumption would rise with every rise of producing power, for human needs are illimitable, and there could be no excess of saving.

This solution and the statement of the problem overlook the importance of money and its characteristics of liquidity. But more important, he overlooks deepening of capital and other aspects already indicated. Every buyer or seller is marginal with respect to his last unit and thus the same problem would exist even aside from the marginal pair fallacy.

The valid part of this statement by Hobson lies in the first proposition that under modern conditions, sellers as a group possess superior bargaining power, rather than in the second proposition. The

---

[1] Marginal buyer and seller do not determine price. Rather, after every price is determined we find a marginal buyer and seller. This Hobson later recognized in *The Industrial System* (New York: Longmans, 1909), at p. 102.

maldistribution argument can be rested on the superior position of sellers under modern economic organization, but to the extent that the second proposition attempts to add anything, (assuming buyers and sellers have *equal bargaining power*) there is no reason to believe over-saving will result where human wants are assumed illimitable.

Since the mother country is the selling country, Hobson can use the first proposition as a basis for his theory of imperialism.

Hobson has summarized his theory and solution of the imperialist problem by an analogy of 'intensive versus extensive cultivation'. 'A rude or ignorant farmer' when land is plentiful is apt to spread his capital and labor over a large area (the foreign markets) whereas a 'skilled scientific farmer' will cultivate less land more intensively for the most remunerative markets (the home markets). The true answer, of course, is to exploit both extensively and intensively to the point of equal returns at the margin. Hobson does not recognize this principle in his theory of imperialism.

The only legitimate criticism of the evidence and arguments marshalled by Hobson to support his theory of imperialism rests upon the lacunae of his logic already pointed out: the failure to incorporate into his system the role of monetary expansion as a creator of demand; his neglect of interest rate adjustments and of deepening of capital; his use of constant coefficients of production, particularly through time; his gratuitous assumption of the existence of surplus in exchanges between parties of equal bargaining power under the market system. These theoretical limitations do not affect affirmatively the validity of the evidence used by Hobson.

Hobson and Underconsumption, Amsterdam, North Holland Publishing House, 1956; pp. 38–43, 48.

25 Hobson's Misapplication of the Theory

A. J. P. TAYLOR

A. J. P. Taylor (1906–   ). Historian and Journalist. Fellow of Magdalen College, Oxford.

Ideas live longer than men; and the writer who can attach his name to an idea is safe for immortality. Darwin will live as long as Evolution; Marx be forgotten only when there are no class-struggles. In the same way, no survey of the international history of the twentieth century can be complete without the name of J. A. Hobson. He it was who found an economic motive for Imperialism. Lenin took over Hobson's explanation, which thus became the basis for Communist foreign policy to the present day. Non-Marxists were equally convinced; and contemporary history has been written largely in the light of Hobson's discovery. This discovery was an off-shoot from his general doctrine of underconsumption. The capitalists cannot spend their share of the national production. Saving makes their predicament worse. They demand openings for investment outside their saturated national market; and they find these openings in the undeveloped parts of the world. This is Imperialism. In Hobson's words, 'the modern foreign policy of Great Britain has been primarily a struggle for profitable markets of investment' – and what applied to Great Britain was equally true of France or Germany. Brailsford put it a few years later in a sharper way:

> Working men may proceed to slay each other in order to decide whether it shall be French or German financiers who shall export the surplus capital (saved from their own wages bill) destined to subdue and exploit the peasants of Morocco.

This idea is now so embedded in our thought that we cannot imagine a time when it did not exist. Yet the earlier Radical opponents of Imperialism knew nothing of it. They supposed that Imperialism sprang from a primitive greed for territory or a lust for conquest. The more sophisticated held that it was designed to provide jobs for the younger sons of the governing classes (a theory which James Mill invented and himself practised and which Hobson did not discard). Marx had no theory of Imperialism. In classical Marxist theory, the state exists solely to oppress the working classes – to silence their grievances, destroy their trade unions, and force them ever nearer to the point of absolute starvation. Marx jeered at the 'night-watchman' theory of the state; but the only difference in his conception was that it stayed awake in the day-time. Hobson added a true Marxian refinement. Marx had demonstrated that the capitalist, however benevolent personally, was condemned by economic law to rob the worker at the point of production. Similarly Hobson showed that the capitalist, however pacific, must seek foreign investment and therefore be driven into imperialist rivalry with the capitalists of other states. Previously Marxists had condemned capitalism as being pacific, and particularly for preventing the great war of liberation against Russia. Now all wars became 'capitalistic', and war the inevitable outcome of the capitalist system. It is not surprising that, when the First World War had broken out, Lenin seized on Hobson's 'bourgeois-pacifist' theory and made it the cornerstone of his neo-Marxism. Like most prophets, he boasted of his foresight only when his visions had become facts.

Hobson wrote his book immediately after the partition of Africa, and when the experiences of the Boer War were fresh in everyone's mind. For him, Imperialism was mainly the acquisition of tropical lands; and what he foresaw next was the partition, or perhaps the joint exploitation, of China. In the spring of 1914 Brailsford applied similar doctrines to a wider field. *The War of Steel and Gold* (1914) is a more brilliant book than Hobson's, written with a more trenchant pen and with a deeper knowledge of international affairs. Though less remembered now, it had probably a stronger influence on its own generation; and American historians between the wars, in particular, could hardly have got on without it. Our own thought is still unconsciously shaped by it. Brailsford speaks more of our condition. The aggressive, self-confident Imperialism of the Boer War seems remote to us; the competition of great armaments is ever-present in our lives.

Both writers wrote with Radical passion. The first sensation in re-reading them is to cry out: 'Would that we had such writers nowadays!' Take Hobson's peroration:

Imperialism is a depraved choice of national life, imposed by self-seeking interests which appeal to the lusts of quantitative acquisition and of forceful domination surviving in a nation from early centuries of animal struggle for existence. . . . It is the besetting sin of all successful States, and its penalty is unalterable in the order of nature.

Or Brailsford's:

> Let a people once perceive for what purposes its patriotism is
> prostituted, and its resources misused, and the end is already in sight.
> When that illumination comes to the masses of the three Western
> Powers, the fears which fill their barracks and stoke their furnaces
> will have lost the power to drive. A clear-sighted generation will
> scan the horizon and find no enemy. It will drop its armour, and
> walk the world's highways safe.

These are heavyweights of political combat. The intellectual diet
of the mid-twentieth century cannot nourish such stamina. But we must
stay the flood of our admiration with some doubting questions. Was
the Hobsonian–Leninist analysis of international capitalism a true
picture either then or now? Has the struggle for overseas investments
ever been the mainspring of international politics?

The export of capital was certainly a striking feature of British
economic life in the fifty years before 1914. But its greatest periods
were before and after the time of ostensible Imperialism. What is
more, there was little correspondence between the areas of capitalist
investment and political annexation. Hobson cheats on this, and Lenin
after him. They show, in one table, that there has been a great increase
in British investments overseas; in another that there has been a great
increase in the territory of the British Empire. Therefore, they say, the
one caused the other. But did it? Might not both have been independent products of British confidence and strength? If openings for
investment were the motive of British Imperialism, we should surely
find evidence for this in the speeches of British imperialists, or, if not
in their public statements, at any rate in their private letters and
opinions. We don't. They talked, no doubt quite mistakenly, about
securing new markets and, even more mistakenly, about new openings
for emigration; they regarded investment as a casual instrument. Their
measuring-stick was Power, not Profit. When they disputed over
tropical African territory or scrambled for railway concessions in
China, their aim was to strengthen their respective empires, not to
benefit the financiers of the City. Hobson showed that Imperialism
did not pay the nation. With longer experience, we can even say that
it does not pay the investors. But the proof, even if convincing, would
not have deterred the advocates of Imperialism. They were thinking in
different terms.

The economic analysis breaks down in almost every case which has been examined in detail. Morocco has often been treated as a classical case of finance-imperialism, by Brailsford himself and in more detail by E. D. Morel. In fact, the French financiers were forced to invest in Morocco, much against their will, in order to prepare the way for French political control. They knew they would lose their money; and they did. But Morocco became a French protectorate. Again, Brailsford made much play with the British investments in Egypt, which Cromer had promoted. But Cromer promoted these investments in order to strengthen British political control, and not the other way round. The British held on to Egypt for the sake of their empire; they did not hold their empire for the sake of Egypt. Even the Boer War was not purely a war for financial gain. British policy in South Africa would have been exactly the same if there had been no gold-mines. The only difference is that, without the profits from the dynamite-monopoly, the Boers would have been unable to put up much resistance. Rhodes was a great scoundrel in Radical eyes, and quite rightly. But not for the reasons that they supposed. Rhodes wanted wealth for the power that it brought, not for its own sake. Hence he understood the realities of politics better than they did.

Those who explained Imperialism in terms of economics were rationalists themselves; and therefore sought a rational explanation for the behaviour of others. If capitalists and politicians were as rational as Hobson and Brailsford, this is how they would behave. And of course a minority did. They took their profits; agreed with their enemy in the way; and died quietly in their beds. But they did not set the pattern of events. It is disturbing that, while Hobson and Brailsford were so penetrating about the present, they were wrong about the future. Hobson ignored Europe altogether – rightly, since he was discussing colonial affairs. He expected the international capitalists to join in the exploitation of China and even to recruit Chinese armies with which to hold down the workers of Europe. Brailsford looked at Europe only to reject it. He wrote – this in March 1914: 'the dangers which forced our ancestors into European coalitions and Continental wars have gone never to return'. And again, 'it is as certain as anything in politics can be, that the frontiers of our modern national states are finally drawn. My own belief is that there will be no more wars among the six Great Powers.' Even if there were a war, 'it is hard to believe that . . . German Socialists would show any ardour in shooting down French workmen. The spirit which marched through Sedan to Paris could not be revived in our generation.' It may be unfair to judge any writer in the light of what came after. Yet men with far less of Brailsford's knowledge and intellectual equipment foresaw the conflict of 1914, and even the shape that it would take. The true vision of the future was with Robert Blatchford, when he wrote his pamphlet, *Germany and England*, for the *Daily Mail*.

This is a sad confession. Hobson and Brailsford are our sort. We think like them, judge like them, admire their style and their moral values. We should be ashamed to write like Blatchford, though he was in fact the greatest popular journalist since Cobbett. Yet he was right; and they were wrong. Their virtues were their undoing. They expected reason to triumph. He knew that men love Power above all else. This, not Imperialism, is the besetting sin. Lenin knew it also. Hence, though a rationalist by origin, he turned himself into a wielder of power. Thanks to him, there is nothing to choose between Rhodes and a Soviet commissar. Nothing except this: the capitalist may be sometimes corrupted and softened by his wealth; the Soviet dictators have nothing to wear them down. If the evils which Hobson and Brailsford discovered in capitalism had been in fact the greatest of public vices, we should now be living in an easier world. It is the high-minded and inspired, the missionaries not the capitalists, who cause most of the trouble. Worst of all are the men of Power who are missionaries as well.

Englishmen and Others, Hamish Hamilton, 1956; pp. 76–80.

III

The Neo-Marxist Theories

26 True and False Elements

W. H. B. COURT

W. H. B. Court (1904–   ). Professor of Economic History, University of Birmingham.

The Communist Doctrines of Empire

The communist literature upon imperialism is enormous. So too is the literature of criticism and counter-comment upon it. I shall therefore be forced to confine myself to stating, as clearly as is possible within a brief space, the nature of the doctrines concerned and some of the questions to be solved, if we are to reach a settled opinion upon them.

Certainly no judgement on such a topic can be final. The communist interpretation of empire is in essence a view of political human nature and of the motives which govern it. It follows that such a theory can neither be wholly proved nor wholly disproved by resort to historical or statistical arguments, or, shortly, by the appeal to experience. When it is the interpretation of experience itself which is the problem, it is clear, an accurate determination of the facts of experience can form only a part of the process by which the truth is reached. To become intelligible, these facts must be related according to some principles of economic or political theory; and into our choice of such principles there will enter assumptions about human nature which depend on the experience, conscious and unconscious, of each one of us. A true understanding of history must consequently always be far more limited and subjective than either the political or economic theorist, or the historian, usually cares to believe.

Yet the matters concerned are so important that discussion upon them cannot be wasted, even if we believe that the correctness of any opinion that can be reached must be to no small extent dependent on a sort of general balance of considerations, which every one is free to strike for himself or herself and to re-strike from time to time.

Present-day communist views about the economic origins of empire may be said to be a systematization of certain general ideas which were already alive in the minds of educated men a century or more ago. It is their association with communist politics and with the materialist philosophy of history which has cut them off so to speak from their origins and given them their modern eminence. . . .

So far as the argument can be summarized, it might perhaps be stated thus. The economic essence of modern imperialism is monopoly-capitalism. Monopoly arose out of free competition, in accordance with the Marxian laws. Production has become concentrated in cartels, syndicates, and trusts of all kinds. At the same time, equally important monopolies have arisen in credit; and the extension of the influence of the banks over industry has tended to form great national financial monopolies. Concentration of control, however, has only postponed the fall of profits, and consequently opportunities for investment abroad have become vitally important. Imperialism therefore is nothing but monopoly-capitalism. It is, however, the last stage of capitalism. Competing economic empires bring war, war brings revolution, and revolution will finally overthrow capital and imperialism together.

Lenin wrote during the world war; so too did Bukharin, who set forth similar ideas. Both men express the hopes and convictions of practical revolutionaries, who were certain that the war was about to bring the movement they represented to victory.

Lenin's book was a practical politician's pamphlet, not a scientific treatise. The author's success in the political sphere has given it such a reputation, however, that it stands to other communist theories concerning empire as orthodoxy to heterodoxy in the early ages of the Christian Church. Nevertheless, a consideration of Lenin's theory is bound to suggest several limitations springing partly from the materials at his disposal, partly from the nature of the theory itself.

The history of the hundred years before 1914 – the greatest lending age in the world's history – certainly has shown over and over again that loans may be fatal to borrowing people and States. The British occupation of Egypt and the French conquest of Morocco are familiar instances of financial assistance first entangling and finally destroying weak governments. Just as in the Indian village the money-lender, that indispensable member of eastern society, profits from the cultivator both when he is prosperous and when he starves, and is well hated for doing so (not only as a usurer but often also as a man of alien faith and race) so in the nineteenth century world the money-lender of western blood conducts his operations often in a tangle of intrigue and conflicting interests which has materially contributed to inflame international relations. Many of his transactions were innocuous, but the influence of investors did from time to time deflect the policy of states, and the chanceries have often converted international finance into a sinister interest.

The most distinct, not to say glaring, example of the impact of finance upon politics in British experience is to be found in the history of the South African War, when leaders in the investment of British capital in South Africa exerted a real personal influence over both South Africa and British politics. . . .

There is, therefore, forceful proof in the history of the nineteenth century for Lenin's thesis. Investment helped to make the empires, and investors often cultivated political interests. It will be remembered, however, that Lenin's book professed to be much more than the exhibition of empiric facts. It set forth a body of economic and social theory of extremely comprehensive character and described capitalist accumulation and collapse as general laws of society.

Lenin's book was written largely out of continental experience. Great Britain, however, as the largest foreign investor known, is the best test of his theory. He takes no account of the very large investments of the first half of the nineteenth century in an age when the economic organization of England was intensely competitive and colonial expansion much out of fashion with its people. Capital flowed abroad in vastest volume when active development was proceeding at home and slowed down with the onset of internal depressions; so that 'saturation' was clearly a highly relative thing; nothing more than a relation between two expectations – of future yield on investments at home and abroad – strongly influenced by the slowness with which a once peasant people accustomed itself to the idea of a rising standard of life.

Neither does his thesis ride more firmly to the facts of the great age of colonial expansion, in the last quarter of the century. The houses handling foreign investment remained independent of the rest of the London money-market and the money-market remained divorced from manufacturing industry, which financed itself in the provinces, down to and after the war of 1914–18. During the same period vast masses of our investment continued to go, as before, to countries outside the British empire and largely beyond the control of British policy.

The issues are certainly more complicated than Marxian writers have been willing to suppose. Experience shows that the wealthy countries of the west have lent money throughout the world. It does not follow that such capital would have continued accumulating in those countries, if it had never been lent. Foreign lendings were not born necessarily of monopoly or of accumulation which would in any case have gone on. Great Britain in the last century lent enormously, long before her industry or her credit-system showed the least tendency in the world towards monopoly; but had there been no openings abroad for her capital, much of that capital would never have been saved at all. She had so much to lend, because she lent indefatigably; only the economic developments abroad made possible by her loans brought about the further increases in her wealth out of which new loans were raised. And she lent chiefly when she was herself making full calls upon her capital for home-development, not – as some may suppose – when development at home drooped unprofitably. These well-known things are not perhaps inconsistent with the communist case, if it is contended simply that investment abroad was necessary for such an accumulation of capital as Victorian England had come to regard as 'natural', and that such investments often brought political consequences; but they are seriously inconsistent with that case as it is usually stated, among others by Lenin.

There was already a communist theory of empire in the field when Lenin wrote. This was Rosa Luxemburg's, published in 1912 [sic]. It, too, was a variant of the law of accumulation, based upon Karl Marx.

How is capitalist accumulation practically possible? This was the question that Rosa Luxemburg posed. She sought the answer to it throughout economic literature. Her own solution was based upon classical economics and Marx. It also represented an attempt to correct errors in Marx's reasonings, as she conceived, and this earned her the stern disapprobation of more orthodox Marxians, among them Lenin.

Rosa Luxemburg discovered the secret of accumulation and of empire in the demand of non-capitalist peoples for goods capitalistically produced. She satisfied herself that the accumulation of capital was impossible, if the goods turned out by the capitalist machine could find a market only among the capitalists and their workers. The money turned into fresh investments of capital by the capitalists could only be realized by the sale of goods to those who stood outside of capitalist organization – to the peasant populations of Europe and, above all, to the colonial worlds outside Europe. Empire was consequently essential to the continuance of capitalism; and again, it was a curse to the capitalist countries that possessed it. The area of the globe is limited. Empires consequently mean imperialist wars and war threatens the very foundations of capitalism.

The great similarity between the idea of Lenin and Rosa Luxemburg arises out of their common preoccupation with the problem of the accumulation of capital. The division is a difference of emphasis, since no hard and fast line can be drawn between export of capital and export of consumable goods. Lenin stresses the element of monopoly and the search for additional profit by investing capitalists; Luxemburg, rather, the competitiveness of capitalists and the necessity of markets. Both have had a wide influence and have opened important questions of economic theory and history.

Memory . . . will suggest numerous examples of the influence which traders in primitive countries have exerted in modern times upon the overseas expansion of the states of Europe. In this connexion it is worth recollecting that the trade incentive to colonial empire remained operative throughout the period described by Lenin as the period of financial capitalism.

To take a single instance – few imperial moves of modern times have been more clearly instigated by the trader than Bismarck's annexation in 1885 of the Cameroons – a part of the world where there was no white capital whatever beyond the floating capital of traders of various nationalities. . . .

Similar instances might be drawn from French and British history of about the same period; but without pursuing the matter further, one must grant the truth of empirical observation behind Rosa Luxemburg's work. It will be recollected, however, that that book claimed the truth of a comprehensive theoretical system, not merely that of historical observation. Nevertheless, the economic theory employed is probably far more limited in its scope than the author supposed.

The relation between accumulation and lack of purchasing-power, which we all are tempted to treat as simple, is pretty certainly complex. Experience shows that shortages of purchasing-power do from time to time occur throughout the highly industrialized communities of the western world, although the causes are still unsettled, notwithstanding a century of discussion of the trade-cycle. In any case, it appears that a persistently low level of consumption in society is far more likely to slow up or check altogether the accumulation of capital, than to bring about an over-supply of it. An over-supply of capital does appear from time to time in particular industries, but this is a different matter, and merely represents the error of investors.

All of this, once more, is possibly not inconsistent with the communist explanation of imperial expansion; yet it fits ill with the fundamental causes of expansion as they are often conceived in simple terms of underconsumption and over-saving.

The theories outlined above deal at length with problems of international relations; but the original question which they set themselves to answer was very different – in what way and at what point will capitalism destroy itself, so as to show itself subject to the Marxian conception of social development.

It was for this purpose that there was evolved the law of capitalist accumulation and the variations of it created by Rosa Luxemburg and Lenin.

In these discussions the heirs of Marxian thought showed themselves fully aware of difficulties which orthodox political economy skated over or altogether avoided. There is much that is penetrating and true in their views of history, in their handling of the trade-cycle and other major questions of economic theory.

That the 'laws of motion of capitalist society', however, have been conclusively established and verified either by Marxian or by orthodox economics cannot be admitted, notwithstanding a century of debate. The existence of at least two communist theories proves that the Marxians are not agreed and orthodox economics is not more united. Many important things have been established and differences no doubt are less than they seem, but the existence of a large body of instructive thought is very different from the one great logical and inductive law which Marxian thought set out to find, which was to predict the course of western civilization.

The original quest of such a law was perhaps a mistake. The development of economics first among the social sciences and its early and natural entanglement with political positions of opposing kinds, has called out everywhere a spirit of dogmatism over its findings. The natural presumption is that the explanation of society requires many social sciences, not one, even if that one numbered among its founders men as able as Adam Smith and Karl Marx.

Over a century ago a new social law was described, which was comparable in its domination over educated men with the influence of the 'law of capitalist accumulation' to-day. The Malthusian law was thoroughly scientific in its origins; it was logically argued, laboriously verified, publicly detested, and ardently believed. For two generations the law governed English social theory and even English politics, so far as an idea can rule men. Yet no one to-day imagines that Malthus, fine scientist as he was, so fathomed society that its problems can be understood and controlled by a simple recital of his formulae.

The theories which we have been discussing already show some of their limits and may be supposed to be in process of being reduced from the level of dogma to the more tolerable standing of fertile thought.

Cast wholly in economic terms they omit the political elements which are essential to war and colonial empire. It is reasonable to believe that man is a political as well as an economic animal. The war of 1914–18 was perhaps, as Croce says, a war of historical materialism, but this materialism was political as well as economic; State and business-community together schooled the world to put wealth and power above peace. The European state system, as a quasi-independent and self-perpetuating force, is excluded from the Marxian picture. Yet the State shook itself free of law and authority a century and a half before public thinkers were prepared to give the same sanction to economic competition, and one of the earliest uses of its modern freedom was for overseas dominion.

Politics and economics are not yet wholly annexed to the kingdom of rational behaviour; yet for the utilitarian psychology which unites Marxian with the classical political economy, the broad instinctive life of man remains like a river underground, not so much unheard as unexplored. In the daily life of societies it constantly bursts to the surface and leaves little in history of the simple patterns of our theories. Where is the ground for supposing that war and domination are always the consequence of economic or political calculation?

The domination of one society over another is a social and not an economic phenomenon, although it is often in large part the result of superior economic organization. Imperialism is the result of the exploitation of advantages of every kind, in a world where races and peoples seem no more equal in resources or civilization or ability than are individuals.

In some of the remote parts of China adjoining Thibet the thoroughly medieval society of Thibet exercises a kind of imperialism over the mountain valleys, where it steadily expands as against the primitive mountain tribes. It is carried forward by wealth, for it is usurer to the poor peasants; by population, for it settles; by the victories of its religion and clearer intellectual life over the confused superstitions and ignorance of the mountaineers. Exactly similar forces have given western society control of modern Africa. But if this is so, then, however great the influence of the western trader and investor in the modern world, imperialism is likely to continue long after capitalism has been forgotten; for differences of national income and resources, culture, and social organization will survive the private capitalism of the west. Societies unequal in strength in many ways will still meet and out of their conflicts of interest imperialism of new kinds will arise.

Appendix I in *Survey of British Commonwealth Affairs*, Vol II, *Problems of Economic Policy 1918–1939, Part 1*, by w. k. HANCOCK, Oxford University Press, 1940; pp. 293, 298–304.

27 The Basic Fallacy behind Marxist Theories

J. A. SCHUMPETER

J. A. Schumpeter (1893–1950). Economist. Austrian Minister of Finance, 1919–20. Professor of Economics, Harvard University, 1932–50.

Two outstanding examples will illustrate both the merits and the demerits of the Marxian synthesis considered as a problem-solving engine.

First we will consider the Marxist theory of Imperialism. Its roots are all to be found in Marx's chief work, but it has been developed by the Neo-Marxist school which flourished in the first two decades of this century and, without renouncing communion with the old defenders of the faith, such as Karl Kautsky, did much to overhaul the system. Vienna was its center; Otto Bauer, Rudolf Hilferding, Max Adler were its leaders. In the field of imperialism their work was continued, with but secondary shifts of emphasis, by many others, prominent among whom were Rosa Luxemburg and Fritz Sternberg. The argument runs as follows.

Since, on the one hand, capitalist society cannot exist and its economic system cannot function without profits and since, on the other hand, profits are constantly being eliminated by the very working of that system, incessant effort to keep them alive becomes the central aim of the capitalist class. Accumulation accompanied by qualitative change in the composition of capital is, as we have seen, a remedy which though alleviating for the moment the situation of the individual capitalist makes matters worse in the end. So capital, yielding to the pressure of a falling rate of profits – it falls, we recall, both because constant capital increases relative to variable capital and because, if wages tend to rise and hours are being shortened, the rate of surplus value falls – seeks for outlets in countries in which there is still labor that can be exploited at will and in which the process of mechanization has not as yet gone far. Thus we get an export of capital into undeveloped countries which is essentially an export of capital equipment or of consumers' goods to be used in order to buy labor or to acquire things with which to buy labor.[1] But it is also export of capital in the ordinary sense of the term because the exported commodities will not be paid for – at least not immediately – by goods, services or money from the importing country. And it turns into colonization if, in order to safeguard the investment both against hostile reaction of the native environment – or if you please, against its resistance to exploitation – and against competition from other capitalist countries,

[1] Think of luxuries to be traded to chieftains against slaves or to be traded against wage goods with which to hire native labor. For the sake of brevity, I do not take account of the fact that capital export in the sense envisaged will in general arise as a part of the total trade of the two countries which also includes commodity transactions unconnected with the particular process we have in mind. These transactions of course greatly facilitate that capital export, but do not affect its principle. I shall also neglect other types of capital exports. The theory under discussion is not, and is not intended to be, a general theory of international trade and finance.

the undeveloped country is brought into political subjection. This is in general accomplished by military force supplied either by the colonizing capitalists themselves or by their home government which thus lives up to the definition given in the *Communist Manifesto*: 'the executive of the modern State [is] . . . a committee for managing the common affairs of the whole bourgeoisie'. Of course, that force will not be used for defensive purposes only. There will be conquest, friction between the capitalist countries and internecine war between rival bourgeoisies.

Another element completes this theory of imperialism as it is now usually presented. So far as colonial expansion is prompted by a falling rate of profit in the capitalist countries, it should occur in the later stages of capitalist evolution – Marxists in fact speak of imperialism as a stage, preferably the last stage, of capitalism. Hence it would coincide with a high degree of concentration of capitalist control over industry and with a decline of the type of competition that characterized the times of the small or medium-sized firm. Marx himself did not lay much stress on the resulting tendency toward monopolistic restriction of output and on the consequent tendency toward protecting the domestic game preserve against the intrusion of poachers from other capitalist countries. Perhaps he was too competent an economist to trust this line of argument too far. But the Neo-Marxists were glad to avail themselves of it. Thus we get not only another stimulus for imperialist policy and another source of imperialist imbroglios but also, as a by-product, a theory of a phenomenon that is not necessarily imperialist in itself, modern protectionism.

Note one more hitch in that process that will stand the Marxist in good stead in the task of explaining further difficulties. When the undeveloped countries have been developed, capital export of the kind we have been considering will decline. There may then be a period during which the mother country and the colony will exchange, say, manufactured products for raw materials. But in the end the exports of manufacturers will also have to decline while colonial competition will assert itself in the mother country. Attempts to retard the advent of that state of things will provide further sources of friction, this time between each old capitalist country and its colonies, of wars of independence and so on. But in any case colonial doors will eventually be closed to domestic capital which will no longer be able to flee from vanishing profits at home into richer pastures abroad. Lack of outlets, excess capacity, complete deadlock, in the end regular recurrence of national bankruptcies and other disasters – perhaps world wars from sheer capitalist despair – may confidently be anticipated. History is as simple as that.

This theory is a fair – perhaps it is the best – example of the way in which the Marxian synthesis attempts to solve problems and acquires authority by doing so. The whole thing seems to follow beautifully from two fundamental premises that are both firmly embedded in the groundwork of the system: the theory of classes and the theory of accumulation. A series of vital facts of our time seems to be perfectly accounted for. The whole maze of international politics seems to be cleared up by a single powerful stroke of analysis. And we see in the process why and how class action, always remaining intrinsically the same, assumes the form of political or of business action according to circumstances that determine nothing but tactical methods and phraseology. If, the means and opportunities at the command of a group of capitalists being what they are, it is more profitable to negotiate a loan, a loan will be negotiated. If, the means and opportunities being what they are, it is more profitable to make war, war will be made. The latter alternative is no less entitled to enter economic theory than the former. Even mere protectionism now grows nicely out of the very logic of capitalist evolution.

Moreover, this theory displays to full advantage a virtue that it has in common with most of the Marxian concepts in the field of what is usually referred to as applied economics. This is its close alliance with historical and contemporaneous fact. Probably not one reader has perused my résumé without being struck by the ease with which supporting historical instances crowded in upon him at every single step of the argument. Has he not heard of the oppression by Europeans of native labor in many parts of the world, of what South and Central American Indians suffered at the hands of the Spaniards for instance, or of slave-hunting and slave-trading and coolieism? Is capital export not actually ever-present in capitalist countries? Has it not almost invariably been accompanied by military conquest that served to subdue the natives and to fight other European powers? Has not colonization always had a rather conspicuous military side, even when managed entirely by business corporations such as the East India Company or the British South Africa Company? What better illustration could Marx himself have desired than Cecil Rhodes and the Boer War? Is it not pretty obvious that colonial ambitions were, to say the least, an important factor in European troubles, at all events since about 1700? As for the present time, who has not heard, on the one hand, about the 'strategy of raw materials' and, on the other hand, of the repercussions on Europe of the growth of native capitalism in the tropics? And so on. As to protectionism – well, that is as plain as anything can be.

But we had better be careful. An apparent verification by prima facie favorable cases which are not analyzed in detail may be very deceptive. Moreover, as every lawyer and every politician knows, energetic appeal to familiar facts will go a long way toward inducing a jury or a parliament to accept also the construction he desires to put upon them. Marxists have exploited this technique to the full. In this instance it is particularly successful, because the facts in question combine the virtues of being superficially known to everyone and of being thoroughly understood by very few. In fact, though we cannot enter into detailed discussion here, even hasty reflection suffices to suggest a suspicion that 'it is not so'. . . .

We shall now consider the question whether, if the Marxian interpretation of capital export, colonization and protectionism were correct, it would also be adequate as a theory of all the phenomena we think of when using that loose and misused term [imperialism]. Of course we can always define imperialism in such a way as to mean just what the Marxian interpretation implies; and we can always profess ourselves convinced that all those phenomena *must* be explainable in the Marxian manner. But then the problem of imperialism – always granting that the theory is in itself correct – would be 'solved' only tautologically.[1] Whether the Marxian approach or, for that matter, any

---

[1] The danger of empty tautologies being put over on us is best illustrated by individual cases. Thus, France conquered Algeria, Tunisia and Morocco, and Italy conquered Abyssinia, by military force without there being any significant capitalist interests to press for it. As a matter of fact, presence of such interests was a pretense that was very difficult to establish, and the subsequent development of such interests was a slow process that went on, unsatisfactorily enough, under government pressure. If that should not look very Marxist, it will be replied that action was taken under pressure of potential or anticipated capitalist interests or that in the last analysis some capitalist interest or objective necessity 'must' have been at the bottom of it. And we can then hunt for corroboratory evidence that will never be entirely lacking, since capitalist interests, like any others, will in fact be affected by, and take advantage of, any situation whatsoever, and since the particular conditions of the capitalist organism will always present some features which may without absurdity be linked up with those policies of national expansion. Evidently it is preconceived conviction and nothing else that keeps us going in a task as desperate as this; without such a conviction it would never occur

purely economic approach yields a solution that is not tautological would still have to be considered. This, however, need not concern us here, because the ground gives way before we get that far.

At first sight, the theory seems to fit some cases tolerably well. The most important instances are afforded by the English and Dutch conquests in the tropics. But other cases, such as the colonization of New England, it does not fit at all. And even the former type of case is not satisfactorily described by the Marxian theory of imperialism. It would obviously not suffice to recognize that the lure of gain played a role in motivating colonial expansion.[1] The Neo-Marxists did not mean to aver such a horrible platitude. If these cases are to count for them, it is also necessary that colonial expansion came about, in the way indicated, under pressure of accumulation on the rate of profit, hence as a feature of decaying, or at all events of fully matured, capitalism. But the heroic time of colonial adventure was precisely the time of early and immature capitalism when accumulation was in its beginnings and any such pressure – also, in particular, any barrier to exploitation of domestic labor – was conspicuous by its absence. The element of monopoly was not absent. On the contrary it was far more evident than it is today. But that only adds to the absurdity of the construction which makes both monopoly and conquest specific properties of latter-day capitalism.

Moreover, the other leg of the theory, class struggle, is in no better condition. One must wear blinkers to concentrate on that aspect of colonial expansion which hardly ever played more than a secondary role, and to construe in terms of class struggle a phenomenon which affords some of the most striking instances of class cooperation. It was as much a movement toward higher wages as it was a movement toward higher profits, and in the long run it certainly benefited (in part because of the exploitation of *native* labor) the proletariat more than it benefited the capitalist interest. But I do not wish to stress its *effects*. The essential point is that its *causation* has not much to do with class warfare, and not more to do with class structure than is implied

---

to us to embark upon it. And we really need not take the trouble; we might just as well say that 'it must be so' and leave it at that. This is what I meant by tautological explanation.

[1] Nor is it sufficient to stress the fact that each country actually did 'exploit' its colonies. For that was exploitation of a country as a whole by a country as a whole (of all classes by all classes) and has nothing to do with the specifically Marxian kind of exploitation.

in the leadership of groups and individuals that belonged to, or by colonial enterprise rose into, the capitalist class. If however we shake off the blinkers and cease to look upon colonization or imperialism as a mere incident in class warfare, little remains that is specifically Marxist about the matter. What Adam Smith has to say on it does just as well – better in fact.

The by-product, the Neo-Marxian theory of modern protectionism, still remains. Classical literature is full of invectives against the 'sinister interests' – at that time mainly, but never wholly, the agrarian interests – which in clamoring for protection committed the unforgivable crime against public welfare. Thus the classics had a causal theory of protection all right – not only a theory of its effects – and if now we add the protectionist interests of modern big business we have gone as far as it is reasonable to go. Modern economists with Marxist sympathies really should know better than to say that even now their bourgeois colleagues do not see the relation between the trend toward protection-ism and the trend toward big units of control, though these colleagues may not always think it necessary to stress so obvious a fact. Not that the classics and their successors to this day were right about protection: their interpretation of it was, and is, as one-sided as was the Marxian one, besides being often wrong in the appraisal of consequences and of the interests involved. But for at least fifty years they have known about the monopoly component in protectionism all that Marxists ever knew, which was not difficult considering the commonplace character of the discovery.

And they were superior to the Marxist theory in one very important respect. Whatever the value of their economics – perhaps it was not great – they mostly[1] stuck to it. In this instance, that was an advantage. The proposition that many protective duties owe their existence to the pressure of large concerns that desire to use them for the purpose of keeping their prices at home above what they otherwise would be, possibly in order to be able to sell more cheaply abroad, is a platitude but correct, although no tariff was ever wholly or even mainly due to this particular cause. It is the Marxian synthesis that makes it inadequate or wrong. If our ambition is simply to understand all the causes and

---

[1] They did not always confine themselves to their economics. When they did not, results were anything but encouraging. Thus, James Mill's purely economic writings, while not particularly valuable, cannot be simply dismissed as hope-lessly substandard. The real nonsense – and platitudinous nonsense at that – is in his articles on government and cognate subjects.

implications of modern protectionism, political, social and economic, then it is inadequate. For instance, the consistent support given by the American people to protectionist policy, whenever they had the opportunity to speak their minds, is accounted for not by any love for or domination by big business, but by a fervent wish to build and keep a world of their own and to be rid of all the vicissitudes of the rest of the world. Synthesis that overlooks such elements of the case is not an asset but a liability. But if our ambition is to reduce all the causes and implications of modern protectionism, whatever they may be, to the monopolistic element in modern industry as the sole *causa causans* and if we formulate that proposition accordingly, then it becomes wrong. Big business has been able to take advantage of the popular sentiment and it has fostered it; but it is absurd to say that it has created it. Synthesis that yields – we ought rather to say, postulates – such a result is inferior to no synthesis at all.

Matters become infinitely worse if, flying in the face of fact plus common sense, we exalt that theory of capital export and colonization into the fundamental explanation of international politics which thereupon resolves into a struggle, on the one hand, of monopolistic capitalist groups with each other and, on the other hand, of each of them with their own proletariat. This sort of thing may make useful party literature but otherwise it merely shows that nursery tales are no monopoly of bourgeois economics. As a matter of fact, very little influence on foreign policy has been exerted by big business – or by the *haute finance* from the Fuggers to the Morgans – and in most of the cases in which large-scale industry as such, or banking interests as such, have been able to assert themselves, their naive dilettantism has resulted in discomfiture. The attitudes of capitalist groups toward the policy of their nations are predominantly adaptive rather than causative, today more than ever. Also, they hinge to an astonishing degree on short-run considerations equally remote from any deeply laid plans and from any definite 'objective' class interests. At this point Marxism degenerates into the formulation of popular superstitions.[1]

[1] This superstition is exactly on a par with another that is harbored by many worthy and simple-minded people who explain modern history to themselves on the hypothesis that there is somewhere a committee of supremely wise and malevolent Jews who behind the scenes control international or perhaps all politics. Marxists are not victims of this particular superstition but theirs is on no higher plane. It is amusing to record that, when faced with either doctrine, I have always

Capitalism, Socialism, and Democracy (1942), 3rd edn. Allen and Unwin, 1950; pp. 49–55.

---

experienced great difficulty in replying in anything like a fashion satisfactory to myself. This was not only due to the circumstance that it is always difficult to establish denial of factual assertions. The main difficulty came from the fact that people, lacking any first-hand knowledge of international affairs and their personnel, also lack any organ for the perception of absurdity.

IV

Other Interpretations

28 Capitalists and Others

E. STALEY

E. Staley (1906–). Economist. Professor of International Development Education, Stanford University, U.S.A.

A crude or naïve form of the economic interpretation of history some-times used to explain investment friction between capital-exporting powers, posits some such pattern as the following in the origin of these disputes: Bankers, business men, speculators, scour the earth looking for profitable opportunities to invest what is often called 'surplus capital'.[1] They seek railway concessions in China, establish banks in Persia, acquire mining rights in Morocco. In all these undertakings they seek, and secure, the support of their national governments. Rival investors of different nationalities are attracted by these supposedly lucrative opportunities, and they enter into competition, each per-suading his government to back him diplomatically in his quest for profits. Soon the governments find themselves involved in con-

[1] This concept of 'surplus capital' needs critical analysis. As with all notions of a surplus in economics one must inquire 'Surplus at what price?' Pursuit of this question leads in the present instance to the discovery that the situation usually described by the phrase 'surplus capital' does not involve a surplus in the absolute sense that the exported capital could not be used at home, assuming the rate of return was made low enough. A more precise description of the circumstances would be that, after due allowance for the expected risks, a greater return is looked for abroad than at home. Response to this differential in the expected rate of return is a more accurate description of the forces which cause capital migration than such phrases as 'surplus capital', implying as they do a sort of squeezing out of redundant capital for which there is no use regardless of price. The differential in the expected rate of return arises not only out of conditions affecting the supply of capital in the exporting country, but also out of demand factors there and abroad, including developments in communication and transportation which make it possible to manage investments abroad more efficiently and to market their products more cheaply.

troversies over the investment opportunities sought by their respective capitalists, or over the protection of capital investments once made. Pushed on by the influence of profit-seeking investors, who continue to demand vigorous support of their financial enterprises, the governments come to sharp political clashes, which may prepare the way for war.

Now, there is nothing logically wrong with this theory. It is perfectly plausible. And events very close to the description it provides have occurred in the actual world. But the facts of investment friction between capital-exporting nations have usually been a good deal more complicated than this theory implies, and especially is this true of those difficulties that have been really serious threats to international peace. The vice of this crude theory is its dangerous over-simplification – dangerous because the half-truths it presents in easy tabloid form divert attention from some vital factors in investment friction and lead to false conclusions regarding the policies of control that might promise most success in minimizing such friction.

The theory rests on half-truths in three important respects. In the first place, it is true that investors do put pressure on governors to influence state policy in ways favorable to the formers' profit interests. . . . But it is definitely untrue that many cases can be found where immediate pressure of this kind has pushed governments so far as to provoke really serious clashes with other strong powers. . . . In the second place, it is true that the ends sought by governmental policies which lead to clashes with other governments often do include expansion of opportunities for the profitable investment of capital. It is not true, however, that the impulse to such purposes on the part of the governors comes necessarily, or even usually, from the pressure of persons with direct economic interest in investment outlets. As a matter of fact, it is a striking circumstance that governments, journalists, colonial zealots, and patriotic societies have often been more avid than the owners of capital in the promotion of investments abroad. Third, and finally, while it is true that the immediate economic interests of rival investing groups come into conflict over desirable investment opportunities, the crude theory fails to give adequate weight to the fact that such conflicts are ordinarily subject to solution with reasonable ease on the basis of the business techniques of compromise, buying and selling, *so long as purely profit-making considerations are involved.* If simply the direct pressure of profit-seeking business were behind the investment frictions between capital-exporting powers these would be much less dangerous. Business interests can be compromised much more readily than can strivings for national power, prestige, and glory. The process by which the latter come to be bound up with the former is not adequately explained in the over-simplified theory we have been discussing. . . .

If the reader desires a typical pattern of events for cases in which investment friction has arisen between capital-exporting countries, the following might be offered as more realistic than the over-simplified one criticized earlier in this chapter: Explorers, traders, travellers, and missionaries establish contact with an undeveloped region. They spread reports, often extravagant, of its wealth and potentialities. Colonial and geographic societies may even be formed, and if so their membership will consist not only of business men with interests in foreign trade or investment, but their most active elements are likely to be ardent young journalists, military and naval men, members of the aristocracy, romantic geographers, explorers, government officials, 'national' economists, and nationalistic patriots in general. The government comes to be inspired by certain economic and political ideas which call for extension of the national sovereignty, or at least the national influence, over foreign territories. In the meantime, a few citizens have established more or less important economic interests, mainly of a trading nature, in the undeveloped country and have perhaps applied for concessions. Their home government now gives these citizens energetic support, urges others in, perhaps subsidizes some firms. It takes every opportunity to assert the national interest, economic and political, in the territory now vaguely marked out for national expansion. It makes diplomatic bargains with other powers looking toward ultimate control of the territory. Bankers who hesitate to risk funds in the region are urged to do so on patriotic grounds. Concessions representing investment opportunities are extracted from the native government of the territory now being consciously 'penetrated' – in many cases before any capitalists can be found who are willing to accept the 'opportunities' so assiduously sought out by the diplomats. Meantime, some other great power has started to pursue similar ambitions in the same region, or has become alarmed lest the territory be seized by the first power and then closed to its traders and investors, or feels that the political balance of power is being disturbed, or that the acquisition of political influence in this region by the first power is a threat to 'vital interests' of its own, such as lines of communication and the like. This second power endeavors to oppose the process of penetration by political and economic means, often including the urging in of its own capitalists and demands for concessions to them. Thus political friction over investments and investment opportunities in the undeveloped country arises, and its intensity will depend largely upon the 'vital' national interests thought to be at stake. A good many outside observers, whose attention is now drawn to the matter for the first time and who see the two powers quarreling over concessions, railways, and economic advantages, will at this point draw the obvious, but erroneous, conclusion that the main conflict is between the immediate economic interests of rival investing groups. . . .

In order to put the immediate, economic conflicts of rival investing groups into proper perspective . . . this chapter has dwelt at length upon the generalized description of the processes by which such friction originates. The complex of ideas, interests, attitudes, and doctrines here called 'expansionism' has received much emphasis in this connection. In fact, the tendency of the argument – representing conclusions which seem unavoidable in view of the concrete evidence – has been to substitute expansionism for the pressure of immediate private investment interests as the villain of the drama . . . But this is in one sense simply to push the question as to the rôle of private foreign investments one step further back, for expansionism has been pictured as the resultant of many social forces, among them some connected with private investment interests or the activities of private investors. To what extent has the pressure of capital for profitable opportunities abroad, or the influence of actual and would-be investors, been responsible for expansionism and thus indirectly for investment friction? . . .

Perhaps the causation of complicated social phenomena like expansionism can never be determined with certainty. Be that as it may, despite these reservations there are two conclusions which seem to emerge with sufficient distinctness so that they deserve mention here. First, the investment pressure in which we are interested cannot be regarded as an indispensable element in the causation of expansionism, for certain modern nations where such pressure has been absent or minimal have nevertheless developed most vigorous outward drives of a sort which we must accept as falling within our definition, since they have involved the use of investments as tools and have led to investment friction with other powers. Second, investment pressure has been a factor in the origin of expansionism in certain other countries, to a degree impossible to evaluate accurately, but differing from country to country and apparently quite important in some. In all such cases it has been intertwined with other factors of the most diverse kinds. . . .

The pre-war histories of Russia and Italy lend no support whatever to the hypothesis that the pressure of 'surplus capital' for investment abroad is an essential element in the origin of modern national expansionism. Tsarist Russia was capital-poor, a heavy borrower when possible, and yet it sprawled over Northern Asia, contested Korea and Manchuria with Japan, and sought to extend its sway southward to Constantinople, and engaged in such an aggressive politico-economic penetration of Persia that England was alarmed for the safety of India. These were typical activities of the sort which has been called 'capitalistic imperialism'. . . . The causes of Russian expansionism have to be sought in political ambition, dynastic megalomania, military lust for conquest. Capital was distinctly a tool, not a cause.

The case of Italy is only slightly less clear than that of Tsarist Russia. Italy, too, was a nation poor in capital, borrowing abroad for its own needs. Yet it engaged in the struggle for acquisition of territory and spheres of influence which characterized the decades before the World War. A rising spirit of nationalism seeking to assert itself in the world, the quest for prestige and glory, were more effective causes of Italian conquest in Tripoli, the establishment of colonies elsewhere on the African coast, the attempt to extend Italian influence over Abyssinia, and the dispute over Tunis with France, than were any investment factors. . . .

It can surely be concluded from these cases that the existence of 'surplus' investment capital pressing for opportunities abroad is not a necessary element in the origin of nationalistic imperialism, colonialism, or – in the general term used here – expansionism. On the other hand, the quest for desirable investment opportunities has undoubtedly been a factor of varying magnitude in the development of expansionism on the part of other powers. . . . The conclusion with respect to the United States must be much like those reached for France, England and Germany: private foreign investments have figured in national expansionism, but as one among many factors, some of which have been more important than the investment influence.

War and the Private Investor, University of Chicago Press, 1935, pp. 419–33.

29 Investments in Africa

S. H. FRANKEL

S. H. Frankel (1903–   ). Economist. Professor of the Economics of Under-developed Countries and Fellow of Nuffield College, Oxford.

From 1870 to 1914, Europe, and in particular Great Britain, played the role of the world's financier to an extent which had not been reached previously, and may not for long be reached again. The London financial market, which occupied pride of place in this new development in international economic relations, derived its power from the great wealth, diversity of experience and world connections built up with growing momentum towards the end of the nineteenth century. At the same time British dominance in world commerce finally led also to direct penetration into tropical areas, most of which had previously been connected with the mother country only by a series of strategic outposts and trading stations.

Up to the last decades of the century the desire to avoid entanglements which might prove costly to the mother countries remained the dominant feature of colonial policy. . . . At the end of the nineteenth century a new era was inaugurated in which both new objectives of colonial policy were conceived, and owing to the growth of wealth in Europe, fresh means of realizing them were available. The widespread industrialization led to rising income levels which could find their expression only in the development and satisfaction of new wants. The potential wealth of the tropics, therefore, suddenly assumed a new importance which was expressed in the political rivalry that marked the partition of the African continent. When the European powers assumed control of their new African possessions, they inaugurated colonial policies based on the deliberate economic exploitation of the natural resources previously neglected. Many complex factors contributed to this new development of colonial policy. Basically, however, it was made possible owing to the fact that the accumulated wealth of Europe, and in particular of Great Britain, began in the seventh decade of the nineteenth century to grow at a rate incomparably faster than ever before. . . .

The growth of accumulated wealth went hand in hand with, and was in large measure due to, a unique confidence in the maintenance of international, commercial and financial contracts and obligations – whether these were entered into by individuals or by Governments. . . .

A remarkable complex of financial institutions was evolved to further the process of international investment. The huge British commercial banks, financing commodity movements throughout the world, had long been the greatest source of short-term credit. Alongside of them there developed the banks, public, private and Imperial, of the British dominions. Around them grew up that unique security market for investment in long-term ventures which functioned through highly specialized groups of financial, promoting, underwriting, and investment companies.

Overseas investment was influenced by the spirit and institutions of the time; by the combination of sentiment, patriotism and opportunities for gain; by the large scope, often indirectly combined with national support, given to the promoters of enterprises in virgin territories; by the considerable possibilities of profit to particular individuals arising from capital windfalls due to the discovery of valuable resources; by the speculative opportunities arising from the creation of numerous enterprises, whose market valuation fluctuated considerably with the psychological propensities of the security markets and with changes in monetary policy; by the large gains that could be hoped for, and frequently accrued, through the appreciation of values in land or natural resources as a result of the movement of population to them. Only against such a background can the almost incredible financial exploits of a Rhodes be understood, or the spasmodic, and at times exaggerated, bursts of capital investment which created the mineral industries of Africa be explained.

It is true that in Great Britain, up to the outbreak of the Great War, the regulation of foreign investment was rare as compared with that exercised in continental Europe – particularly in France – where it was considerably interfered with for political and diplomatic purposes. Yet the influence of non-economic considerations on capital investment in Africa must not be underestimated. Once European powers had committed themselves to establish sovereignty over, and permanent administrations in vast territories, capital had to be diverted to them in order to make their rule effective. In British territories a considerable part of the early investment was directly financed by Government loans and grants-in-aid. Whenever this was done it was invariably because, without Government intervention, the capital could not have been made available. Apart from these loans and the powerful influence of the Colonial Stock Acts, there was no direct control of investments. Nevertheless the direction it took was influenced in many ways. The diversion did not take place through definite regulations, but by the process of consciously or unconsciously influencing public opinion and the expectations of the investor.

The general atmosphere of optimism engendered by glowing descriptions of, and imperialist propaganda about the potentialities of the new African possessions had a powerful effect in making not only the loan issues of Colonial Government, but also the shares of innumerable exploration, mining and financial companies acceptable to the investor. That Rhodes could continue for years to get money from a large circle of shareholders in the Chartered Company, in spite of the fact that the payment of even a single dividend was successfully deferred for half a generation, illustrates how the direction of investment could be affected by vague and general expectations combined with patriotic and sentimental considerations. . . .

Much confusion in current discussions of colonial policy arises from the fact that trade and international investment are considered abstractly. In practice, the provision of capital, the development of new products and the expansion of commerce are not processes that occur *in vacuo*. Their success inevitably depends on innumerable personal and political connections of, and on the vast store of accumulated knowledge and experience possessed by countless special groups in the metropolitan countries and their commercial or financial representatives in Africa. It is on the combined activity of these that the success and the direction of African development depends. For this reason the economic progress of any particular African territory cannot be discussed as if it were something divorced from that whole complex of economic experience and business tradition, which has moulded the economic structure of the metropolitan country itself. Capital investment in colonial territories is, therefore, not merely a quantitative question, but also a qualitative one. Those responsible for the direction, type and application of the investment, and for creating the administrative and social structure through which alone it can be applied, must possess special individual and national qualities.

To represent the development of Africa in the last fifty years as the result merely of financial or imperialist greed is to miss the real implications of the vast changes which this period has inaugurated. The motives of individuals and of western nations were doubtless mixed, but the main outcome was that, by the end of the nineteenth century,

Europe found itself irretrievably engaged in the task of incorporating the African continent into the income-creating stream and the economy of the world. For this purpose, it was necessary to divert enormous resources to Africa in order, first, to obtain access to the interior, and, secondly, to commence the arduous task of revitalizing the habits and work of its backward peoples.

Capital Investment in Africa, Oxford University Press, 1938; pp. 16–29.

30 Did Foreign Investment Pay?

A. K. CAIRNCROSS

A. K. Cairncross (1911–   ). Economist. Economic Adviser to H.M. Government.

Public opinion has almost always been biased in favour of investment of capital at home and against investment in other countries. Even in England, from the eighteenth century onwards, there has generally been an undercurrent of feeling against the right of investors to hazard capital freely in the bonds of foreign governments or in enterprises situated abroad. . . .

It is not easy to say how far this bias is justified. Questions of investment are so wrapped up in human institutions – in private property, in capitalism, in imperialism, and in war – that judgements of national advantage cannot be based simply upon money yields. Those who encouraged the French rentier in his folly may have thought the cementing of a political alliance vastly more important than the sacrifice which they were foisting on him, or the profits which they were able to net for themselves. It is not even possible to say that there is a necessary money advantage or disadvantage in the export of capital. The experience of different countries – and of different generations – has varied too widely for any definite presumption that foreign investment does or does not pay to be established. It is only possible to offer a catalogue of some of the circumstances in which foreign investment should be looked upon with favour or disfavour; or to try, from a recital of the gains and losses of some particular country at some particular time, to form a balanced judgement of probable gains and losses at some future time. . . .

The dangers of foreign investment can readily be illustrated from French experience. By 1914 France had embarked close on £500 m. in Russian bonds bearing 4 and 5%. It was known – although not to the French investor – that the Russian government was spending half of its borrowings on armaments, and that it was relying to an increasing extent upon profits from the sale of alcohol in order to meet its ordinary expenses. It had, in fact, been more or less on the verge of bankruptcy ever since the nineties. A war or a revolution – and neither was altogether unforeseen – would bring certain default. In the event, the loans were repudiated outright, and not a penny of the whole £500 m. has ever been recovered. The loans which France had made, with equal craziness, to Turkey, Greece, Austria-Hungary, the Balkans and South America, were also repudiated. In all, France lost two-thirds of the net total of her foreign investments, or about six times the amount of the German indemnity of 1870. . . .

The interest received, in spite of the difference in risk, was not appreciably greater than the market rate on similar French securities. It has been estimated that in 1899 the yield on domestic securities at the price of issue averaged 4·28%, while the yield on foreign securities was no more than 3·85%. At the *market* price in 1900 the yields were 3·23 and 3·84% respectively. The difference, whether positive or negative, was trifling. It must be remembered, too, that the type of investment in which France specialized – bonds of European governments – paid the lowest interest. The French rentier – the most cautious of capitalists and the most credulous – was content with a gilt-edged return on securities in which no self-respecting gambler would have dabbled. He was financing the warmongers for a mere pittance. He was starving French industry of capital. And he was doing little or nothing to promote French commerce or to reduce the cost of imported products.

On the other hand, there is at least a *prima facie* case for believing that British investment in other countries has been economically advantageous to the investors themselves and to the nation as a whole. In the nineteenth century there were constant defaults – chiefly by South American countries – but, for the most part, with the exception of those of the twenties and seventies, of a comparatively minor character.

The return, in profits and interest, was substantial. And the opening-up of new countries with British capital – the building of railways, the provision of banking and insurance facilities, the financing of public utilities of all kinds, the operation of mining ventures and so on – was attended with solid advantages to this country over and above the pickings of judicious investment. There were, of course, many 'unsavoury incidents' – exploitation of the weakness and credulity of foreign peoples and governments, and of the ignorance and folly of investors. But political injustice and polite fraud were not peculiar to *foreign* investment, and would presumably exist in the absence of any investment whatever. And it was remarkably rare – everything considered – for any of the countries most heavily indebted to us to find in its reliance upon foreign capitalists a source of irritation or a matter for regret. . . .

In all, British capitalists earned some £4000 m. in just over forty years in interest and dividends on their foreign investments. An average income from overseas of almost £100 m. a year was a tidy contribution to the National Dividend, which at that time was ranging between, say, £900 m. in 1870 and £2300 m. in 1913. During the period, moreover, there was a steady improvement in the credit of our debtors and in their power to buy back (at enhanced prices) their own bonds. There was a secular capital appreciation to add to the high dividend yield.

The actual return on our foreign investments is something quite definite. The earnings on the home investment that (presumably) would have gone on if foreign investment had been less popular, are altogether incalculable. How far the rate of interest would have fallen one can only guess; how much more rash investors would have become is also a matter for speculation. The available statistics do not show any very pronounced change in the trend of interest rates when there was a burst of foreign investment, but this cannot by itself be taken to prove that the demand for capital for investment at home was highly elastic. There may have been a simultaneous decline (e.g. because of emigration) in the demand *schedule* for capital for home investment; or a very rigid, and more or less unanimous, view of the future course of interest rates.

Some check to the National Dividend would certainly have taken place. The earnings of capitalists would presumably have been less, because of a lower rate of interest, or because of a check to accumulation, or for both reasons. These earnings being the main source for the provision of fresh capital, the check to the National Dividend might have been cumulative. Indeed, a gloomier view may be taken. The alternative may have been to accumulate capital abroad or none at all. Our foreign investments were made largely in times of boom out of the abundance of high profits, and when nearly the whole employable population was at work. Is it certain that, if there had been no convenient 'sinks' for British capital in foreign countries, the income from which that capital was provided would ever have been created? It is only those who think of savings (or of investment) as something apart from the income-creating process who can lightly deny that the depressions of the Victorian age would have dragged themselves out, or that the wealth of Great Britain would have been little augmented had foreign investment been unpopular or impracticable. We might have had to put up with a lower level of world investment, and of employment and income in Britain, if the difficulties in the way of foreign investment had been greater.

This is largely a matter of speculation: the gain to our export industries was one of simple observation. There was an expansion of buying power in their markets, increased orders for equipment, with the prospect of additional orders later for replacements, and increased sales to consumers. Now, in many of the export industries, there were economies of scale – both in marketing and production – whereas in the chief import-competing industry, agriculture, there were few economies. There was thus a national gain to be derived from an extension of the export industries, quite apart from any increase in employment or rise in export prices that might result.

A second source of gain lay in the spread of information of profitable openings for investment. The commercial ties of Britain with other parts of the world opened our eyes to the credit-worthiness of borrowers, enabled us to take sane risks, and gave us the inside track in the negotiation of attractive propositions. Moreover, the projects which traders sought to finance brought good customers to our export industries. Companies promoted here, however controlled, were often staffed by British engineers or British managers who, through goodwill, prejudice, or actual arrangement, tended to specify British machinery for new construction and for replacement. Thus the market imperfections which allowed us to dominate the business of exporting capital (for industrial purposes, at any rate) worked also in the Victorian age to put large sections of our export industry in a semi-monopolistic position.

We gained also through a cheapening of imports. The heavy fall in the price of imported foodstuffs between 1880 and 1900 was largely the result of railway-building with British capital in the United States, Argentine, India, Canada, and Australasia. In 1870 there were no more than 62,000 miles of track in these countries. By 1900 there were 262,000 miles of track. In the seven years 1907–14 Britain provided £600 m. for the construction of railways in countries supplying us with foodstuffs and raw materials.

At a time when the population was increasing rapidly it was vital that foodstuffs should be obtained as cheaply as possible. By 1870 the home supply was clearly approaching a limit, and our dependence on imports was increasing. For an improvement in the standard of living the rapid opening-up of fresh sources of supply was obviously imperative. The change took place rather abruptly in the seventies, and from then on the course of real wages in Britain was dominated by the terms on which we were obtaining imports. These terms in turn depended upon what sums we had placed abroad in new countries in the recent past. The course of real wages was thus closely dependent upon our willingness to finance railway building abroad.

On the other hand, in 1914 the future prospects of foreign investment were by no means rosy. Those governments whose credit had improved could re-borrow on progressively better terms. What was more important, the chief sanction on which British investors relied for the enforcement of their claims – namely, the financial power of London – was certain to become gradually less effective in bringing recalcitrant debtors to heel. So long as foreign countries found it necessary to pile up debts to Britain, there was some guarantee that they would honour these debts: but once the time came for repayment and no fresh debts were being contracted, they might not be so scrupulous. Companies owned by British capital might with more impunity be harassed by heavy taxation or by discriminatory legislation. The chief bargaining counter in trade agreements might become the observance rather than the conclusion of loan contracts.

It would be a mistake to suppose that all our foreign investments were in this precarious position. We had an enormous sum (probably £700 m.) in the United States – a rich country unlikely to stoop to default. Half of our investments were in the Empire, in which default was practically unknown. Much of the remainder was in foreign companies, controlled by the citizens of foreign countries, and not particularly open, therefore, to discriminatory treatment.

Secondly, a latent divergence of interest between workers and capitalists was coming more and more to the front. Though capitalists had not been alone in gaining from the export of capital, the working class participated more by accident than design. It was only by a rare coincidence of interests that the most profitable risks happened to fructify in cheaper and cheaper foodstuffs and raw materials. Capitalists were ready enough, at a price, to finance schemes of less advantage to their countrymen – the building of sultans' palaces, the mining of diamonds, the purchase of warships, the construction of strategic railways. At the same time, a rising standard of living amongst wage-earners was not entirely dependent upon reductions in the cost of imports. More investment at home would have meant better houses, better travelling facilities, and better public amenities of all kinds. Had the rate of interest fallen, there would have been, in addition, a redistribution of income in favour of wage-earners, and it is possible that the slowing down in the rate of capital accumulation would not have been great.

The more new countries were opened up, the more apparent did the sectional conflict become. The likelihood that foreign investment would reduce the cost of British imports was less overwhelming, the fear that industries competing with our own would be fostered was more intense. Cheap capital for other countries and improving terms of trade and real wages were no longer synonymous. Foreign investment, it was apparent, might lower the standard of living instead of raising it.

Finally, there was the danger that capital abroad might be lost through revolution either in Britain or in the country in which the assets were situated. There was no guarantee that, if the export of capital gave way to an export of capitalists, the title-deeds to foreign property could be easily seized or would be readily honoured. Tangible assets at home can be lost to the nation only through invasion, destruction, depreciation, or obsolescence. But assets abroad may be beyond the reach of expropriation.

Up till 1914 there was a sufficient coincidence of private profit and social gain in Britain's export of capital to prevent the government from exercising more than a minimum of control over investment. Broadly speaking, British foreign investment paid. But it was far from evident that uncontrolled investment would be equally advantageous in the future.

Home and Foreign Investment, 1870–1913, Cambridge University Press, 1953; pp. 222–35.

31 Capital Export as the Product of Trade

R. NURKSE

R. Nurkse (1907–59). Economist. Professor at Columbia University, U.S.A., 1947–59.

Trade was an 'engine of growth' in the 19th century. . . . As I see it, it was also a means whereby a vigorous process of economic growth came to be transmitted from the center to the outlying areas of the world. . . .

This pattern of 'growth through trade' affected particularly the new countries, or, as the late Folke Hilgerdt used to call them, the 'regions of recent settlement' in the world's temperate latitudes: Canada, Argentina, Uruguay, South Africa, Australia, New Zealand. No doubt the United States, too, belongs substantially to this group. . . . These regions had certain essential characteristics in common, but in the present context what matters is their high, though varying, dependence on growth through primary commodity exports and on the private foreign investment which, directly or indirectly, was thereby induced. . . .

While trade all over the world was expanding at a rapid pace, there is no doubt that the exports of the new countries enjoyed a particularly vigorous increase in demand. Correspondingly the outflow of British capital went mostly to these favored areas. The year 1870 is the earliest for which we can determine with any degree of confidence the geographical distribution of British capital invested overseas. The share of the 'regions of recent settlement' in the British foreign-investment total outstanding rises from less than one-third in that year to just about two-thirds in 1913. Again the share of the United States in that total remains constant at about one-fifth, while that of the other new countries shoots up from about 10 per cent in 1870 to 45 per cent in 1913. But again we must remember that the rise in the U.S. share in British capital exports occurred in the earlier part of the century, for which the data are too poor to permit any confident statistical estimates.

The growth in British imports of primary products induced British capital exports to most if not all primary producing countries, but it is clear that the R.R.S. group was specially favored by the flow of capital as well as the rise in demand for its exports. Evidently there was a connection between the two phenomena. Private international investment in undeveloped areas was fundamentally, if not directly, induced by the growth in demand for essential foodstuffs and raw materials. The connection was not always a close one with regard to timing. Thus the 1880's were a period of active capital exports even though trade in agricultural products was relatively depressed. All the same, in that decade and on other occasions also, foreign investment was supported by a long-run prospect of expanding demand in the industrial centers for the raw materials whose supply it went out to augment.

These circumstances illustrate the essentially cumulative nature of economic growth. 'To those who have shall be given': there is good reason for calling this 'the first law of development'. . . .

Areas that had natural resources whose products were in growing demand abroad received capital with which to exploit those resources and to increase the supply of those products. An increase in export demand alone is a favorable factor: it may improve the terms of trade, but even if it does not, it draws any increments in local capital and labor into lines in which the country enjoys a comparative advantage, so that increased supplies of imported goods in great variety can be got in exchange. If on top of this foreign capital comes in, this may lead not only to an enlargement of the export sector itself but also to the building of overhead facilities essential to the expansion of domestic activities as well. In fact, railways were the principal object of external investment in the areas of recent settlement. These areas include countries that are now among the most prosperous in the world. It is not suggested that the trade-and-investment relationship is the only explanation of their rapid growth in the past. There are other factors, but these lie outside our present subject.

Economists like Marshall and Robertson in contemplating the 19th century scene spoke of the old countries (in Europe) and the new countries (overseas) as the world's workshops and granaries respectively. This was of course an incomplete view of the world. It ignored the exotic countries, the 'outsiders'. Such areas as China, India, tropical Africa and central America were not unaffected by the forces of growth through trade, but compared with the newly settled countries they were relatively neglected by the expansion of export demand as well as the flow of capital. And in places where both trade and capital flows were exceptionally active, as in parts of South-East Asia, the outcome was sometimes a 'dual economy' in which a well-developed export sector coexisted with a primitive domestic economy. This lopsided pattern of development was surely better than no growth at all, yet it did show up the limitations of the external trade-and-investment engine when other conditions of progress were absent.

It is interesting to notice that J. A. Hobson in his influential study on *Imperialism* was perfectly aware that, with one exception (Malaya), the British colonies acquired in the second half of the nineteenth century – the products of the 'New Imperialism' – took a relatively insignificant share in the expansion of Britain's trade. In the course of a dispassionate study of statistical evidence he found that Continental Europe and the new countries overseas took the major share in this expansion. What, then, he asked, was the economic motive of the New Imperialism? His answer was: foreign investment – the desire of a capitalist society to find an offset to its surplus savings, to gain exclusive control of colonial markets and to dump excess supplies in primitive economies. This is his economic explanation of imperialism.[1] But it contradicts in effect his earlier analysis of the pattern of trade expansion. Here the spirit of rational empiricism forsakes him; he cites no evidence. Had he tried to do what he did for trade, that is, to show the geographical distribution of overseas investment, he would have found that British capital tended to bypass the primitive tropical economies and flowed mainly to the regions of recent settlement outside as well as inside the British Empire.

These fertile temperate regions, though now all more or less industrialized, became indeed, and still are, the world's principal granaries. They dispelled the Malthusian spectre of world food shortage, at any rate for a century or two. This turns out to have been the main object and achievement of British capital exports.

Patterns of Trade and Development, Basil Blackwell, 1961; pp. 14–19.

[1] To Hobson, the underconsumptionist, it looked as if a part of Great Britain's current saving had to be continually invested abroad – so as to maintain business profits and activity at home – because oversaving and underconsumption kept down investment incentives in Great Britain. In reality a part of British saving was invested abroad because the growth of British consumption expenditure, including expenditure on imported goods, created inducements to invest overseas as well as at home.

Part Four

APPLICATION OF
THE THEORY

The Historians

The importance of theories of this kind lies largely in the influence they exert over public attitudes; and the link between the theorist and the non-specialist is often the historian, who applies the theory to actual events. The Theory of Capitalist Imperialism exerted a very great influence on historians during the first half of the twentieth century, and, partly through them, on general attitudes to the colonial empires. Gradually, however, as the Theory was criticized along the lines illustrated in Part Three, and as historians began to do detailed work on the events of the period 1870–1914, discrepancies became apparent. Doubts about the truth, or in some cases the completeness, of this explanation of imperial expansion became more evident in historical accounts as time went on, until by the 1960's it is doubtful whether any Western historian not absolutely committed to Lenin's dogma would use the Theory without very many reservations. The course of this historical reappraisal is a fascinating study in its own right. Here it is possible only to give short extracts from four well-known writers, chosen to illustrate the trend of attitudes over some forty years. Beginning with complete acceptance they end with virtual rejection. At the same time alternative interpretations were being evolved – though many proved as vulnerable as the Theory of Capitalist Imperialism itself. Shortage of space makes it impossible to give examples of other approaches, but these are represented in other books listed in the bibliography.

32 Economic Imperialism

LEONARD WOOLF, 1921

L. S. Woolf (1880–). Author and Critic. Ceylon Civil Service, 1904–11. Member of the 'Bloomsbury Circle' and husband of the late Virginia Woolf.

About 1870 Europe had just become ripe for economic imperialism. It already believed that economics were the greatest of all interests and it was slowly acquiring the belief that the power of each state should be used in the world outside the State to promote the interests of its own citizens and against the interests of citizens of other States. Two events combined to bring about the sudden flowering and fruiting of these beliefs and desires in the subjection of Asia and Africa to the economic interests of Europe. Between 1870 and 1880 the interior of Africa and its apparently inexhaustible riches were finally opened to the world by the well-advertised explorations and discoveries of Stanley. At the same moment there was beginning the change from the policy of Free Trade to the policy of protectionism. It was the beliefs and desires contained in this policy of protectionism, which, when applied to the problem of the newly opened lands of Africa, and then by analogy to Asia, produced economic imperialism. For the theory and practice of protectionism which established themselves between 1870 and 1880, implied that the organization of the State should be used as a weapon against the industrial and commercial interests of the citizens of other States. A ring fence of tariffs and administrative regulations was to be drawn round the territory under the control of the State in order to reserve within it for its own citizens the markets and the stores of raw materials. These new conceptions, or rather this return to the old conceptions of mercantilism, roused in the capitalist, industrial, and commercial circles of every European nation mingled emotions of cupidity and fear, and since those circles were beginning to exercise great influence upon the policy of the Great Powers, the emotions and the beliefs behind them were clearly reflected in European policy between 1870 and 1914. The fear was the fear of being shut out from the profitable markets of Europe with its growing population, and of being shut out from the stores of raw materials and food supplies essential for large scale industrial production in towns; the cupidity lay in the desire for profit resulting from success in shutting out your foreign rivals.

The policy of protectionism began on the continent of Europe and in the United States of North America, but it was soon seen that its implications stretched out to embrace Asia and Africa. Men turned, again with fear and cupidity, to the markets composed of the potential demands of millions of Asiatics and Africans and to the vast stores of raw materials lying in the rich lands of those two continents. No one knew when the shutter of a protectionist tariff might not descend and shut him off from some European market or from some essential raw material for his industry, and it was natural that the captains of trade and industry should seek to insure themselves against such European disasters by making their position secure in the markets, the mines, and the forests of Asia and Africa. But the nemesis of economic cupidity and fear cannot be confined to one of the world's continents. If industry and trade were to be converted into a struggle and war between organized national States in Europe, what was to prevent it becoming a war too outside Europe? If the French capitalist and manufacturer, using the power and organization of his State, shut the British out of France, would he not also do the same in Algeria? And what France had done in Algeria, in northern Africa, she or some other State might proceed to do again in the Eldorado which Stanley was rumoured to have discovered in central Africa, or in the vast, rich, thickly populated countries of Asia. Why, it was already whispered that King Leopold of Belgium, under the pretence of science and philanthropy, was using Stanley and his explorations to win the new Eldorado for himself and Belgium.

So men began to argue about the year 1880. The effect upon foreign policy was instantaneous. The 'Great Powers', France, Germany, and Britain fell upon Africa and Asia, seizing territory wherever they could lay hands on it. In the ten years 1880-1890, five million square miles of African territory, containing a population of over sixty millions, were seized by and subjected to European States. In Asia during the same ten years Britain annexed Burma and subjected to her control the Malay peninsula and Baluchistan; while France took the first steps towards subjecting or breaking up China by seizing Annam and Tonking. At the same time there took place a scramble for the islands of the Pacific between the three Great Powers.

The next two chapters will show in some detail the immense part which economic causes played in this outburst of imperialist activities.

Here two points may be noticed. First, over and over again the immediate impulse towards the European State's intervention in Asia and Africa, its annexations, protectorates, or penetration, came from financiers or capitalist joint-stock companies. In German East Africa, British East Africa, Nyasaland, South Africa, German West Africa, Nigeria, the Congo, British North Borneo, chartered or unchartered companies paved the way to empire by extracting treaties from native chiefs and rulers purporting to hand over the sovereignty in these vast territories to the joint-stock companies. Elsewhere in Cameroon and Togoland, Italian Somaliland, and the French Congo, financiers, traders, and companies laid the foundations and supplied the impetus of the subsequent annexation. Thus the economic beliefs and desires can be seen to have been completely different in their effects from the sentimental, moral, and military causes which we examined above: they supplied the original motive power which set in motion the power of the State.

But that is not all. The policies of States emanate from Governments, and Governments are composed of statesmen and politicians. If we turn to the speeches of the statesmen who were responsible for this imperialist policy during 1880 to 1914, we can learn the reasons for that policy which they gave in defending it and explaining it to the peoples of France, Britain, and Germany. In France the protagonists in that policy were Jules Ferry, Saint-Hilaire, and Etienne. All three agree in affirming that the main motives of their policy were economic. It was essential, they said, that France should acquire an empire in Asia and Africa in order to provide outlets for her industries and capital (débouchés pour nos industries, nos exportations, nos capitaux) and in order to ensure her food supplies and her supplies of raw material. In Britain the spokesmen of the new imperialism were Joseph Chamberlain and Lord Rosebery. Mr Chamberlain declared that the care of his Government was that 'new markets shall be created, and that old markets shall be effectually developed', and he explained that there was therefore 'a necessity, as well as a duty, for us to uphold the dominion and empire which we now possess', and a 'necessity for using every legitimate opportunity to extend our influence and control in that African continent which is now being opened up to civilization and to commerce'. Lord Rosebery expressed the same view in a sentence when he described the subjection of territory outside Europe to the British State as a necessary process by which the British were 'pegging out claims for posterity'. In Germany the first steps towards a colonial empire were taken by Bismarck, though he was no imperialist. He took those steps under pressure from commercial and industrial circles, and he made it perfectly clear that his action was governed by economic reasons: he wanted, he said, outside Europe 'not provinces, but commercial enterprises'.

The motive power, therefore, behind modern imperialism is economic; it springs from economic beliefs and desires. There are other ingredients in the ferment which has caused the Europeanization of Africa and Asia, but if they had all been absent and the economic causes and motives had remained, the same effects would have resulted. That is why we are justified in calling this process economic imperialism.

Note

The reader will find the subject of this chapter much more fully developed in my book *Empire and Commerce in Africa*.

Economic Imperialism, The Labour Publishing Co., 1921; pp. 29–36.

33 Why Europe Shouldered the White Man's Burden

P. T. MOON, 1926

P. T. Moon (1892–1936). Historian. Professor at Columbia University, U.S.A., 1915–36.

The Logic of Economic Necessity

Europe was converted to imperialism not by logic alone, nor by economic 'necessity' alone, but by a combination of argument and interest, arising from an almost revolutionary alteration of economic and political conditions. The old order, the good old mid-Victorian order, has passed away, and if not a new heaven, at least a new earth was seen by the keen eye of business and politics.

First consider the alteration of economic conditions. Four signal changes appear, and first of these is the waning of the comfortable supremacy which English cotton mills and iron works had achieved by the inventions of the Industrial Revolution. As long as other nations worked with their hands, while Englishmen worked with machines and steam, England was secure from serious competition. And other nations were slow to install machinery. . . . But during the last quarter of the century the industries of Germany, United States, France, and other powers, after a long period of infancy, suddenly waxed mighty. England's share of the iron industry diminished with startling rapidity until, before the close of the century, United States had won first place and Germany was about to forge ahead of England into second place....

This situation meant cut-throat competition. Each of the great industrial nations was making more cloth, more iron and steel, or more of some other manufacture, than its own inhabitants could possibly consume. Each had a surplus which must be sold abroad. 'Surplus manufactures' called for foreign markets. But none of the great industrial nations was willing to be a market for the other's surplus, at least in the major competitive fields. All except Great Britain built around themselves forbidding tariff walls. United States, solicitous for 'infant industries', took the lead in establishing a protective tariff during and after the Civil War, and raised it still higher in 1890 and 1897. Russia built up her tariff by degrees from 1877 onward. Germany began the erection of her tariff wall in 1879; France in 1881; and other countries followed the lead. Business men and statesmen were not slow to take alarm. A French prime minister, Jules Ferry, described the situation in 1885 clearly enough:

> What our great industries lack . . ., what they lack more and more, is markets. Why? Because . . . Germany is covering herself with barriers; because, beyond the ocean, the United States of America have become protectionist, and protectionist to an extreme degree.

There appeared, however, one bright ray of hope, one solution – colonies. How earnestly the rulers of Europe in the eighties and nineties viewed this situation and how hopefully they sought to acquire colonies whose markets could be monopolized by the mother-country's industries, cannot fail to impress any reader of the political debates and imperialistic literature of the period. . . .

'Surplus manufactures', then, provided the chief economic cause of the imperialistic expansion of Europe in the last quarter of the nineteenth century. . . .

The second great change in the economic world, to be noted as an explanation of Europe's conversion to imperialism in the last quarter of the nineteenth century, was the revolution in means of communication. To make colonial produce profitable, on a large scale, steamships were needed. To make commercial and military penetration of the interior wilds of Africa and Asia possible, railways were required. To bind colonies close to mother-countries, the telegraph had to be invented. To be sure, steamship, locomotive, and telegraph were invented long before the age we are considering; but their effect was not felt, in the world at large, until the last two or three decades of the nineteenth century. The following table offers the reason:

	1850	1873	1880	1890	1900
Railways (thousands of miles). .	24	—	224	—	500
Steam shipping (as per cent of world's total shipping) . . .	—	25	—	59	77
Telegraphs (thousands of miles) .	5	—	440	—	1,180

The victory of steam and electricity over space made possible the gigantic increase of colonial trade between 1870 and the present; it also made possible the extension of empires, by transporting the troops that conquered the tropics. Incidentally, as it will later appear more clearly, the building of railways, the laying of cables and telegraphs, the operation of shipping lines, were economic enterprises which themselves were and still are prizes of imperialism.

The third economic factor to be examined is the demand of industrial nations for tropical and subtropical products. Cotton factories in Lancashire, England, are one of the reasons for British troops in Egypt and India. The millions of bales of raw cotton devoured by busy British spindles and looms had to be produced in southern United States, or in colonies. When the American Civil War cut off supplies of American cotton, England and other countries looked about for other sources of supply, and since that time colonies have become increasingly important as cotton-producers. Egypt, for example, produced only 87 thousand bales in 1850, but by 1865 this quantity had been multiplied by five; by 1890 it had been multiplied by nine, and Egypt had become the chief producer of fine, long-staple cotton. British India likewise multiplied its production, and in many another colony plantations were laid out.

Rubber affords another instance, spectacular in its effects. When the civilized world began to wear rubbers and raincoats, to put tires on its wagons and bicycles and automobiles, Europeans had to invade tropical jungles and, by persuasion or by force, induce the natives to tap the wild rubber trees and vines which grew in the Congo and Amazon valleys. The Congo became a colony, where natives were compelled to labor, and its rubber output increased from about thirty thousand dollars in 1886 to eight million in 1900. The Amazon, protected by the Monroe Doctrine against European annexation, was subjected to economic imperialism, almost as if it were a colony. And as the demand for rubber grew still more insatiable, vast rubber plantations were established in British colonies in the Malay Peninsula and Ceylon, and in the Dutch East Indies. Rubber means imperialism.

Coffee, cocoa, tea, and sugar have also founded empires. Coconuts and coconut oil provided motives for the conquest of sunny islands in the South Pacific. The use of phosphate for fertilization of the soil in France is one of the reasons why France prizes her North-African colonies. To obtain tin the French endeavored to dominate [the] southernmost part of China. Gold mines caused the British conquest of Transvaal. The universal hunger of industrial states for coal, iron, and oil has been a *leitmotif* in world politics.

Perhaps, one speculates, these objects of desire might have been bought in the normal manner of trade, without imperialism or conquest. Perhaps. But in fact they were not. Sometimes the complaint was that African Negroes failed to appreciate the dignity of labor and preferred their accustomed life of sloth; or that South Sea islanders were unwilling to toil; conquest and compulsory labor were demanded. Or sometimes when Europeans laid out plantations, or opened mines, or drilled oil wells, in a backward country, they found the native government little to their liking, and desired the protection of their own imperial flag. Or in another case, one European government believed that only annexation of coconut-bearing islands would secure the output to its own citizens. In short, the northern world's desire for tropical products has been one of the conditions causing imperialism.

One more economic factor, the fourth, must be added. It is 'surplus capital'. (Although, as a careful reading of imperialist utterances in the eighties and nineties clearly shows, 'surplus manufactures' rather than 'surplus capital' provided the chief incentive at the outset, the latter has become the dominant force in twentieth-century imperialism.)

That anyone can possess too much capital will perhaps be denied by impecunious readers, if this volume should have such. But by 'surplus capital' is meant a superfluity too great for profitable reinvestment at home. That such surpluses must be created by the industrial expansion of the last century was an inevitable result of the economic laws governing capitalist production. The large incomes from factories, mines, rentals, return a profit on the capital; owners of the capital receive larger profits than they care to spend; wealthy capitalists reinvest most of their income. Fortunes accumulated from rents and finance must also be invested. Now it is a commonplace business law that the capital investment in an industry cannot be indefinitely increased by reinvestment of earnings, and still obtain a profitable return, unless the industry can be indefinitely expanded. But unlimited expansion is usually impossible; the world's demand for cotton stockings or for steel girders cannot be arbitrarily increased. If capital accumulation is proceeding more rapidly than industrial and agricultural expansion, the excess of capital must either be invested in relatively unprofitable enterprises, such as the construction of new railways along comparatively undesirable routes, at a profit lower than in the past, or lent out at lower rates of interest to be used in relatively unprofitable enterprises, or invested in less advanced countries, where capital is scarcer and returns larger. . . .

Why investments have so often led to annexations needs just a word of explanation. French bankers lend money, let us say, to Morocco; it is a speculative venture, but the rate of interest is attractive. Morocco, being inefficiently governed by its native rulers, fails to pay interest. The French bankers appeal to their own government. And presently Morocco is a French protectorate, a French colony, in which efficient French officials make sure that French investors receive their due. Whether there is any other way one may well ask; but the question of solutions must be left for consideration after we have mastered the facts.

The Logic of Nationalism

The economic stage is now set for imperialism, with surplus manufactures, steam transportation, raw materials, and surplus capital ready to play their rôles. The cast is not complete, however, until we add another actor – the new doctrine of politico-economic nationalism. Upon this all the plot hinges. For if most men still believed, as they did a half-century or so ago, that the state has no concern with economics, the economic factors mentioned above would have been impotent to spur national governments to imperialist deeds. But the mid-Victorian doctrine of liberalism, which brooked no governmental intervention in business affairs, was after all a mid-Victorian doctrine, and it soon yielded the center of the stage to the rival doctrine of economic nationalism or Neo-Mercantilism, a reincarnation of that early modern Mercantilism which we have been at pains to describe.

If ever there was a 'spirit of the age', the spirit of the second half of the nineteenth century was political nationalism. Germany achieved national unity 'by blood and iron'; by blood and iron was Italy welded into nationhood; the Civil War cemented the American union; the Balkan nations emerged from Near Eastern turmoils; the Poles valiantly but vainly fought, in 1863, to regain national independence; Russia began to practise the nationalist policy of 'Russification'; Disraeli revived British patriotism; the same ferment was at work among the Czechoslovaks and Yugoslavs and Magyars of Austria-Hungary; and in France nationalism became a bitter passion after the loss of Alsace-Lorraine. The nationalist wars of the period from 1848 to 1878 were succeeded by imperialist conquests.

Nationalism means that people considering themselves similar in language, 'race', culture, or historical traditions, should constitute a separate sovereign state; imperialism, on the contrary, means domination of non-European native races by totally dissimilar European nations. Antithetical as these two principles may seem, the latter is derived from the former through economic-nationalism or neo-mercantilism. German economists in the middle of the nineteenth century were peculiarly prominent in developing this doctrine. If Adam Smith's *Wealth of Nations* laid the theoretic foundations for free-trade England, Friedrich List's *National System of Political Economy* (*Das Nationale System der Politischen Ökonomie*, 1841) offered a basis for the protectionist policies of Continental nations. List boldly blasphemed against the first article in the creed of the orthodox or 'classical' British and French economists, namely, that by the working of natural law, the free pursuit of self-interest by each individual would produce the greatest welfare for society collectively. Instead, List offered the dogma that the nation is a continuous and supremely important entity, whose well-being must be promoted by wise regulation of business. Private interests must bow to national needs. Nations with infant industries should adopt 'educational tariffs', until industry, agriculture and commerce reached the mature development and harmonious balance. List is cited as one among a host of European theorists who led the movement of ideas in favor of economic nationalism.

And such doctrines fitted in well with practical exigencies of politics. The votes of working men demanded labor legislation; industrialists demanded tariff protection; humanitarians pleaded for social reform; and each of these urgent political forces made for greater control over economic matters by the national state. In tariffs, in labor legislation, in social reforms, economic nationalism became the order of the day in the waning years of the century. Imperialism naturally ensued, once it was assumed that government should promote business. For then it follows that nations may legitimately reach out for colonial empire, in order to pre-empt markets for their surplus manufactures, protect investments of their surplus capital, obtain business and coaling stations for their shipping, and secure raw materials. Such is the logic which combined with economic facts makes imperialism a necessity.

More humanly interesting, doubtless, than the abstractions and statistics through which it has been necessary to make our way thus far, is the story of the actual conversion of England, France, Germany, and other nations to imperialism. Conversions are always interesting. And this one is a peculiarly intriguing display of man's ability to combine egotism and altruism in a plausible amalgam.

On the eve of conversion individual sinners often possess a dual personality: an unregenerate dominant ego, and a more devout but suppressed self struggling to gain the upper hand. Without carrying over the ethical implications of this metaphor, we may say that the conversion of a nation to imperialism meant not an instantaneous *volte-face* on the part of the entire people, but the triumph of a hitherto submerged imperialist agitation reinforced by general economic and political changes, over a gradually weakening anti-imperialist party.

Imperialism and World Politics (1926), New York, Macmillan Company, 1947, pp. 25-34.

34 Bases of a New National Imperialism

C. J. H. HAYES, 1941

C. J. H. Hayes (1882–1964). Historian. Professor at Columbia University, U.S.A., 1910–50.

Synchronizing with the revival of protective tariffs and the extension of socializing legislation toward the close of the 1870s, was a tremendous outburst of imperialistic interest and activity. The outburst was common to all great powers of Europe (except Austria-Hungary); and it was so potent that during the next three decades greater progress was made toward subjecting the world to European domination than had been made during three centuries previous.

This may seem odd in view of the fact that the immediately preceding era of Liberal ascendancy, say from the 1840's into the 1870's, had witnessed a marked decline of European imperialism. There had been, to be sure, some spasmodic additions to British India, some scattered efforts of Napoleon III to resuscitate a colonial empire for France, some continuing Russian expansion in central and northeastern Asia. Although China and Japan had been forcefully opened to European (and American) trade, the opening had been for practically everybody on free and equal terms and had been unattended by any considerable expropriation of territory. The surviving farflung British Empire had ceased to be an exclusive preserve for British merchants since the 1840's, and in 1861 France had freely admitted to her colonies the commerce of all nations. In 1870–1871 European colonialism appeared to be approaching its nadir. Gladstone was Prime Minister of Great Britain, and he was notoriously a 'Little Englander'. The provisional French government so slightly esteemed the colonies it had inherited that it offered them all to Bismarck at the end of the Franco-Prussian War if only he would spare Alsace-Lorraine. Bismarck spurned the offer, as he had recently refused Portugal's offer to sell him Mozambique. A colonial policy for Germany, he said, 'would be just like the silken sables of Polish noble families who have no shirts'.

A favorite explanation of why European imperialism turned

abruptly within a decade from nadir to apogee, has been the economic. It was advanced originally by publicists and statesmen to win the support of business interests for imperialistic policies, and it received classical treatment, at the time of the Boer War, by John A. Hobson. Latterly it has been taken up by Marxian writers and integrated with their dogma of materialistic determinism, so that the argument now runs in this wise: Imperialism is an inevitable phase in the evolution of capitalism, a phase in which surplus capital, accumulated by the exploitation of domestic labor, is obliged by diminishing returns at home to find new outlets for investment abroad. Hence it seeks non-industrialized areas ever farther afield where it may dispose of surplus manufactures, obtain needed raw materials, invest surplus capital, and exploit cheap native labor. The resulting 'new imperialism', unlike the old, is not primarily a colonizing or a simple commercial imperialism, but rather an investing one in regions ill-adapted to European settlement. Conditions are alleged to have been ripe for it about 1880, when tariff protection restricted customary markets of European capitalists and impelled them to seek new ones.

Doubtless large-scale mechanized industry, with accompanying improvement of transportation facilities, did immensely stimulate an ever-widening quest for markets where surplus manufactures might be disposed of, necessary raw materials procured, and lucrative investments made. Nor can there be any doubt that by the 1870's, when industrialization on the Continent was beginning seriously to vie with England's, the quest was being as eagerly pursued by commercial and banking houses of Hamburg and Bremen, Marseilles and Paris, as by those of London and Liverpool. In Germany, for example, at the very time when Bismarck was disdaining the French proffer of colonies, his banking friends, Bleichröder and Hansemann, were helping to finance distant trade ventures of various Hanseatic firms – O'Swald's in East Africa, Woermann's in West Africa, Godeffroy's in Samoa and other South Sea islands. In 1880 some 335,000 marks' worth of German goods were shipped to West Africa alone, while 6,735,000 marks' worth of African products entered the port of Hamburg.

Yet the only novel feature of all this was a relatively greater importation of tropical and sub-tropical products and hence a special concern with Africa, southern Asia, the Indies, and Oceania. Surplus manufactures from industrialized countries of Europe, even after the imposition of protective tariffs, still found export markets principally within that Continent or in temperate zones outside, notably in

America, Australasia, northern India, and the Far East. What actually started the economic push into the 'Dark Continent' and the sun-baked islands of the Pacific was not so much an overproduction of factory goods in Europe as an undersupply of raw materials. Cotton grew finer in Egypt than in the United States, and with the partial cutting off of the latter's copious supply by the American Civil War it was but natural that dealers in raw cotton should enter the Egyptian field and raise its yield ninefold during the next twenty years. Rubber was now needed also, and it could be got from the Congo and from Malaysia more cheaply and plentifully than from Brazil. Copra, with its useful oil, was to be had in the South Sea islands, and the Godeffroy firm at Hamburg made a specialty of going for it. Tin was essential for the new canning industry, and gold, for measuring the new industrial wealth; rich supplies of the former were obtainable in the East Indies, and of the latter in Guinea and the Transvaal. Sugar cane and coffee, cocoa and tea, bananas and dates, if not directly serviceable to industrial machinery, were very palatable to the enlarging European multitude that tended it.

But commercial expansion into the tropics was a novelty of degree rather than of kind and hardly suffices to explain the political imperialism of the '70's and '80's. This was inaugurated prior to any general resort to tariff protectionism in Europe, and prior also to any universal export of capital. Neither Russia nor Italy had surplus manufactures to dispose of or surplus wealth to invest; yet both engaged in the scramble for imperial dominion, the one with striking success and the other not. Germany exported little capital until after she had acquired an extensive colonial empire, and France secured a far more extensive one while her industrial development lagged behind Germany's. Great Britain had long had all the supposed economic motives for imperialism – export of manufactured goods, demand for raw materials, supply of surplus capital – and yet these did not move her in the '60's as much as they did in the '70's.[1] On the other hand, Norway, whose ocean-borne commerce was exceeded only by Great

[1] It should be remarked, however, that the depression which began in 1873, by limiting opportunities for profitable investment in countries already largely industrialized, probably stimulated investment in 'backward' regions and may thus have contributed to a revival of imperialistic interests and ambitions. Nevertheless, this was truer of Great Britain than of any nation on the Continent, and it scarcely suffices to explain why with almost all the great powers (and only with them) political imperialism preceded any substantial financial investment in particular regions appropriated.

Britain's and Germany's, remained consistently aloof from overseas imperialism.

Apparently the flag of a European nation did not have to follow its trade – or its financial investments. But once flag raising became common and competitive in Africa and on the Pacific, economic considerations undoubtedly spurred most of the European participants to greater efforts and keener competition in those regions. Then the tariff protectionism of Continental nations was applied, in one form or another, to their respective colonies, and the more colonies each one had the greater were its opportunities for favorable trade and investment and the closer it approached to the ideal of all-round self-sufficiency. And to prevent too much of the world from being thus monopolized by France, Germany, Italy, or any other protectionist power, Great Britain moved mightily to gather the lion's share into her own free-trade empire. In other words, neo-mercantilism, once established, had very important imperialistic consequences.

The fact remains, nevertheless, that the founding of new colonial empires and the fortifying of old ones antedated the establishment of neo-mercantilism, and that the economic arguments adduced in support of imperialism seem to have been a rationalization *ex post facto*. In the main, it was not Liberal parties, with their superabundance of industrialists and bankers, who sponsored the outward imperialistic thrust of the '70's and early '80's. Instead, it was Conservative parties, with a preponderantly agricultural clientele notoriously suspicious of moneylenders and big business, and, above all, it was patriotic professors and publicists regardless of political affiliation and unmindful of personal economic interest. These put forth the economic arguments which eventually drew bankers and traders and industrialists into the imperialist camp.

Basically the new imperialism was a nationalistic phenomenon. It followed hard upon the national wars which created an all-powerful Germany and a united Italy, which carried Russia within sight of Constantinople, and which left England fearful and France eclipsed. It expressed a resulting psychological reaction, an ardent desire to maintain or recover national prestige. France sought compensation for European loss in oversea gain. England would offset her European isolation by enlarging and glorifying the British Empire. Russia, halted in the Balkans, would turn anew to Asia, and before long Germany and Italy would show the world that the prestige they had won by might inside Europe they were entitled to enhance by imperial exploits outside. The lesser powers, with no great prestige at stake, managed to get on without any new imperialism, though Portugal and Holland displayed a revived pride in the empires they already possessed and the latter's was administered with renewed vigor. . . .

Most simply, the sequence of imperialism after 1870 appears to have been, first, pleas for colonies on the ground of national prestige; second, getting them; third, disarming critics by economic argument; and fourth, carrying this into effect and relating the results to the neo-mercantilism of tariff protection and social legislation at home.

A Generation of Materialism, 1871–1900, Harper, 1941, pp. 216–23.

35 Britain and the Partition of Africa

R. E. ROBINSON and J. A. GALLAGHER, 1961

R. E. Robinson (1920–). Historian. Smuts Reader in Commonwealth Studies and Fellow of St John's College, Cambridge.

J. A. Gallagher (1919–). Historian. Beit Professor of The History of The British Commonwealth and Fellow of Balliol College, Oxford.

Did new, sustained or compelling impulses towards African empire arise in British politics or business during the Eighteen eighties? The evidence seems unconvincing. The late-Victorians seem to have been no keener to rule and develop Africa than their fathers. The business man saw no greater future there, except in the south; the politician was as reluctant to expand and administer a tropical African empire as the mid-Victorians had been; and plainly Parliament was no more eager to pay for it. British opinion restrained rather than prompted ministers to act in Africa. Hence they had to rely on private companies or colonial governments to act for them. It is true that African lobbies and a minority of imperialists did what they could to persuade government to advance. Yet they were usually too weak to be decisive. Measured by the yardstick of official thinking, there was no strong political or commercial movement in Britain in favour of African acquisitions.

The priorities of policy in tropical Africa confirm this impression. West Africa seemed to offer better prospects of markets and raw materials than east Africa and the Upper Nile; yet it was upon these poorer countries that the British government concentrated its efforts. These regions of Africa which interested the British investor and merchant least, concerned ministers the most. No expansion of commerce prompted the territorial claims to Uganda, the east coast and the Nile Valley. As Mackinnon's failure showed, private enterprise was not moving in to develop them; and they were no more useful or necessary to the British industrial economy between 1880 and 1900 than they had been earlier in the century. Territorial claims here reached out far in advance of the expanding economy. Notions of pegging out colonial estates for posterity hardly entered into British calculations until the late Eighteen nineties, when it was almost too late to affect the outcome. Nor were ministers gulled by the romantic glories of ruling desert and bush. Imperialism in the wide sense of empire for empire's sake was not their motive. Their territorial claims were not made for the sake of African empire or commerce as such. They were little more than by-products of an enforced search for better security in the Mediterranean and the East. It was not the pomps or profits of governing Africa which moved the ruling *élite*, but the cold rules for national safety handed on from Pitt, Palmerston and Disraeli.

According to the grammar of the policy-makers, their advances in Africa were prompted by different interests and circumstances in different regions. Egypt was occupied because of the collapse of the Khedivial *régime*. The occupation went on because the internal crisis remained unsolved and because of French hostility which the occupation itself provoked. Britain's insistent claims in east Africa and the Nile Valley and her yielding of so much in west Africa were largely contingent upon the Egyptian occupation and the way it affected European relations. In southern Africa, imperial intervention against the Transvaal was designed above all to uphold and restore the imperial influence which economic growth, Afrikaner nationalism and the Jameson fiasco had overthrown. Imperial claims in the Rhodesias, and to a lesser extent in Nyasaland, were contingent in turn upon Cape colonial expansion and imperial attempts to offset the rise of the Transvaal. The times and circumstances in which almost all these claims and occupations were made suggest strongly that they were called forth by crises in Egypt and south Africa, rather than by positive impulses to African empire arising in Europe.

To be sure, a variety of different interests in London – some religious and humanitarian, others strictly commercial or financial, and yet others imperialist – pressed for territorial advances and were sometimes used as their agents. In west Africa, the traders called for government protection; in Uganda and Nyasaland, the missionaries and the anti-slavery groups called for annexation; in Egypt. the bondholders asked government to rescue their investments; in south Africa, philanthropists and imperialists called for more government from Whitehall, while British traders and investors were divided about the best way of looking after their interests. Ministers usually listened to their pleas only when it suited their purpose; but commercial and philanthropic agitation seldom decided which territories should be claimed or occupied or when this should be done, although their slogans were frequently used by government in its public justifications.

It is the private calculations and actions of ministers far more than their speeches which reveal the primary motives behind their advances. For all the different situations in which territory was claimed, and all the different reasons which were given to justify it, one consideration, and one alone entered into all the major decisions. In all regions north of Rhodesia, the broad imperative which decided which territory to reserve and which to renounce, was the safety of the routes to the East. It did not, of course, prompt the claiming of Nyasaland or the lower Niger. Here a reluctant government acted to protect existing fields of trading and missionary enterprise from foreign annexations. In southern Africa the extension of empire seems to have been dictated by a somewhat different imperative. Here the London government felt bound as a rule to satisfy the demands for more territory which their self-governing colonials pressed on them. Ministers did this in the hope of conserving imperial influence. Nevertheless, the safety of the routes to India also figured prominently in the decision to uphold British supremacy in south Africa. It was the same imperative which after impelling the occupation of Egypt, prolonged it, and forced Britain to go into east Africa and the Upper Nile, while yielding in most of west Africa. As soon as territory anywhere in Africa became involved, however indirectly, in this cardinal interest, ministries passed swiftly from inaction to intervention. If the papers left by the policy-makers are to be believed, they moved into Africa, not to build a new African empire, but to protect the old empire in India. . . .

An essentially negative objective, it had been attained hitherto without large African possessions. Mere influence and co-operation with other Powers had been enough to safeguard strategic points in north Africa; while in south Africa control of coastal regions had sufficed.

The ambition of late-Victorian ministers reached no higher than to uphold these mid-Victorian systems of security in Egypt and south Africa. They were distinguished from their predecessors only in this: that their security by influence was breaking down. In attempting to restore it by intervention and diplomacy, they incidentally marked out the ground on which a vastly extended African empire was later to arise. Nearly all the interventions appear to have been consequences, direct or indirect, of internal Egyptian or south African crises which endangered British influence and security in the world. Such an interpretation alone seems to fit the actual calculations of policy. Ministers felt frankly that they were making the best of a bad job. They were doing no more than protecting old interests in worsening circumstances. To many, the flare-up of European rivalry in Africa seemed unreasonable and even absurd; yet most of them felt driven to take part because of tantalizing circumstances beyond their control. They went forward as a measure of precaution, or as a way back to the saner mid-Victorian systems of informal influence. Gloomily, they were fumbling to adjust their old strategy to a changing Africa. And the necessity arose much more from altered circumstances in Africa than from any revolution in the nature, strength or direction of British expansion.

Hence the question of motive should be formulated afresh. It is no longer the winning of a new empire in Africa which has to be explained. The question is simpler: Why could the late-Victorians after 1880 no longer rely upon influence to protect traditional interests? What forced them in the end into imperial solutions? The answer is to be found first in the nationalist crises in Africa itself, which were the work of intensifying European influences during previous decades; and only secondarily in the interlocking of these crises in Africa with rivalries in Europe. Together the two drove Britain step by step to regain by territorial claims and occupation that security which could no longer be had by influence alone. The compelling conditions for British advances in tropical Africa were first called into being, not by the German victory of 1871, nor by Leopold's interest in the Congo, nor by the petty rivalry of missionaries and merchants, nor by a rising imperialist spirit, nor even by the French occupation of Tunis in 1881 – but by the collapse of the Khedivial *régime* in Egypt.

From start to finish the partition of tropical Africa was driven by the persistent crisis in Egypt. When the British entered Egypt on their own, the Scramble began; and as long as they stayed in Cairo, it continued until there was no more of Africa left to divide. Since chance and miscalculation had much to do with the way that Britain went into Egypt, it was to some extent an accident that the partition took place when it did. But once it had begun, Britain's over-riding purpose in Africa was security in Egypt, the Mediterranean and the Orient. The achievement of this security became at the same time vital and more difficult, once the occupation of Egypt had increased the tension between the Powers and had dragged Africa into their rivalry. In this way the crisis in Egypt set off the Scramble, and sustained it until the end of the century. . . .

So much for the subjective views which swayed the British partitioners. Plainly their preconceptions and purposes were one of the many objective causes of the partition itself. There remain the ultimate questions: how important a cause were these considerations of government? What were the other causes?

The answers are necessarily complicated, because they can be found only in the interplay between government's subjective appreciations and the objective emergencies. The moving causes appear to arise from chains of diverse circumstances in Britain, Europe, the Mediterranean, Asia and Africa itself, which interlocked in a set of unique relationships. These disparate situations, appraised by the official mind as a connected whole, were the products of different historical evolutions, some arising from national growth or decay, others from European expansion stretching as far back as the Mercantilist era. All of them were changing at different levels at different speeds. But although their paths were separate, they were destined to cross. There were structural changes taking place in European industry cutting down Britain's lead in commerce. The European balance of power was altering. Not only the emergence of Germany, but the alignment of France with Russia, the century-old opponent of British expansion, lessened the margins of imperial safety. National and racial feelings in Europe, in Egypt and south Africa were becoming more heated, and liberalism everywhere was on the decline. All these movements played some part in the African drama. But it seems that they were only brought to the point of imperialist action by the idiosyncratic reactions of British statesmen to internal crises in Africa. Along the Mediterranean shores, Muslim states were breaking down under European penetration. In the south, economic growth and colonial expansion were escaping from imperial control. These processes of growth or decay were moving on time scales different from that of the European expansion which was bringing them about.

By 1882 the Egyptian Khedivate had corroded and cracked after decades of European paramountcy. But economic expansion was certainly not the sufficient cause of the occupation. Hitherto, commerce and investment had gone on without the help of outright political control. The thrusts of the industrial economy into Egypt had come to a stop with Ismail's bankruptcy, and little new enterprise was to accompany British control. Although the expanding economy had helped to make a revolutionary situation in Egypt, it was not the moving interest behind the British invasion. Nor does it seem that Anglo-French rivalry or the state of the European balance precipitated the invasion. It was rather the internal nationalist reaction against a decaying government which split Britain from France and switched European rivalries into Africa.

But the cast of official thinking profoundly influenced the outcome of the emergency. Moving instinctively to protect the Canal, the Liberals intended a Palmerstonian blow to liberate the progressives and chasten the disruptive elements in Egyptian politics. But instead of restoring their influence and then getting out, the need to bottle up anarchy and stave off the French forced them to stay on. This failure to work the mid-Victorian techniques, by coming to terms with the nationalists and finding Egyptian collaborators, meant that Indian solutions had to be applied to Egypt as well. The disenchantment of the 'Guardians' was replacing the liberal faith in voluntary co-operation; and Gladstone's sympathy with oppressed nationalities was hardening into Cromer's distrust of subject races. For similar reasons, official pessimism deepened about the reliability of the Turkish bastion in the Mediterranean; and as the balance tilted against Britain in the inland sea, her rulers realized that they were in Egypt to stay. Weighing the risks of Ottoman decay and the shifts in the European balance, remembering Indian experience and distrusting Egyptian 'fanatics', England's rulers pessimistically extended the search for security up the Nile to Fashoda, and from the Indian Ocean to Uganda and the Bahr-el-Ghazal. . . .

The notion that world strategy alone was the sole determinant of British advances is superficial. For strategy is not merely a reflection of the interests which it purports to defend, it is even more the register of the hopes, the memories and neuroses which inform the strategists' picture of the world. This it is which largely decides a government's view about who may be trusted and who must be feared; whether an empire assumes an optimistic or pessimistic posture; and whether the forces of change abroad are to be fostered or opposed. Indeed any theory of imperialism grounded on the notion of a single decisive cause is too simple for the complicated historical reality of the African partition. No purely economic interpretation is wide enough, because it does not allow for the independent importance of subjective factors. Explanations based entirely on the swings of the European balance are bound to remain incomplete without reference to changes outside Europe.

Both the crises of expansion and the official mind which attempted to control them had their origins in an historical process which had begun to unfold long before the partition of Africa began. That movement was not the manifestation of some revolutionary urge to empire. Its deeper causes do not lie in the last two decades of the century. The British advance at least, was not an isolated African episode. It was the climax of a longer process of growth and decay in Africa. The new African empire was improvised by the official mind, as events made nonsense of its old historiography and hustled government into strange deviations from old lines of policy. In the widest sense, it was an offshoot of the total processes of British expansion throughout the world and throughout the century.

How large then does the new African empire bulk in this setting? There are good reasons for regarding the mid-Victorian period as the golden age of British expansion, and the late-Victorian as an age which saw the beginnings of contraction and decline. The Palmerstonians were no more 'anti-imperialist' than their successors, though they were more often able to achieve their purposes informally; and the late-Victorians were no more 'imperialist' than their precedessors, though they were driven to extend imperial claims more often. To label them thus is to ignore the fact that whatever their method, they were both of set purpose engineering the expansion of Britain. Both preferred to promote trade and security without the expense of empire; but neither shrank from forward policies wherever they seemed necessary.

But their circumstances were very different. During the first three-quarters of the century, Britain enjoyed an almost effortless supremacy in the world outside Europe, thanks to her sea power and her industrial strength, and because she had little foreign rivalry to face. Thus Canning and Palmerston had a very wide freedom of action. On the one hand, they had little need to bring economically valueless regions such as tropical Africa into their formal empire for the sake of strategic security; and on the other, they were free to extend their influence and power to develop those regions best suited to contribute to Britain's strength. Until the Eighteen eighties, British political expansion had been positive, in the sense that it went on bringing valuable areas into her orbit. That of the late-Victorians in the so-called 'Age of Imperialism' was by comparison negative, both in purpose and achievement. It was largely concerned with defending the maturing inheritance of the mid-Victorian imperialism of free trade, not with opening fresh fields of substantial importance to the economy. Whereas the earlier Victorians could afford to concentrate on the extension of free trade, their successors were compelled to look above all to the preservation of what they held, since they were coming to suspect that Britain's power was not what it once had been. The early Victorians had been playing from strength. The supremacy they had built in the world had been the work of confidence and faith in the future. The African empire of their successors was the product of fear lest this great heritage should be lost in the time of troubles ahead.

Because it went far ahead of commercial expansion and imperial ambition, because its aims were essentially defensive and strategic, the movement into Africa remained superficial. The partition of tropical Africa might seem impressive on the wall maps of the Foreign Office. Yet it was at the time an empty and theoretical expansion. That British governments before 1900 did very little to pacify, administer and develop their spheres of influence and protectorates, shows once again the weakness of any commercial and imperial motives for claiming them. The partition did not accompany, it preceded the invasion of tropical Africa by the trader, the planter and the official. It was the prelude to European occupation; it was not that occupation itself. The sequence illuminates the true nature of the British movement into tropical Africa. So far from commercial expansion requiring the extension of territorial claims, it was the extension of territorial claims which in time required commercial expansion. The arguments of the so-called new imperialism were *ex post facto* justifications of advances, they were not the original reasons for making them. Ministers had publicly justified their improvisations in tropical Africa with appeals to imperial sentiment and promises of African progress. After 1900, something had to be done to fulfil these aspirations, when the spheres allotted on the map had to be made good on the ground. The same fabulous artificers who had galvanized America, Australia and Asia, had come to the last continent.

R. E. ROBINSON and J. A. GALLAGHER, with ALICE DENNY *Africa and the Victorians*, Macmillan, 1961, pp 462–7, 470–2.

Part Five

SOME CONCLUSIONS

The Historian and the Historicists

What conclusions emerge from this collection of documents, and what significance have they for the student of history?

The obvious conclusion is that the Theory of Capitalist Imperialism is of little value to the historian whose aim is simply to explain why the colonial empires expanded so widely and so fast in the period after about 1870. To support this statement let us recapitulate the Theory in its various forms and then survey its defects from the historian's point of view.

In every form in which the Theory is represented in these documents – and in others also – its central theme is that overseas colonies were acquired primarily because of their relevance to the internal economic characteristics or problems of European countries or of the United States. English liberals such as Robertson, Hobson and Brailsford took the driving force to be 'underconsumption', by which they meant that the unequal distribution of wealth in capitalist countries so deprived the mass of workers of buying power that the capitalist could not profitably invest his surplus capital in industry at home. Hence his anxiety to acquire colonies as alternative fields for profitable investment. The neo-Marxists had other arguments. Rosa Luxemburg thought that capitalist countries depended on trade with non-capitalist places at all stages of their development, and that colonial acquisitions were primarily the result of a shortage of such necessary extra-European commercial balancers. By contrast, Hilferding, Bukharin and Lenin, followed thereafter by most orthodox Marxists, thought imperialism was the product of the special economic problems of capitalism in its last, monopolistic, phase, when 'finance capital' had absorbed competitive capital. Such differences of interpretation are important; yet they do not destroy the essential unity of the Theory of Capitalist Imperialism in its assumption that imperialism was the product of factors within Europe and that colonies were acquired primarily to save capitalism from a moribund condition in which the further accumulation of capital within Europe was becoming impossible.

Turning from the Theory to its critics, the documents in Part Three suggest that there are two main ways in which to dissect and evaluate such concepts. First it is possible to consider the basic premise that capitalist societies have been forced by economic factors to invest abroad rather than at home: that capital was forced out and had to find a home in dependent territories or 'semi-colonies'. On purely theoretical grounds this is highly dubious; and it is perfectly possible to construct a model for the economic development of modern Europe on the assumption that the continent had no possibility of outside investment without necessarily accepting as a consequence a stop to the process of investment or the accumulation of capital. Economic development would certainly have been very different and might have been slower; but it could still have taken place. Conversely it is possible to explain the fact of capital exports without accepting the premise that capital was forced out. It is equally arguable that capitalists merely chose to invest part of their capital overseas because at particular times such investment seemed more attractive than investment at home – that it was pulled out by higher interest or dividends, or to develop commodities needed in Europe. While such eclectic investment might well have led to colonial annexation, and so does not make it impossible that colonization might be economic in aim, it does emasculate the Theory of Capitalist Imperialism by making overseas investment a voluntary rather than a necessary phenomenon, and so eliminates the element of inevitability. At the same time such a modification leaves it open to the historian to decide whether, in particular cases, the attractive power of such overseas investment seems to have been the motive behind the process of colonial expansion.

A rather different approach to the Theory in its full form is to concede its economic premises, but to test its historical validity against facts and chronology. On this test also the critics have found it vulnerable. The key period for the establishment of the tropical colonial empires was during the 1880's and 1890's, when the partition of Africa and the east was virtually completed. If the main force behind imperialism was indeed the need of capitalism for new fields for investment, then this need must have been felt acutely during these twenty years. Yet the neo-Marxist argument based on finance capital simply does not fit this requirement. Lenin expressly dated the predominance of finance capital in Germany from about 1900. Germany was certainly more advanced along this line than any other great power, so that it would be unreasonable to look for similar conditions in, say, Britain or France, which were certainly not dominated by monopoly capitalism at any time before 1914. Hence it seems undeniable that the Lenin hypothesis, whatever its possible relevance to European attitudes to empire once the process of colonial expansion had taken place, cannot be used to explain the expansion itself.

If the neo-Marxist version of the Theory falls down most obviously on chronology, both this and the liberal Hobsonian version break on the test of geography. As most of the critics have indicated, the Theory can only be accepted as an historical explanation if it can be shown that there was in fact some direct connection between the desire of Europe to export capital and those parts of the world where capital was invested during the period of annexation or shortly after: which would suggest that the new colonies really did offer special attractions to the investor as against existing colonies or comparable independent states. In fact this was not so. The facts of European overseas investment, which were for the most part not available at the time when the Theory was being formulated, now make it clear that there was very little geographical correlation between capital export and the new colonies. In some places there was, of course, an apparent link. Europe had invested heavily in Tunis, Morocco, Egypt and the Transvaal before these were acquired by France and Britain respectively. In fact, these were the basic examples which convinced men like Hobson that their argument was demonstratively true. Moreover, in the years before 1914, significant amounts of capital were invested in new colonies, such as the Gold Coast, Malaya, the newly occupied parts of Indonesia and elsewhere. So far the Theory would seem correct. But in fact this is misleading. First, these places were not typical of the greater part of those areas acquired during the 'imperialist' grab. They were the plums, the exceptionally favoured areas, which would almost certainly have attracted capital because of the opportunities they offered even if the possibility of political annexation had not existed. It was reasonable for the observer to assume that imperial control was imposed on these in order to safeguard or stimulate capital investment under the most favourable conditions: but what of the rest, which had previously attracted no keen attention from the investing capitalist and in fact never did so? Unless we accept the view that European capital was so desperate for future fields for investment that it was prepared to annex even the most unpromising regions of the world as a long-term precaution – a view which Lenin would have accepted, but which seems historically improbable – it is difficult to see the relevance of the Theory in explaining their annexation. In short, it is one major weakness of the Theory that capital exported on a large scale and tropical colonies annexed only rarely coincide.

Nevertheless, at first sight, the correlation of these two factors in certain of the new colonies would seem to give the Theory some historical basis. It is only when the historian investigates the evidence as to why obvious places like Egypt or the Transvaal were annexed that even this element of probability disappears. While few would deny that the fact of existing investment gave these regions heightened significance, it seems increasingly clear that 'political' rather than economic considerations were decisive. Thus the British were more interested in the strategic relevance of Egypt to the security of India than in their holdings in the Canal Company; the Transvaal was annexed less to satisfy investors in the gold mines than to prevent the absorption of the Cape by an unfriendly Boer republic; France saw Tunisia in terms of the security of Algeria rather than as a place where French bankers had made large loans, and was determined to forestall an Italian takeover; and so on. In fact, although it would be out of place here to put forward alternative explanations of particular annexations, few historians would now concede that European motives, even in these apparently blatant examples of capitalist activity, were simply based on financial questions.

We are left, then, with clear evidence that the Theory has historical defects. Imperial expansion occurred too early to fit the chronology of the emergence of 'finance capitalism'; many 'imperialist' powers – notably Russia, Italy, Portugal and Spain – far from having an embarrassing surplus of capital, were net importers of capital and must have had other motives for making annexations. The greater proportion of capital exports after about 1870 did not go to the regions involved in the grab for new colonies, but either to existing European possessions – Canada, Australia, New Zealand, India – or to independent states, such as Russia, China, the Argentine or the United States. Capital went where it was most strongly attracted by economic conditions. There was no shortage of such places, and it is impossible to think that European capitalists were embarrassed by lack of fields for investment along traditional lines. Even where there does seem to to be some correlation between capital export and the annexation of a new colony, as often as not there is inconvenient evidence that the statesmen of Europe had reasons for acting other than merely to further the interests of high finance.

But these conclusions leave us with a major historiographical problem. Why is it that the Theory of Capitalist Imperialism, despite the mauling it has received from critics, remains dogma in Marxist countries and influential almost everywhere? Although any answer must be speculative, it is important to provide one because this Theory is one of many quasi-historical concepts which have survived equally devastating analysis, often for analogous reasons. In this case there would appear to be two distinct explanations for its survival in different circumstances. The first is special to Marxists who accept the basic premises of Lenin's theory. If one accepts the hypothesis that capitalism at a certain stage in its development must either export capital or be strangled by lack of the opportunity to accumulate more capital, then the tests applied by the historian to see whether this need was the direct cause of colonial expansion become irrelevant. Once a capitalist country has become 'imperialist' in Lenin's sense it is not only bound to export capital but also to protect that capital by political means. Whether these means include formal annexation or informal pressures is largely irrelevant, for imperialism is infinitely adaptable to changed conditions, preserving its essential control over its economically dependent territories even when these eventually became sovereign states after decolonization. In the face of such certainty historical quibbles over the exact chronology of partition or the precise motives of a few statesmen become irrelevant. The essential truth remains that the colonial empires were the product of the socio-economic condition of the imperialist states and were an inevitable outcome of their historical evolution. Hence any evidence to the contrary must be regarded as misleading.

But the Theory also won acceptance from many who were not Marxists, and we must therefore look for a more general explanation of its popularity. This is probably the simple fact that it provided a straightforward and apparently convincing explanation of what at first sight seemed an intractable question. Until the Theory is examined in detail it carries conviction. As has been seen in Part One of these documents, the classical economists and their successors postulated the need of all capitalist societies to export capital to preserve the rate of profit on investments. In the later nineteenth century and during the twentieth there was no doubt that Europe was exporting capital in very large amounts, some of it to the newly acquired colonies. Leading statesmen and enthusiasts for empire, such as Leopold II, Jules Ferry and Leroy-Beaulieu, supported by propagandists in many countries of Europe, deliberately justified colonization in economic terms. The rough chronology of colonization seemed to indicate that the rapid expansion after 1870 coincided with the unprecedented economic growth of Europe and North America. Some colonies, if not the majority, became important annexes of the European and American economies. On all counts the facts appeared to support the Theory, and it seemed pointless to look beyond it for an explanation of the modern colonial empires.

Thus the main reason for the general popularity of the Theory has been its sheer probability, coupled with its neatness and universality. Conversely, the difficulty of the critic has been that in rejecting or modifying it he seems to be merely captious. The onus is on him to show that the Theory is misleading, and he can do so only by a tedious examination of individual cases through which few are prepared to follow him. Yet by now the work done has largely demolished the foundations of the Theory. It remains possible still to say that imperialism might possibly have worked that way. Capital was being exported, colonies were being acquired, the two might well have been linked as cause and effect. Yet the evidence, perhaps surprisingly, points in the other direction. Despite the obvious explanation, colonization was more the product of political ambitions, international rivalries, and complex situations in the non-European world than of simple and universal economic forces. The Theory of Capitalist Imperialism might have been true, but in fact it was not. Sooner or later the sheer volume of the evidence and argument marshalled on the other side will convince the majority that imperialism was not the simple product of advanced capitalism.

Yet to eliminate the Theory of Capitalist Imperialism from the historian's stock creates a vacuum. How are we to explain the second expansion of Europe if not in these terms? No serious attempt has been made in selecting these documents to provide other types of historical approach or explanation, for the problem is too complex to be dealt with so briefly. But, in conclusion, two general points may be made about alternative ways of interpreting the same facts and answering the same problems.

First, given the scope of the problem, no single theory or explanation of imperialism is satisfactory. It is quite as inaccurate to say that imperialism was entirely the product of a desire for power or prestige, the result of European rivalries, the outcome of trading competition or of missionary enterprise (to mention a few alternatives) as to put it all down to capital exports. To replace the Theory of Capitalist Imperialism by any single alternative theory is merely to substitute one vulnerable hypothesis for another. For the historian who really wants to know why these things happened there is only one possible approach: to begin by studying as fully as possible the general forces operating within Europe and in other parts of the world; to study each particular case of annexation as a special problem; and finally to reach a tentative conclusion about why colonization occurred in each case. The result will certainly be untidy and often contradictory. In some cases economic motives may seem to have predominated; in others political or idealistic motives. But the sum of these multiple investigations is the nearest the historian can come to achieving a general explanation of the tendency of Europe to expand after about 1870. Anything more comprehensive will almost certainly be misleading.

Second, it now seems evident to historians that their investigations should be as much concerned with the periphery – with the world in which colonization occurred – as with Europe. The idea that empire was the product merely of the needs or impulses of Europe was common to most theorists and historians until quite recently; and the extracts from historians in Part Four of these documents suggest that some even of those who rejected the Theory felt bound to replace it by other 'Eurocentric' explanations. More recently, however, it has been realized that empire was as often as not due primarily to the 'pull' of forces operating outside Europe, though often connected with the activities of Europeans operating at the circumference. Hence the emergence of those 'peripheral' interpretations of imperialism which were mentioned in the Introduction and are reflected in the concluding chapter of Robinson and Gallagher's detailed study of British policy, *Africa and the Victorians* (No. 35). Again, caution is necessary. By no means all colonial acquisitions resulted from crises at the perimeter, and where the peripheral approach fails, the historian must turn back to Europe for his explanation. Yet the effort of studying the periphery is not wasted, for it ensures that the historian is doing his job properly. Instead of starting with a general hypothesis and leaping from there to a general explanation, he is forced to begin with the specific and detailed and then to pace out the way to a broader hypothesis step by step. Treated in this pedantic way imperialism ceases to be a mystical force and becomes the sum of so many established facts. At the same time it is transferred from the speculative field of the historicist and becomes part of the proper study of the historian.

FURTHER READING

Other Exponents and Critics of the Theory and its Origins

M. B. BROWN. *After Imperialism.* Heinemann, 1963.

M. A. DOBB. *Studies in the Development of Capitalism.* Routledge, 1946.

W. K. HANCOCK. *Wealth of Colonies.* Cambridge University Press, 1950.

L. ROBBINS. *The Theory of Economic Policy in English Classical Political Economy.* Macmillan, 1952.

J. STRACHEY. *The End of Empire.* Gollancz, 1959.

P. M. SWEEZY. *The Theory of Capitalist Development.* Dennis Dobson, 1946.

G. S. L. TUCKER. *Progress and Profits in British Economic Thought, 1650–1850.* Cambridge University Press, 1960.

E. VARGA and L. MENDELSOHN. *New Data for V. I. Lenin's Imperialism.* New York, International Publishers, 1940.

D. WINCH. *Classical Political Economy and Colonies.* G. Bell, 1965.

Further Historical Accounts of Imperial Expansion

M. BAUMONT. *L'Essor industriel et l'Impérialisme colonial, 1878–1904,* 2nd edn. Paris, Presses Universitaires de France, 1949.

M. BELOFF, P. RENOUVIN, F. SCHNABEL and F. VALSECCHI, eds. *L'Europe du XIXe et du XXe Siècle.* 2 vols. Milan, 1962.

H. BRUNSCHWIG. *French Colonialism, 1871–1914* (1960). English edn. Pall Mall Press, 1966.

D. K. FIELDHOUSE. *The Colonial Empires.* Weidenfeld & Nicolson, 1966.

E. HALEVY. *Imperialism and the Rise of Labour,* 2nd revised edn. Benn, 1951.

W. L. LANGER. *European Alliances and Alignments, 1871–90.* New York, Alfred A. Knopf, 1931.

W. L. LANGER. *The Diplomacy of Imperialism.* 2 vols. New York, Alfred A. Knopf, 1935.

P. RENOUVIN. *Histoire des Relations Internationales.* vol VI. *Le XIXe Siècle. II. De 1871 a 1914. L'apogée de l'Europe.* Paris, Librairie Hachette, 1955.

A. J. P. TAYLOR. *The Struggle for Mastery in Europe, 1848–1918.* Clarendon Press, Oxford, 1954.

The New Cambridge Modern History, Vol. XI. *Material Progress and World-Wide Problems, 1870–1898.* Cambridge University Press, 1962.

The Cambridge History of the British Empire. Vol III. *The Empire-Commonwealth, 1870–1919.* Cambridge University Press, 1959.

Index

Index